C000113699

Human Interference

An Out of Control Novel

Donald L Reavis

DonaldLReavis.com

ISBN 978-1-64007-306-7

HUMAN INTERFERENCE

ACKNOWLEDGEMENTS

I would like to acknowledge the following people who were instrumental in the writing of this book. First to my wife, Sharla who endured countless hours of listening to ideas and stories, then proof reading the manuscript early on. We give special thanks to a couple of our editors Aurora my daughter and Doddie Messick.

I will always be indebted to my advisors, Doctor Roger H. Morgan, co-author of "The Parent Project" who has more than 20 years experience treating high risk adolescents and their families. To my childhood friend, Captain Kurt Hufford, who has experience flying numerous types of aircraft and is currently is captain on the CRJ700.

To my coworkers who had no idea I was writing this book during the latter years of my career. Thank you for the great conversation we had bouncing around ideas of future air traffic control.

To the rest of our family and friends who were both critical and supportive during the years I spent writing and editing Human Interference. For the confidence they gave from their feedback. I will always be grateful to my parents who have given me the stability of a strong Christian home and the ability to see beyond the horizon. Above all I thank God for giving me the strength to carry on through times of doubt and discouragement.

Glossary and Acronyms

FAA – Federal Aviation Administration – Controlling agency of the National Airspace System here in the United States and is part of the Department of Transportation.

NTSB – National Transportation Safety Board

TMU – Traffic Management Unit – In theory see the "big picture"

Ops Manager – Individual in charge of the control room.

URET – User Request Evaluation Tool – Replaced the antiquated flight progress strips and allows the controller to evaluate an altitude or route change prior to issuing the clearance.

NextGen – The largest transformation of air traffic control ever attempted, while thousands of planes and millions of passengers continue to fly safely.

TSA – Transportation Security Agency – Protects the nation's transportation system to ensure freedom of movement of people and commerce. The TSA is an agency of the Department of Homeland Security.

Air Traffic Control Tower – The tower centrally located at an airport where the controllers can control the airplanes on the taxiways, runways and normally within five miles of the airport.

Approach Control – Controls the airplanes into and out of busy airports using radar. This is usually within approximately forty miles of the primary airport.

Air Traffic Control Center – Consist of a facility established to provide air traffic control service to aircraft operating on IFR flight plans within controlled airspace, principally during the enroute phase of flight.

Unicom - An air-ground communication facility operated by a private agency to provide advisory service at uncontrolled airports.

Minimums – Lowest altitude and or visibility allowed on a given instrument approach to a runway.

Operational error – When two aircraft lose standard separation. In the centers that is normally five miles lateral or 1000 feet vertical. It is reduced to three miles with approach control.

Operational deviation – When an aircraft enters another sector or facility's airspace without approval.

ATO - The Air Traffic Organization (ATO) is the operations arm of the Federal Aviation Administration. All air traffic controllers are in the organization.

ITT - A diversified leading manufacturer of highly engineered critical components and customized technology solutions for growing industrial end-markets in energy infrastructure, electronics, aerospace and transportation.

ADS-B - Automatic Dependent Surveillance-Broadcast will be replacing radar as the primary surveillance method for controlling aircraft worldwide. When using this system both pilots and controllers see the same radar picture.

ERAMS - En Route Automation Modernization System replacing the Host computer. The computer system used at the FAA's high altitude en route centers is considered the backbone of the nation's airspace system. It processes flight radar data, provides communications and generates display data to air traffic controllers.

D-side – Is an assistant to the radar controller, entering data into the computer and with communicating with other sectors or facilities.

ETA – Estimated time of arrival

AGL – Above ground level

IFR – Instrument flight rules

PDA - Personal digital assistant

LAN – Local area network

GPS – Global positioning system

SBC – Satellite based communications

4 DT – Four dimensional trajectory - The program designed to perform automated control of aircraft.

FMS – The flight management system is a specialized computer system that automates a wide variety of in-flight tasks, reducing the workload on the flight crew.

VOR - VHF omnidirectional radio range is a type of radio navigation system for aircraft.

TALC - Terminal automated-landing control is the four dimensional program used in the terminal environment.

TCAS – Terminal collision avoidance system

FOREWORD

Technology has always been an integral part of the aviation industry. For years air traffic control lagged in the industry at the constraints of bureaucracy. In 2003 the signing of the Century of Aviation Reauthorization Act, started the wheels rolling to change the future of the air traffic control system.

I have always been a proponent of advance technology in our field and am pleased with the moves the FAA has made over the last decade. While the air traffic controller mentality will not let me be in complete agreement, it is still refreshing to see the energy being expended on a safe and efficient system.

The stories told in this book may appear real and have some validity, but let me emphasize, this is a novel. As a retired controller I have complete confidence in safety of the National Airspace System. That being said, as with all things involving human life, we need to move forward with caution in implementing our future programs.

PROLOGUE

Charlie had just finished lunch when the buzz of his cell phone startled the aging, and retired air traffic controller. Having retired just three years ago, Charlie was trying to find his place in life without the constant stress of controlling the skies above southern California. He had run a few marathons since his unexpected retirement and worked out constantly to keep in shape. His part time job of working for O'Leary & Associates, an aviation consulting company, kept him as busy as he cared to be. Charlie had just turned fifty-five and had noticed his hairline was sliding further back on his furrowed forehead. Due to high blood pressure, Charlie had cut back on red meat and recently settled into a vegetarian lifestyle. A glance at his phone revealed an almost forgotten era. The number brought back memories of the times he had refused to answer the calls for overtime. The added stress of additional hours during the last few years had been more than his blood pressure and his family could handle.

Puzzlingly looking at the number, he answered with a resentful, "What?"

"Mr. Beckler?" asked an unfamiliar shaky voice.

Charlie, in his candor-retired attitude, replied with, "Depends, why are you asking?"

"Mr. Beckler, I am from the Department of Homeland Security. All I can tell you at this time is that we have a national emergency and we need your help. A car will pick you up shortly, and pack a bag; this may take a few days."

Charlie did not ask any more questions; he knew it would be a worthless endeavor. He ran upstairs and quickly threw together an overnight bag as all kinds of scenarios were running through his head. Why do they need him? He had refused to go along with the new administration when the controllers' cry for safety had gone unheeded. Why was Homeland Security calling him? He no longer worked for the FAA. He had been a rebel throughout his career, never a conformer but he was one of the last few who could control a scope full of airplanes, while at the same time eating lunch and listening to the latest fishing report from his coworkers.

He stopped by the kitchen and grabbed a couple of energy bars and a banana before pausing long enough to text a note to his wife, Carrie. He had been anxious for her and Mitzy to get home. What could he tell her? Charlie quickly typed about the strange phone call and said he would call her as soon as he had more news.

"I guess that will have to do," he mumbled hearing the sound of a horn outside their two-story suburban home. Idling in the driveway was a navy blue Lincoln Navigator with an impatient driver sitting behind the wheel. Opening the door, he was surprised to see his old coworker Jim in the back seat.

"What's going down?" asked Charlie as he fastened the seatbelt and the Navigator backed out of the drive. Jim Gallagher, an Air Force veteran, had served as an air traffic controller in Iraq during the early part of the century.

"Don't know," he replied as he shrugged his shoulders and revealed that he knew absolutely nothing more than Charlie. Silently they rode through town and out towards the Western Center for Air Traffic Services located thirteen miles north of Ely, Nevada south of the village of McGill. As Charlie looked out the window, his thoughts drifted, as they often did, back over his twenty-three year career.

Chapter 1

It had been a blistering day in the southwest as the controllers arrived in room 210A. The heat, along with moisture moving up from the Sea of Cortez, had thunderstorms popping all over the Nevada and southern California deserts. This had created havoc on their day, with unbelievable deviations. Ever since the regional jets had started flying and Las Vegas had become a mega resort destination, the volume of air traffic had multiplied to an almost unmanageable level. It had been just twenty-six years since the president had fired a generation of controllers. The aging work force was retiring in alarming numbers. A new generation was coming onboard, and training was going nonstop in order to prevent an airspace crisis. It was these days of sheer terror in the minds of the controllers, unnoticed in the eyes of the flying public and only briefly noticed by the pilots, which caused the veteran controllers to call it quits. While a lot of the controllers were retiring, many were also looking for other careers and swearing off flying as a plausible form of transportation.

To the controllers, briefing day meant one less hour in front of the scopes. It happened every week on the last hour of the controllers' fourth day of their work week. Normally Air Space and Procedures or Quality Assurance would have some tidbit of information to share. Sometimes it was even interesting and noteworthy.

Overall, controllers are a strange lot. Most do not like being told what to do as it conflicts with their type A personality. They are opposed to change, but they will embrace

it if brought into the decision making process. This had been
the way business was done prior to the FAA imposing work
rules upon the controllers. The concerns of the controllers were
no longer a factor. These actions caused morale to hit an all-
time low as more and more changes were thrown at the
controllers with no regard to the emotional impact. The
controllers became very leery of any "new ideas" management
came up with, as many of these new managers had never
controlled an airplane in their lives. With the controller
shortage being a critical issue, many of these new managers had
crossed over from other branches of the government to fill
vacancies left by the retirees.

It was supposed to be just another weekly briefing. That
was until Barney, the administrative manager, and Ted, a
supervisor, walked in and brought the group of thirty
overworked, tired controllers to a distinctively disgusting groan.

"Everyone, sit down and shut up," commanded Barney.
"We have a lot to go over, and we are not paying you
overtime."

Charlie figured this would just be another boring
meeting with an IWH (idiot without headset) telling us
controllers what to do.

For the next hour, Barney entertained the controllers
with fairy-tale plans to build an air traffic control system that
would revolutionize the aviation industry. In the near future, no
longer would the controllers actually separate the airplanes.
Their job would be diminished to merely that of an observer.
The new technology would allow aircraft to fly closer together
without any controller intervention. The super computer called
NextGen would keep the aircraft apart and get them to their
destination more quickly and safely. Barney droned on with an
almost nauseating smirk about how this NextGen air traffic
management system would work more efficiently than its
human counterpart without complaining or requiring time off
for vacations and sick leave.

"We are replacing you. And we don't care if you like it or not!" explained Barney as he half-heartedly opened the room or questions. By now, Charlie and his teammates had had about all they could handle from this moron, and walked out of the room.

Thirty minutes later, they were at the local watering hole and loudly recalling the obnoxious information they had just received. The general consensus being who in their right mind would come up with this kind of pea-brained idea. As the controllers attempted to put together the pieces of the NextGen plan, questions filled their minds. What happens when the weather gets bad? What happens when there is an emergency? And God forbid, what would happen if another 9/11 were to take place?

Leaving the watering hole even more disturbed and confused, Charlie headed home. Should he question NextGen as he had justifiably questioned URET? The user request evaluation tool was implemented two years earlier to assist in separation of airplanes and did away with the antiquated paper flight plans. The system had been somewhat a disappointment as it had been only about 95 percent successful in warning of potential conflicts and had a mind of its own. The controllers were not comfortable with these odds and would only use the system as an extra set of eyes. How could a program of the magnitude of NextGen handle all the variables necessary to assure perfect performance? The stress of the day was heavy on his mind as he pulled into the drive and his young wife and little daughter came out to meet him.

Chapter 2

Charlie and Carrie had met in the spring of 1992 while attending Georgia State College. Charlie was working on a degree in engineering, and Carrie was majoring in liberal arts. Soon after graduation, Charlie joined the Navy and attended the Great Lakes Naval Academy for boot camp and then on to Memphis for his "A" school training. Here, he was first introduced to air traffic control. After graduation Charlie was stationed at NAS North Island in San Diego, California. He and Carrie continued their long-distance relationship throughout his military career as Charlie went to sea for six months then transferred to the East Coast where he was stationed at Norfolk, Virginia.

After a second tour at sea, this time in the Mediterranean, Charlie waived his reenlistment and moved to Atlanta, where Carrie had been working as a program director for a local resort. Shortly after his arrival in Atlanta, Charles Beckler and Carrie Shoemaker were married in a small church northeast of Atlanta where Carrie's grandfather was the pastor. After the wedding they flew off to Cancun for a two-week honeymoon. Upon arriving home, a letter was waiting from the Federal Aviation Administration advising Charlie his application had been accepted and he was to report to work the following week at the Mike Monroney Aeronautical Center in Oklahoma City. If he completed the screening program, he would be working at the Los Angeles Air Route Traffic Control Center which is located in Palmdale, California. The next two

15

days were hectic in preparation for the move. After some teary-eyed good-byes they were on their way to Oklahoma. Three months later, they again loaded up their belongings in Oklahoma and headed for the west coast.

It was a long drive across the country as the newlyweds drove their over packed Ford Ranger across Texas and on through New Mexico. Carrie had never been to California and Charlie had never heard of Palmdale.

"Why is Los Angeles Center located in Palmdale?" he had asked. That is when he found out the history. Around 1960, the FAA moved the center from a hanger at LAX to the desert town as a safety precaution during the cold war. He found that this had happened to many centers throughout the country.

They were looking forward to seeing this paradise. With a name like Palmdale, they were sure the streets would be lined with palm trees and music of the tropics would be whistling through the branches. They drove through the heat of Arizona and then down Interstate 10, up through the Cajon Pass and down Highway 138. As they passed Littlerock, Charlie was looking for the palm trees when he heard Carrie sobbing.

"What's wrong?" he asked already knowing the answer.

Through the tears, she softly whispered, "I can't live in this God forsaken place. Charlie, I love you and will never leave you but please do what you can to get us out of here."

That had been seven years earlier, and Charlie had put in for every transfer that opened up and for every promotion possible. Many times he had been accepted for another position only to have it shot down by management. His facility was just too short staffed to let anyone go. While these frustrations continued to occupy his mind, his daughter brought him back to reality.

"Daddy, Daddy!" yelled little Mitzy as Charlie crawled out of his Toyota Landcruiser. "How was your day, Daddy?

Did you control airplanes today? Are you happy to see me, Daddy? Can we go to the park? Huh, Daddy, huh? Please!"

It was all Charlie could do not to scream. Carrie quickly picked up Mitzy and shushed her, as she knew from years of experience this was not the time to talk to Daddy. Charlie needed his space, even if just for a few minutes. He needed to change from Charlie the certified professional controller to Charlie the husband and father. He suppressed his desire to scream. Instead he leaned over and kissed his little girl on the forehead with a quick thank-you kiss for his wife.

"See you in a few," he whispered as he headed for the house and a few minutes of solitude. Charlie had learned long ago that stress from the job did not mix with his family. He realized the first twenty minutes at home needed to be spent alone. This time allowed him to rid himself of the day's challenges and prepare his heart to respond in a positive manner to his family. First he looked back over the day. What situations had caused him the most grief? How could he avoid these situations in the future? Had he done his best? Once these questions were answered, he would silently thank God for His help throughout the day. He would ask God to give him peace with his family, as he did not desire to alienate them.

Charlie walked into the kitchen, just as Carrie was finishing dinner. "How was your day, darling?" he asked as he wrapped his arms around her.

She turned with a smile and said, "Welcome home. It's always so good to see you once you're rested. Everything was status quo today. Mom called and was wondering when you're going to take a vacation so she could spend some time with us. I really think she's more interested in spending time with that little granddaughter of hers."

"Doesn't sound like a bad idea to me," Charlie replied. "We could drop her off in Atlanta and fly over to your parents' summer home for a few days. It will probably be Thanksgiving before we can go, but I'll see what they can give me," Charlie added, knowing time off would be limited at best.

Charlie was thinking how great it would be just to get a few days off, let alone a real vacation. Ever since the FAA had blind-sided the union, vacations were hard to come by. Even though he had earned a lot of vacation time, staffing was so short that management was not inclined to schedule time off. Because of this style of management, sick leave usage had sky rocketed.

Charlie knew that early September, as the Mojave Desert cooled, the thunderstorms subsided and the monsoon season was finally over. Things settled down to the normal hectic pace at Los Angeles Center. Over the years, it seemed the traffic count continued to climb and still no word on the pay raise the controllers had been promised two years earlier. The union continued to fight with management over this issue. Then came the word that the supervisors and managers would be getting their raise but the senior controllers were out of luck and would not be receiving even a plugged nickel. So morale moved from bad to worse. Controllers started resigning, and those who were able, retired.

After dinner, Charlie informed Carrie that they would be spending Thanksgiving with her folks. He would immediately submit his request for his much over-due time off.

Monday afternoon Charlie found his leave request in his mailbox with a big red "Denied" stamped across the middle of it.

"So much for trusting the FAA!" Charlie complained as he planned his next move. "Sick leave is out of the question since I'm already on a sick leave letter for abuse. So I guess if they want to play hardball, hardball is what I will play."

Thanksgiving was rapidly approaching as Charlie and Carrie made preparation for their trip to the East Coast. On Friday morning, after the working the night shift, Charlie handed his supervisor a COP form requesting continuation of pay for the next two weeks and walked out the door. This was Charlie's ace in the hole as it allowed him to take up to forty-five days of unspecified leave that, if proven was job related, would not count against his vacation time. If turned down by the labor review board, he would be charged vacation time or sick leave.

"Exactly what I wanted anyhow," Charlie said to himself as he was driving home, "but now I get two weeks instead of one."

"Gotta love loopholes," he said to Carrie as he walked in the door and grinned. "Let's get packed. We are out of here."

Two hours later, they were in the car headed for the airport. "Going to see Grandma, going to see Grandma," sang Mitzy as LAX came into view and the jets screamed overhead with gear and flaps down. The frustration of getting through security was only magnified by the fact that Charlie had worked two eight-hour shifts without sleep. Now having to tolerate inept TSA agents left the disgruntled controller tired and grumpy.

"Behave, darling," Carrie smiled, "you're scaring the other passengers."
Charlie settled down to a post-mid-shift stupor and made it to the gate without further incident.

As the flight attendant was giving the pre-takeoff briefing, Charlie drifted off to sleep with a scope full of airplanes on his mind.

The mid-shifts were unique in that only two controllers worked from midnight until six in the morning. Whereas during the day shift a controller would have help if he worked more than a handful of airplanes, now he found himself with twenty to twenty-five targets working alone. No one wanted to complain about the amount of traffic, or the stress, because if they did, then management would be there all night monitoring their every move. This kind of attention created even more stress and challenges.

"Cactus 475, climb and maintain flight level three five zero. USAir 432 cleared. Direct Dove Creek climb and maintain flight level three three zero and do not exceed two-eight-zero knots."

Even in his sleep Charlie was busy controlling the airplanes from the night before. It seemed like an hour of constant control instructions and listening to readbacks when conflict alert started flashing. All Charlie could see was two aircraft coming together. He keyed his mic and opened his mouth, but no words would come out. As the targets merged, he sat frozen in time looking for the aircraft to appear on the other side.

Charlie was startled awake as the speaker blared, "Flight attendants please take your seat, we are next in line for departure."

Delta Airlines Flight 101 nonstop to Atlanta was uneventful, and Charlie was able to get some quality sleep. Landing in Atlanta just in time for the evening rush hour, they picked up a rental car and headed northeast on Interstate 85, arriving at Carrie's parents' farm outside of Maysville just as the sun was casting its final ray of light over the Georgia pines.

"Grandma!" Mitzy yelled as she jumped out of the car and ran to the porch of the beautiful southern mansion which Carrie's parents had recently restored. Sarah Shoemaker had heard the car drive up and had just opened the large hand carved mahogany door as Mitzy leaped into her arms.

"Where's Grandpa?" Mitzy asked as she looked around. Grandpa Will always told Mitzy exciting tales and read bedtime stories; however, the most fun was when Grandpa would hitch up the wagon to the old horse and they would ride around the farm.

"Right here behind you, Cupcake," Will spoke up as he walked up the flagstone walkway that led from the tool shed.

"Daddy!" This time it was Carrie who ran to meet the man she had adored all her life.

"Dinner is ready," Grandma said as she hugged everyone. "Get your stuff upstairs and clean up. Charlie, I fixed your favorite," she added as if unnecessarily trying to win over her son-in-law.

"Oh! Do we have to eat pot roast again?" Charlie moaned, winking at Sarah as he grabbed the suitcases and headed upstairs.

Dinner consisted of Grandma's succulent pot roast, freshly mashed potatoes, green beans from the summer garden, and a delicious fresh baked peach pie topped with vanilla ice cream. After dinner Will and Charlie excused themselves from the kitchen and retired to the family room where the overstuffed recliners were the answer to the end of a long day. By the time Carrie and Sarah had cleaned up the table, both men were sound asleep. Carrie quickly gave Mitzy a much-needed bath and got her off to bed before heading back downstairs and reviving her man. It wasn't long before they both headed upstairs for a good night's sleep. It had been thirty-eight hours since Charlie had any real sleep and it did not take long before it showed.

As Carrie slipped into her favorite nightgown and sat down to read from her Bible, she was drawn back to a time not more than twenty years ago when, as a young teenage girl, this had been her room. It was here in this bed she had dreamed of someday being a wife and a mother. She had tried many times to imagine what it would be like. Would she be a good wife? Could she raise a child with the same level of respect and ethics that her parents had raised her? What would her husband be like? What would he do? How would he treat her? Many questions used to go through her mind, as she would lie there awake. Glad to be home once again, she no longer let questions occupy her mind as she was now living the life she had dreamed of. Charlie treated her with utmost love, and as that love continued to fill her life with satisfaction and joy, she in turn

21

showed Charlie the respect he needed to continue the level of competence required in his occupation.

Crawling into bed underneath the hand-sewn quilt, she leaned over and kissed her sleeping husband and softly whispered, "Thank you, my love, thank you for just being you." Carrie drifted off to sleep with memories of her childhood still occupying her mind.

Chapter 3

"Good morning!" greeted Charlie as he walked into the kitchen, "Nothing like waking up to the smell of bacon frying. Sure feels good to be back on the farm."

Carrie greeted Charlie with a big hug and a kiss that made her mother blush.

Carrie smiled at Charlie, "If you liked this then tonight will blow you away. Speaking of tonight, what time are we leaving?"

"I checked the weather and the fog should be gone by nine. If we're airborne by ten, we should get into Kitty Hawk by two. Though if you threaten me with too much of you, we just may bypass Kitty Hawk."

After breakfast, Charlie and Carrie took Mitzy for a walk down to the pond where they skipped stones across the water. Looking at their daughter, it amazed them of the speed at which a child grows. They had never been away from her for more than a couple of hours since she had come into their lives over three years ago.

"Why are you leaving?" Mitzy wanted to know.

"Well, I'm sure your mother can answer that question." Charlie replied, winking at Carrie.

"Daddy and Mommy need some alone time to rest up." Carrie told Mitzy, glaring back at Charlie. "And Grandma and Grandpa want to spend some special alone time with their little princess." That seemed to satisfy Mitzy as she picked up a pebble and tried to imitate Dad who was still skipping stones across the glassy water.

As the fog started to burn off, they headed back to the house. They had a long day ahead and wanted to get on their way to the beach house. Dropping Mitzy off at the house, they gave Grandpa and Grandma hugs and final instructions for their granddaughter.

"Be careful with my airplane," Grandpa Will hollered as they headed out the door.

"You know Charlie's a good pilot, Dad," Carrie shot back with a smile and blew him a kiss.

They turned right out of the drive onto Donahoo Road and headed south on Highway 82, the four miles to Jackson County Airport where Will Shoemaker kept his Cirrus SR22. Will had learned to fly during the Korean War flying F80 Shooting Stars. Once out of the Air Force he had flown for Pan American Airlines. When the airline collapsed in 1991 Will decided it was time to give it up and retire. Turning left on Lyle Field Road, Charlie noticed a couple of deer in the field beside the departure end of runway three four. He and Will had a close call with a deer the last time he had flown out of this airport. Shouldn't be a problem this morning he was thinking as the fog had dissipated and he could see the entire length of the runway. Pulling up to the hangers, they spotted their airplane glistening on the ramp.

"Looks like they have been expecting us," commented Charlie. "I thought we would have to get it out of the hanger ourselves."

A young man Charlie had met last summer greeted them as they walked up to the blue-and-white single engine aircraft.

"Mr. Shoemaker said you would want full tanks today, Charlie. Do you have a long flight ahead?"

"Good morning, Tommy, heading over to Kitty Hawk then down to Hatteras," Charlie replied.

"Well, she's in shipshape and shouldn't cause you any problems," Tommy continued. "Looks like a beautiful day to fly."

With the plane loaded Charlie did one last walk around before they strapped in and started the engine. Slowly taxiing Charlie listened to automated weather before broadcasting on Unicom their intentions of departing on runway three four with a right turnout. After a quick run through the pretakeoff checklist, they taxied onto the runway. Charlie advanced the throttle to max power and N234CD leaped down the runway, rapidly increasing speed. With the airspeed passing through seventy knots, Charlie nudged back on the side stick, the aircraft rotated, and the ground fell away beneath them. Stabilizing the airspeed on one hundred knots for best rate of climb, Charlie made a gentle right turn to heading zero-seven-five and engaged the autopilot. As the autopilot took over the chore of flying, Charlie dialed in Atlanta Center and picked up VFR flight following. Leveling off at fifteen thousand five hundred feet the sleek composite aircraft settled in at 180 knots. Charlie looked down at the Garmin 430 GPS and noted they were only two hours away from Kitty Hawk, the birthplace of aviation.

Eighteen minutes after takeoff they passed over Hartwell Lake in South Carolina and Carrie was already sound asleep. The drone of the engine and gentle motion of the aircraft seemed to have a somnolent effect on her. As Charlie watched the patchwork landscape pass beneath the wing and the miles tick off the GPS, he thought about their destination. Over one hundred years ago on a chilly Thursday morning, Orville Wright slid down the rail and rose into the air. Lasting only twelve seconds, the flight was the beginning of a revolution in travel which over the years evolved from those twelve seconds with limited control to tens of thousands of aircraft crisscrossing the world. From the twelve horses which powered the Wright Flyer to the Airbus 380, carrying up to 853 passengers with Rolls-Royce power plants putting out over seventy-five thousand pounds of thrust. Little did the Wright brothers know that December morning the impact of their accomplishment.

Charlie's thoughts took him through all the stages of aviation over the last hundred years. How the aces of World War I brought aviation into the fighting arena. How the Ford Trimotor and the DC-3 had introduced the idea of air travel for the normal citizens. The mass training of pilots during World War II as men were needed to fly thousands of bombers and fighter planes used to defeat the Axis powers. After the war, the jet engine reduced the nation to five hours and became the standard way to travel. After a century of flying, from that one airplane in the air for twelve seconds to skies that are now saturated with aircraft, a person has to ask what is next. What will the next decade bring? Over the next twenty years, will there be a need for pilots? Or will NextGen transmit data to the autopilot, which will respond accordingly?

"N234CD contact Washington Center 135.3." Charlie read back the frequency and checked in with Washington Air Route Traffic Control Center. One hour and ten minutes later, as they were crossing just south of Swan Bay, Charlie reduced power and started a gradual descent into First Flight Airport.

"Where are we?" Carrie asked wiping the sleep from her eyes.

"Almost there, sleepy head," Charlie responded. "Look just past the bay, you can see the ocean."

A few minutes later crossing over Kitty Hawk Bay, they entered a left downwind for runway two, briefly leveling off at eight hundred feet as Charlie configured the aircraft for landing. Turning base, he reduced the speed to ninety knots. As Buzzard bay moved underneath them, Charlie turned final and lined up with the three thousand feet of asphalt. Applying 50 percent flaps, he corrected for a slight right crosswind coming in off the ocean. Carrie wasn't paying much attention to the landing since she was busy surveying the Wright Brothers National Memorial off to the right. It wasn't long before Charlie squeaked the mains onto the runway rolling to a stop. Turning around, they taxied back to the south end of the runway and parked next to the walkway leading up to the memorial on Kill Devil Hill.

"Why are we here?" Carrie wanted to know as they exited the aircraft.

"It's where it all started," Charlie responded. "Every pilot should walk these grounds at least once in his life time."

Hand in hand, they walked up the sidewalk winding around the grassy knoll known as Kill Devil Hill. Sitting on the wall next to the sixty-foot granite memorial, Charlie looked to the north where the first flights had taken place. A shiver swept through his body as if he himself had been here that very day as the signal flag had gone up and they pulled the Wright Flyer out of the hanger. He could almost feel the biting wind blowing off the ocean and across the sand dunes. Shutting his eyes, he could picture himself standing at the end of the wing, holding it steady as they turned the propeller and fired up the home-built engine. As the engine settled into a steady rumble, Orville crawled onto the flyer facing forward on his stomach, grabbed the controls, and signaled. He was ready for the ride of his life. The throttle opened up, and Charlie saw himself running down the track helping propel the flyer as it lifted into the air. Charlie felt Carrie's hand on his shoulder bringing him back to reality.

To the east, waves were lapping the seashore. Where sand dunes and brush once littered the landscape, hotels and summer homes had taken over. The perfect spot to break the bonds of earth had become a favorite summer haven for thousands of vacationers. Leaving the hot city life up north, they had started coming here to enjoy the cool ocean breeze.

Coming down off the bluff, they headed north to the rail that was still in place over a century later. A rubber mat stretched out in front of them with four granite pillars, the last one off in the distance.

Charlie read the inscription on the first and a feeling of reverence flowed through his spine. "End of 1st Flight, Time 12 Seconds, Distance 120 feet, Dec 17, 1903, Pilot Orville."

After walking through the museum, they made their way back to their airplane with just a little more understanding and respect for the brothers' accomplishments.

"N234CD departing runway two with a right turn out," Charlie announced on Unicom frequency as he took to the runway and advanced the throttle. Ten seconds later, the aircraft left the runway and Charlie made a sweeping right turn around the sacred ground that had made history at the beginning of the twentieth century. Leveling off at fifteen hundred feet, less than a mile off the coastline, they made a sweeping right turn toward Billy Mitchell airport sixty miles south. A few minutes later, Carrie spotted the black-and-white-striped Bodie Island Lighthouse and talked Charlie into circling around it before they continued on to the south. Crossing over the shoreline just north of Cape Hatteras as Brigand Bay passed off the left wing, Charlie descended to pattern altitude. Three minutes later, they entered a left downwind for runway seven. After another perfect landing, Charlie was finally able to exhale. It was not the flying but the accumulative stress of controlling aircraft day after day that built up a destructive emotional bubble. This emotional bubble is best managed by periodic outburst or preplanned periods of relaxation. This was one of those times, and Charlie was well aware of it. Now for a few days on the outer banks of North Carolina, his blood pressure would go down and his jovial attitude would return. After making sure the airplane was secure, Charlie and Carrie climbed in the airport shuttle that took them to the family beach house.

Turning left onto Summer Place Drive brought back memories to Carrie. This was the place she had spent many summers while growing up. Will Shoemaker had always wanted a big vacation home on the beach. So as soon as her dad had the opportunity, he built this six-bedroom bungalow only a stone's throw from the warm Atlantic Ocean. As they pulled into the familiar drive of this three-story turquoise green beach house, Carrie's eyes were drawn to the six-foot cutout of a marlin hanging above the third-floor balcony. She remembered helping her dad cut it out of a piece of old weathered lumber when she was young. Wooden steps with horizontal white railing led from the driveway up to the second-floor porch, which stretched all along the back of this beautiful seaside home.

Carrie ran up the stairs, leaving the luggage for Charlie. Unlocking the door, she let out a squeal, which was more of a tradition than of any actual surprise. She always did the same thing when she arrived at this little piece of paradise on earth. Wasting no time, she slid across the hardwood floor and opened the patio doors. Her gaze took in the ribbon of sand and the waves lapping ever so gently over the few protruding rocks just off shore. Carrie had been to this beach many times with her family, but this time was different. For the first time, she and Charlie would be alone in this big house. And the beach would be practically empty, since most everyone else had gone home for the winter.

She felt Charlie's arms wrap around her. As she turned around, he started to say something but she put a finger to his lips as if to say to be quiet and listen to the sounds of the sea. With that, she pulled him to her and kissed him with such compassion he knew she was at peace with the world and in love with him. Taking advantage of this moment, he took Carrie by the hand and led her back inside and down to the second-floor master bedroom where he hung a "do not disturb" sign on the doorknob and closed the door.

Waking up later in the evening, Charlie looked over at his beautiful wife. She was lying there so peacefully he did not want to wake her, but he knew she would not want to miss dinner. The family had always made it a tradition to eat dinner the first night at Captain Jack's Seafood Restaurant. Thinking he had time for a quick shower before waking his best friend, Charlie slid out of bed and turned on the shower. He had loved this shower since the first time he had laid eyes on it. The white marble, laced with tones of grey, went from the floor all the way to the ceiling. The ceiling had three showerheads, each dispelling a strong blast of steaming-hot water. Along the wall, the vertical spa massaged all the aching muscles accumulated during a hard day of play or, in this case, a long day of flying. As Charlie stepped out of the shower he was surprised to see Carrie already dressed and putting on makeup.

"Nice nap, girlfriend?" he asked as he kissed her cheek messing up the makeup.

"It sure was, but now I'm starving," Carrie replied. "Let's get out of here."

The drive to Hatteras was uneventful, and fifteen minutes later they were being shown to a small booth amidst rope, anchors, and other paraphernalia from the sea. The candlelight flickered as they ordered their favorite dinner of fried grouper, crumb fried shrimp, french fried sweet potatoes, and a side dish of southern coleslaw. After a short walk through town, they headed back to the beach house where they settled in for the night.

Chapter 4

Any morning, especially Sunday morning, had always been surreal for Carrie here on the Outer Banks. She woke up as the first light appeared through the patio door. Slipping on her robe, she noticed that Charlie was already up. *Wonder where he disappeared to*, she thought as she slipped through the door onto the deck. Her thoughts turned to awe as she pondered anew God's creation. That's where Charlie found her.

"Why, good morning, girlfriend!"

"That for me?" she asked as she reached for the cup of steaming-hot coffee in his hands.

"For my one and only," was all he could say as she sipped the hot Columbian brew. The sky, like an ever-changing canvas transforming night into day, was suddenly interrupted by the bright glare of the sun rising out of the sea.

"Anyone can see a sunset," Carrie sighed, "but only the early risers get to see the sunrise."

"Why do we have to go to church this morning?" Charlie asked as they pulled into the Hatteras Island Baptist Church.

"My parents always brought me here, so I wanted to keep up the tradition," Carrie answered. "Anyway, it will do you good.   That is if you listen."

They were greeted at the door by a couple well into their seventies welcoming them to the small island church. They enjoyed the traditional worship service and settled into the sermon.

Charlie was half asleep when something the pastor said caught his attention. He was reading from the first chapter of Proverbs referencing what happens when we ignore wisdom.

"Continuing on at verse twenty-five," the pastor read:

Since you ignored all my advice and would not accept my rebuke, I in turn will laugh at your disaster; I will mock when calamity overtakes you- when calamity overtakes you like a storm, when disaster sweeps over you like a whirlwind, when distress and trouble overwhelm you. Then they will call to me but I will not answer; they will look for me but will not find me. Since they hated knowledge and did not choose to fear the LORD, since they would not accept my advice and spurned my rebuke, they will eat the fruit of their ways and be filled with the fruit of their schemes. For the waywardness of the simple will kill them, and the complacency of fools will destroy them; but whoever listens to me will live in safety and be at ease, without fear of harm.

What could this mean? wondered Charlie as he listened to the pastor continue on about the world we live in and how people in general had challenges with taking advice from those that had the knowledge. He spoke of the pride we tend to let control us in not allowing the experiences of others help us from repeating the same mistakes.

All Charlie could think of was the way his employer had constantly shunned the air traffic controllers in the administration's quest to achieve the new program. Many times the controllers had asked to be involved in the development process only to be denied. Charlie was still tossing this around in his thoughts as they headed back to the beach house. Pulling in the drive with the view of the beach behind the house,

Charlie was able to force himself to forget about the job and all its complications. Finally, he was able to bring himself back to the sensibility of where he was and who he was with.

They spent the next two days resting and playing on the beach. Wednesday, Charlie got the bright idea to take the ferry over to Ocracoke.

"You mean we have to leave this place?" was all Carrie could say, but she knew it would be a fun day no matter what they did. Charlie always made it interesting. It was about noon when they drove down to Hatteras to board the ferry only to find out there was only one ferry running and it would not be back for over an hour. They decided to park the car, grab the beach towels and spend some time on the beach. It was a gorgeous sunny day as they walked hand in hand over the boardwalk to the beach.

"Wow, Charlie, look at this sand!" Carrie exclaimed while tugging his hand.

"Hey, now, slow down! We still have another day together without the Mitzy." Charlie was laughing and secretly enjoying his ability to bring out the little girl in Carrie. He remembered their wedding night, and this vacation seemed to have brought out the same romantic results. It'd been a while since they'd had the ability to get away, just the two of them, and he'd been anticipating the occasion. Charlie loved his daughter, but this reconnection with his wife had desperately been needed. Carrie was embarrassed at how much she felt like a teenage girl on a first date. She loved Charlie so much, but he'd been pretty distant with all the stress from work; she was happy to see the teenage boy come out in him and commune with the teenage girl in her. Carrie winked at Charlie as she pulled him along.

The waves slowly cascaded into the beach as little sand crabs scurried into their holes. The seagulls flying over head caused Carrie to be a little nervous as she recalled the numerous times birds had left their little deposits on the top of her head. Charlie laughed as he watched her scanning the sky.

"What," Carrie asked.

"Oh, nothing," Charlie laughed, "just thinking about the many times I've had to remove those little deposits from your hair."

Carrie couldn't help but giggle with him.

Charlie spread out the beach towel as Carrie removed her shoes. After Charlie slipped off his shoes, they strolled along the beach for a few minutes and reminisced about their lives. Carrie put her head on Charlie's shoulder and her arm around his waist. Charlie pulled her close and kissed the top of her head. It felt good to get away from work. He hated the stupid games that were being played there and the many hours that he had to spend in that hellhole.

Carrie looked up into Charlie's eyes, "Hey, my Mr. Man, know how much I love you?"

"No, but I have a way that you can show me."

Carrie laughed as she punched him on the arm...she knew what he'd like. Then, she got a crazy idea. "Well, how is that exactly?"

Charlie grinned and then leaned over and whispered a few of his ideas into her ear.

"Ok, let's do it."

Charlie was taken aback, "What? Here?"

Carrie ran ahead to their towel, calling over her shoulder, "Sure, why not? There's no one around."

Charlie was pretty excited that he'd found such a secluded spot, but he wasn't sure that it was that secluded. "Well, I guess if you're game, I'm game."

The sun was setting when they came back down from their love making high. It was getting chilly as Charlie pulled Carrie close. "I love you, you're my best friend."

Carrie answered with a contented smile on her face, "I love you too."

With the sun setting in the west, they drove back to the beach house, stopping only to pick up an ice cream cone at Sweet Sam's. "Guess Ocracoke will have to wait," Charlie said, "but I wouldn't trade today for anything."

Thanksgiving morning, Carrie woke up to the voice of Charlie talking on the phone. "So you say we need to go south around the squall line?"

Hanging up, Charlie returned to the bedroom.

"Good morning, my darling! We need to be out of here in an hour if we plan to make Maysville for dinner."

"Who was that on the phone?"

"I just called flight service. We have weather moving into north Georgia. So it looks like we're going to be in the clouds on our flight back to your parents this morning. We will be heading straight across the Pamlico Sound and down through Fayetteville."

An hour later they had the airplane all packed up and Charlie was on the radio with Raleigh Flight Service Station getting their instrument clearance back to Jackson.
"All right, I got it that time. N234CD is cleared from the Billy Mitchell airport via standard instrument departure PUNGO, Victor 290 join Victor Seventy, Kinston, Victor Fifty-four RAEFO, Victor Two ninety-six, join Victor Sixty-six to Athens. Maintain four thousand and squawk four seven seven three."

Through the headset Carrie had just plugged in, she heard the specialist acknowledge Charlie's read back with a southern drawl, "Roger on the read back, N234CD, have a good flight."

With a gentle breeze blowing out of the east the Cirrus lifted off runway seven as they passed the auxiliary parking half way down the runway. Climbing quickly to two thousand feet, they made a left turn crossing over Kings Island. Charlie engaged the autopilot, which turned the aircraft a few degrees farther left to a heading of three-zero-five.

"Cherry Point, N234CD with you out of two thousand five hundred feet for four thousand."

"N234CD, Cherry Point roger, radar contact four miles northwest of Hatteras airport. Climb and maintain one four thousand, Cherry Point altimeter, two-niner-seven-two."

Carrie looked out over the sound at the numerous fishing boats slowly passing under the wing. She was drifting deep in thought over what had transpired these last four days. She cherished the time spent alone with the man she loved. She desperately desired for Charlie to retire so they could spend more time here. Over the last few years she had watched as her cheerful, easygoing husband had changed to one that was easily irritated and spent too much time in seclusion with that distant stare in his eyes. This vacation had shown that with love, compassion and time away from the workplace, the symptoms were reversible. There again was that glint in his eyes showing signs of ambition and excitement. *How much longer?* The thought kept coming across Carrie's mind. *Thirteen years until he is eligible for retirement. Will he stay any longer? By then Mitzy will be in college. What will things be like?*

"You say five hundred feet one mile?" Charlie was talking to the Atlanta Center controller who was describing the weather at Jackson County. "That's almost down to the minimums. Do you have any icing reports?"

"None reported yet," the controller responded. "I had a King Air go in there ten minutes ago. No problem."

Looking out the window, all Carrie could see below them were solid white fluffy clouds that stretched on for miles. She was not too concerned as she had flown with Charlie many times in these conditions. He always seemed to know what to do, and they eventually would find the airport.   Flying Dad's new airplane with all the latest navigational equipment was a piece of cake.

An hour later, Atlanta Approach Control cleared N234CD for the RNAV GPS runway three four approach to

Jackson County airport. Crossing over the town of Athens, Charlie descended to two thousand five hundred feet. At KEKTE intersection, the autopilot made a right turn to a 346-degree heading and Charlie applied 20 percent of flaps. As the speed was bleeding off, he watched intently for the JIRWI intersection to pass under them and the autopilot started them down to 1,233 feet. At about two thousand feet, rain started pelting the windscreen. Charlie looked at the wing for icing and was thankful to see nothing had accumulated yet. Five hundred feet above the ground, all they could see was solid gray-and-white fog rapidly slipping past the windscreen.

"Doesn't look good," was all Charlie could say as the remaining three miles seemed to take forever. Passing over the threshold, Charlie could just make out the runway below. Nothing he could do about it now. Applying power, he cleaned up the airplane and started the climb back up to thirty-three hundred feet direct to the missed approach fix MIJLO.

"Atlanta Approach, Cirrus Two Three Four Charlie Delta back with you on the missed approach."

"N234CD," Atlanta Approach responded, "say intentions."

Charlie looked out at the white fluffy clouds now slowly moving under the wings.
"What did you say the winds were at Jackson?" He asked the Atlanta controller.

"It looks like they are straight across the runway now zero-seven-zero at twelve knots."

Looking over the approach plates, Charlie noticed the runway one six GPS approach had a lower descent altitude.

"Approach, Cirrus Two Three Four Charlie Delta request Runway one six GPS approach to Jackson County, and we have the current weather."

"N234CD, we have your request, stand by."

Two minutes later, the Atlanta Controller cleared Charlie for the approach from the north, this time in hopes they would be able to see the runway a little sooner. One more turn in hold as Charlie finished reprogramming the autopilot and they were again heading towards the runway. The gradual decent took them back into the fluffy white clouds shortly after passing the KUKRE fix. Again the rain droplets pelted the aircraft, streaming across the windscreen reducing visibility. Wiping the fog off the side window, Charlie could see the glistening signs of ice collecting on the leading edge of the wing.

"This will be our last attempt," he told Carrie as they were now only two miles from the airport and only eight hundred feet above the ground. A mile from the runway, and almost at the missed approach point, Charlie was able to make out the precision approach path indicator lights as they came into view. Switching off the autopilot, Charlie took over and landed on a rain-soaked runway and taxied up to the hanger as Tommy sped up in the golf cart.

"I didn't think you'd make it, Mr. Beckler. I've been listening on the radio. We heard you go over and all. Never did see you on the first approach. Now don't worry about the airplane, I'll put it away. You need to get that young lady up to her mom's for dinner or we'll all be in trouble."

"Thanks, Tommy, you sure you don't mind?"

"Not at all! I have to stay here anyhow. It seems a lot of folks are flying in late because of this weather."

Throwing their bags in the car, Charlie and Carrie headed back to the farm and their little girl.

Thanksgiving ended up being picture perfect and Mitzy was excited to see her parents. Carrie's sister and her husband arrived just in time for dinner and the family enjoyed a time of reflection and thankfulness. They shared with each other the blessings they all enjoyed in this great land. Sunday morning came around way too soon, and they all said good-bye. The ride back to Hartsfield-Jackson Atlanta airport would have been silent except for Mitzy chattering in the backseat about all the fun she had at Grandma's house and how much fun Grandpa was. The trip home to California was shrouded in a cloud of discouragement as Charlie's thoughts were again turning towards the week ahead as he returned to work.

On Monday evening, Charlie showed up at the center for his 1600 shift just a few minutes early in order to get caught up on the latest information and rumors. Sure enough, as had become common lately, another operational error had happened at Sector 16. This one, a lot like the one Charlie had a couple of years ago, could have been avoided if the controller had taken a little more time to scan the airspace before descending the aircraft into Las Vegas. There had been twenty operational errors in less than two years in this narrow piece of airspace the controllers refer to as the funnel of death. It ran from Las Vegas northwest along Death Valley and was sandwiched between two restricted areas. Designed twenty-five years ago when Las Vegas was a small desert playground, the airspace had not grown with the now megaresort city. It had become a sector of heartburn and frustration. One-third of the controllers certified on this sector had fallen into the traps it offered. As Charlie plugged in to this godforsaken piece of airspace, he again asked, as many before, "What changes could make this a safe and orderly sector?"

Eight hours later, he signed out and headed home. The vacation was incredible, and the time with Carrie was unforgettable, but it was all too short. These were the times he wondered why he continued on with his career.

Chapter 5

Jim Gallagher had arrived at LA Center two years after Charlie. He had previously been a controller, stationed at NAS North Island and on the USS *Constellation*. Jim resigned from the navy after his enlistment was up and joined the FAA. Jim and Charlie soon became friends and enjoyed weekly rounds of golf at the local country club. During one of these rounds of golf Jim revealed to Charlie the details of his screwed up life. His marriage had ended when he caught his wife in an affair with his best friend. It had really messed him up and he swore never to get involved with another woman. This constant agony had become a detriment in his training, and finally, at Charlie's insistence, Jim met with a counselor, who helped him deal with the empty pain he felt deep inside.

It wasn't long before Jim had the confidence to start dating again. Carrie introduced him to her friend Sandy. Jim and Sandy hit it off from the start, sharing common backgrounds. Both were natives of western Kansas where they were raised by conservative parents on large ranches. While Jim had signed up for the navy to see the world, Sandy's military experience was to further her education and the air force did just that. It became very obvious they were meant for each other. As the two continued to build their relationship, Jim started having doubts. Even though he constantly yearned to be with Sandy, he had the fear of rejection and the "what ifs" that tend to follow a failed relationship. How could he be sure this one would not end in the same way?

Jim in all his stubborn nature decided he had to do something different. He had to find the answer. Maybe his golfing pal could help. After all, he seemed to have the perfect marriage. Jim always listened whenever Charlie told him about date nights with Carrie. It never really mattered to Charlie what play or movie they saw as long as Carrie loved it. Jim was trying to figure out how Charlie knew this was all that mattered.

While on break during work one day, Jim finally got up enough nerve to ask Charlie how he and Carrie were able to have such an incredible relationship.

Charlie sat there for a moment, looking into the setting sun for answers to such a question. He remembered back at the times in their marriage things were different. There was a time when they didn't have a good relationship. Even though they were husband and wife, they were not friends. After moving to California they had started sowing their wild oats. This lifestyle seemed to fit the stereotype of an air traffic controller. It wasn't long before Charlie would stay out late after work, drinking with his coworkers. On weekends, he would watch Mitzy while Carrie would go out partying with her friends. They had not seen the dangers of this action as all their friends were doing the same thing. It was this lifestyle that caused the couple to drift apart. During this time, Carrie had an affair, and even though she came to her senses and terminated the relationship, it was a long time before she had the courage to confess this indiscretion to Charlie.

Charlie slowly drew in his breath and with a sigh spent the next few minutes explaining how their marriage had transformed.

"It was only a couple of years ago that we almost called it quits," Charlie began, "then one day a neighbor invited us to church. We were both raised in Christian homes but had turned our back on God. We knew we were not living right, so it wasn't long before we found ourselves recommitting our lives to each other and to serving God. With the help of our pastor we learned to trust each other again. We took some marriage

41

classes and started spending time with people who were a positive influence on our marriage. It was through them that we learned how to treat each other."

Charlie paused for a moment. Jim looked somewhat agitated as if he wanted to tell Charlie where he could put this "God thing." Instead, he looked at his watch and jumped up to head back inside. Break time was over.

A few nights later, a cool evening breeze softly blew across the Beckler's back porch as the two couples vigorously consumed the steaks Charlie had so expertly grilled.

"I thought seriously about what you said," Jim spoke up.

"What do you mean?" Charlie replied.

"You shared how you had forgiven Carrie for the pain she had caused you. I decided if you two could go through what you have and forgive each other then there is hope that I also may be able to move on with my life. So now Sandy and I have decided we want the same thing."

"What you're saying is that you're getting married," Carrie interjected with a smile.

"You could say that. And we want you two to help us. You know that stuff about how to treat each other," Jim explained. "I really don't want this marriage to turn out like so many other controllers' marriages tend to do. I have seen so many broken marriages in our occupation, and I no longer want to be one of those statistics."

"You don't have to," Charlie softly whispered. "No, you don't have to."

Jim and Sandy got married the first Saturday in August at Table Mountain campground in the San Gabriel Mountains with Charlie and Carrie by their side. They moved into a cabin in the mountain town of Wrightwood. Moving into this small conservative village had been at Charlie's recommendation to help separate this newlywed couple from the lifestyle that so often destroyed marriages.

Chapter 6

Early afternoon, FAA Administrator Randy Culton was in the back of his chauffeured Lincoln Town Car as he rode down Independence Avenue slowly approaching the Capital building. He was deep in thought about the upcoming meeting with his vice presidents and heads of departments. Was it really possible for them to do all the things his predecessor had promised the flying public? Could they come through with the high-powered dream of artificial intelligence controlling the skies? Yes, he had been there in the meetings last year when the programmers and tech heads briefed the management team on the possibilities of current and future technology. He was not all that sure of the plans laid out, but he was willing to push forward. It had been a big surprise when the FAA administrator, his boss, had announced not only were they moving forward with the new systems, but that she would personally be holding a press conference the next week to introduce it to the public.

He could only wonder why. Why it was necessary to do it so soon?" He realized the necessity of moving forward, as air traffic had experienced phenomenal growth, and the controlling work force was struggling to keep up. *We could have just kept it to ourselves for a little longer just to make sure we could follow through. Oh well, cat's out of the bag now, not much we can do about it. And a big thanks to my predecessor for this headache being dropped in my lap.*

The car pulled into Mr. Colton's parking space at the FAA headquarters and he noticed the Chief Operating Officer Hank Voltz had already arrived.

This *will be interesting,* he thought. Hank was new to the FAA, coming in from United Airlines to help air traffic though this transition. Hank, being a common sense guy, would rip his VPs apart if they showed even a slight sign of weakness.

Stopping by his secretary's desk he was informed the others had arrived and were waiting patiently in the conference room. Silently cursing the traffic that had made him late, he walked into the ninth-floor conference room. Immediately the room went silent as he walked to the far end of the mahogany table and slowly lowered himself into the soft leather office chair that, for the last five years, had been occupied by the previous administrator.

"Good afternoon, ladies and gentlemen. I apologize for my tardiness. This traffic seems to get worse every day. Kind of makes a person miss Kansas." Looking around the room, Randy continued, "Well, I heard some rumors this week on software delays. I expect to be brought up to speed on where and why we are not making the deadlines. As you know, the aviation subcommittee will not tolerate any more delays. And don't count on any additional funds either. So let's get started, Bob tell us what you've got."

Bob Burkhammer had been the Air Traffic Organizations vice president leading up an ATO team working with the ITT corporation in developing the automatic dependent surveillance-broadcast system. The ADS-B system would be one of the first programs to be implemented into the NextGen system. Bob was feeling somewhat eminent from their accomplishments since the last meeting. Sitting forward in his chair, and with an air of satisfaction, he explained their achievements and expectations for the upcoming benchmarks.

"The Critical Design Review is complete and will be published in three weeks for your reading pleasure. We ran multiple testing in Alaska, and the system worked as designed. There are currently over two hundred aircraft equipped in the northwest for additional testing. All systems are go for deployment in the Gulf of Mexico next year. I can't foresee any problems from our end on the ADS-B program. About the software glitch, maybe Sean can answer that one."

Sean O'Leary was a wiry gentleman and very much Irish as his name. He was born in Northern Ireland and fell in love with America when he spent a year in Boston as an exchange student. He moved back to Boston three years later, where he received a doctorate in computer science. Sean joined the FAA as a software engineer and rapidly moved up the ranks; never satisfied with his present position and never liked being referred to as a geek.

Now shooting a nasty look back at Bob, he turned to the rest of the team and with a sigh explained. "There is some truth to the rumors you are hearing. We have had numerous glitches with this system. ERAMS, the en route automation modernization system, is giving us fits. We are continually running tests with Lockheed and come up with the same problem every time. It wants to just shut down after twenty minutes of run time. I really don't think the controllers will be thrilled with this reliability factor. Lockheed's tech heads are all over it and have yet to find the answer. I will keep you advised."

Randy Culton could just shake his head and moan. "You know we are under pressure to get the ERAMS out before the end of this year to keep our funding? Congress is really getting disturbed at the way this administration is operating. First the whining controllers, then the aircraft inspectors, and now running over budget and behind schedule on NextGen. It is my recommendation that you get your people off their duffs and find a solution soon. We will move forward with the system at Salt Lake in August. Understand?"

"Yes, sir!" was all Sean could say, feeling he had just been reprimanded for something he seemed to have little control over.

"What about data link communications?" Randy's next question was directed at Amy Blumstein head of communication development.

"We have been progressing on schedule. The people at Sunhillo have assured us they will be ready to run live tests as soon as we get the go ahead from the ADS-B program office."

Knowing what the next question would be Bob Burkhammer quickly spoke up. "That will be the end of March. May be sooner, but don't count on it. Some of our remote sites are on top of mountains, and the weather people don't always cooperate."

"Oh! So now you're blaming the weather people?" John Andrews, team leader for the National Weather Service, spoke up with a grin. "First you blame the software people, now my folks. Do your people walk on water or do they ever screw up?"

"Okay, guys!" Hank cut in. "We don't need to get into a pissing contest. Let's look at problems and setbacks as only challenges to overcome. We all need to work together as a team not only doing our job but also looking at ways of making other peoples' tasks easier. All of you have been through crew resource management training and know we need to look out for each other to keep even small mistakes from taking down a complete program."

The meeting went on through the late afternoon as all the team leaders had their opportunity to bring the executive team up-to-date on where they stood. Security was overly concerned at the number of foreign specialists involved in the software programming, which really brought out the Irish temper in Sean. He assured them they all had been cleared. Then crudely he explained that if security had a problem with his people they could quit sitting on their little squirt guns moaning and bring it to him. It was his department, and he could handle it. Again after being admonished by their leader, they all agreed to get along and move forward.

It was well past dinnertime when Randy was dropped off at his town house in Rosemary Hills. It had been one of those days he hated. It was full of controversy, so many differences in opinion. He knew he would never see the end of the NextGen program. He was very aware of the sentiment in Congress as to his confirmation. They would never give him the five years of a confirmed administrator. With the upcoming election he knew he would most likely be looking for work elsewhere.

So why even try? It had been his wife who had encouraged him to move forward and keep his resolve. She had reminded him of their last trip to Italy when they had visited the small town of Lucca. The village had a wall built around it ten meters high. The wall had taken one hundred years to complete.

"This is why you go on," she had explained. "The stone masons who laid the first stones knew they would never walk along the top of the completed wall, but they started it anyway. They knew that someday a need would come for that wall to protect the villagers. You know that someday, the time will come when NextGen will be complete, and it too will be needed."

This gave Randy some sense of significance. "Well maybe, just maybe, I can somehow stay involved in the program. I just want to live long enough to at least see it come to pass when air traffic will be automated and no longer under the limited capacity of human controllers."

Chapter 7

It was a cold blustery January winter morning as Sean O'Leary boarded the train for Atlantic City. He was not overly thrilled at the idea of confronting his software development team on the setbacks to ERAMS. He had his doubts about Lockheed's ability to fix the problem. He had ordered his engineers to research all possibilities in fixing this Achilles' heel. Now being under the gun from Washington, for what seemed like an incompetent workforce, he knew it would be a tiring day. Arriving at the William J. Hughes Technical Center just before ten, he was told his team had assembled in the conference room awaiting his arrival. Sean stopped by the washroom, taking a couple of minutes to gain his composure for what he expected would be a battle. Stepping into the conference room, he was surprised nobody even noticed. They were all gathered around a computer screen. In front of the computer was a middle-aged man speaking in broken English. Sean ran through his mental data bank trying to recall this guy, but came up blank. Shrugging his shoulders, he just assumed he was from Lockheed.

Finally Scotty looked up, "Greetings, Boss. Have a good trip this morning?"

"Good as a train trip in the winter can be," Sean replied taking a seat at his end of the conference table. "What have you got that can make me happy?"

As the rest of the team took their seats, Scotty introduced the stranger. "Sean, this here is Abdur Rahman. Mr.

48

Rahman is a freelance software engineer and a graduate of MIT. Barney Williams from Los Angeles Center put him into contact with us, thinking he may be able to help. Abdur, this is my boss who I have been telling you about, Sean O'Leary."

Formal greetings accomplished, Sean got right to the point. "Scotty, I need to speak to you alone before we get started. The rest of you take a break and be back in here in ten minutes."

Looking around as the door shut behind him, Sean turned back to Scotty with a very disturbed and intense look. "What about security, Scotty? This guy looks more like a terrorist then a geek. What kind of clearance does he have?"

Scotty had known Sean for over ten years and had never seen him so perturbed. "Relax Sean! First, he came with a recommendation from Barney, who said he had a security clearance, then we had the FBI check him out and he came back clean. He says he has the answers to our ERAMS problem. I have seen his analysis and agree with him, as I'm sure you will also." Letting out a long sigh, Sean leaned back in his chair. "Okay! But this had better work. You know the stress this whole program is under. The last thing I need is a terrorist blowing up the whole place."

Scotty grinned at his old friend and added, "Anyhow, you need to quit stereotyping."

Ten minutes later, they were intently listening as Abdur presented his case to the group. "Gentlemen, as I have already explained to Mr. Morris, I have done my homework. When I first heard about the software glitch in the ERAMS program from my friend Mr. Williams, I contacted Lockheed to offer my services. They did confess to the fact that there is a problem, but they were not interested in my input. After going through the proper protocol, I was able to obtain the test results and found a common denominator. That is when I contacted Barney, who directed me to this office. I know you may be concerned as I am not attached to a major corporation, but let me assure you, I can fix your problem."

Sean, now showing some sort of curiosity asked the question, "What is the common denominator? Is it fairly obvious?"

Slowly looking around at the group of engineers and managers, Abdur locked unto Sean with an intense stare and spoke softly. "Yes, the problem is simple, but the solution is complex. As you are well aware, not all of the centers are going online at the same time. This would be impossible to accomplish considering the vast amount of training required. ERAMS under its current configuration will not communicate properly with non-ERAMS centers. I have located the code where this is happening and have already taken the liberty to write a patch that will fool ERAMS into thinking the adjacent centers have been upgraded."

"So you're ready to go with it now?" Sean was now sitting up in his chair.

"Not yet," Abdur continued, "I still have a lot of work to do, and there is the subject of a contract. I am only a small company and need to make a living also. So if you desire my help in providing the solution to this two-billion-dollar headache I am willing to start negotiations on a contract. If you just think I am full of hot air then no problem. I will be on my way."

"Just wait a minute," Sean snapped back. He was getting just a little irritated with this somewhat-arrogant geek. "What size of contract we talking about? We are already under the microscope and no one wants to ask Congress for more. Anyway, what guarantee do we have that you have the answer?"

"I expected this would come up," Abdur replied. "I understand the concern and lack of faith. My proposal is very unique to your government. I am asking for one million U.S. dollars only to be paid if contract is fulfilled and I solve your problem and bring ERAMS up to operational standards. Considering what you have already spent, this should be a reasonable amount."

The room fell silent, as every one of the FAA employees knew this could not pass the General Accounting Office even if the administrator was willing. Now what! Sean pushed back his chair and stood up. Looking around the room all he saw was a group of empty stares.

Looking back at Abdur, he smiled, "Mr. Rahman, thank you for your time. I am intrigued by your conviction. I regret that my own employees lack the same zeal. Under most circumstances, I would have you escorted out of the building, but we have a problem. In the last six months, neither Lockheed nor our technicians have been able to come up with the answer. Give me one week to secure the funds. Once funds have been secured, our legal department will complete the contract. I have only two stipulations. First, upon signing of the contract, you are required to reveal to this team a synopsis of the solution. Second, I am only willing to give you thirty days from that meeting to have it ready for live testing."

"Fair enough," Abdur said as he stood up, picked up his briefcase, and walked out of the room now filled with stunned software engineers.

"Why would you fold to these unrealistic demands?" Scotty was furious. "He doesn't deserve that kind of compensation. Not for only a month's work. Who does he think he is?"

Sean was now fairly perturbed at the incompetent geeks which criticized the person that had the solution to their challenge, the challenge they were incapable of discovering. Sean looked around the room, taking in the look of disgust on the faces of these unmotivated government employees.

"Each one of you had your chance to make a difference with this program. Nothing was in the road to stop you. Now that time is just about to expire. You have two weeks before the contract is signed. During that time, if you can bring me the solution, it will save us a million dollars, and a bonus will be in your future. After the contract, which in my honest opinion will save the agency millions, is signed, you guys will work hand in hand with Abdur, giving him all the information he needs. Any lack of cooperation will be dealt with appropriately. Scotty, take me back to the train station, we have some things to discuss."

On the way to the train station, Sean admonished Scotty on his attitude towards such a big contract to an individual freelance contractor. "Why are you so worried?" he asked. "If the man can't fix it, no big deal. He doesn't get paid. If he does, then it will be worth it. Think about all the man hours already put into this piece of garbage."

"In all honesty, sir," Scotty shot back, "it is not a piece of garbage. It just has some problems."

"Yes, and they're problems neither your people nor Lockheed can find. So if that holds true, in two weeks we should know why and the logic of a solution."

"I still don't like the idea," Scotty mumbled as they pulled into the station.

"You don't have to. Neither do I, but I don't think we have any other option other than turning in our resignation. Is that something you are ready to consider?"

"Guess you're right. In six weeks we will be either heroes or zeros. Good luck!"

"Another thing," Sean said looking over at Scotty as he exited the car. "No one, I mean no one, is to hear about this contract. It is to be kept confidential. I am sure you're aware of this, and make sure the rest are too. If we're really lucky, one of your geeks will find the answer this week."

"Understood. Have a safe trip, Boss," Scotty answered.

Sean boarded the 12:20 train for the return trip to Washington. After changing trains in Philadelphia he settled down in his seat for the two-hour trip back to the nation's capital. It wasn't long before the sound of the clicking rails caused Sean's mind to drift to his childhood when as a ten-year-old lad, he used to travel with his mother to Waterford from Dublin. Papa never seemed to be available for these trips. His occupation as a fisherman would keep him away from home for days at a time, and when he was home, he drank a lot. Sean had always looked forward to visiting his grandparents. They would take the taxi from the train station up to the large, seven-bedroom home built around 1870 by a wealthy merchant. Grandpa had bought this home as a wedding present for his grandmother forty-five years earlier, and together they had turned it into an immaculate estate. In Sean's eyes, Grandpa was rich. He had hired on at the Bank of Ireland at the age of eighteen as a mail clerk and worked his way up through the ranks, and at the age of thirty-four became the bank manager.

As the taxi would pull through the big black iron gates and up the cobble stone drive, Sean's face would be glued to the window for the first glimpse of his *seanathair*. The purple, white, and red mums along the drive would smile back at him before the car would come to a stop in front of the walkway leading up to the large front door. The fragrance of lilacs filled the air as he jumped out of the car and into the arms of Grandpa. Sean recalled how he and Grandpa would take his suitcase up the big wooden staircase to his bedroom at the end of the hall. How much he wished he could again spend time with the man who not only gave him the dream of coming to America to go to school, but also financed his college education here in the states.

The big house now sat empty. Sean's grandpa had passed away while he was studying in Boston. Grandma, heartbroken, had followed her husband of sixty years only a few months later. In their will, they had left the home to their only grandchild, and Sean had no idea what to do with it. His mind drifted to the times his grandma had run him out of the parlor. The parlor was the most immaculate room in the house.

Grandma always kept the double doors shut, but he would sneak in just to see what was in this room that nobody used. Its rich maroon walls gave sharp contrast to the glossy white trim. The big brick fireplace with its dark oak mantel never had seen a fire as far as Sean knew. A large tapestry rug covered the middle of the hardwood floor. Only four wing backed chairs occupied the room along with a small table and two lamps. It had a smell of pipe tobacco even though he had never seen his granddad smoke in the parlor.

After losing his grandparents and graduating college, Sean broke his parents' hearts by not returning to Ireland. The plans they had for his life were not his. How time flies. That was over twenty years ago. He had only been back to his homeland once since then, and that was to bury his dad.

Now as the train sped down the East Coast of America, Sean wondered what it would have been like had he returned to his homeland and lived the life of the Irish. He may have even married his childhood sweetheart and had a family. Possibly would have gone to the same church where his parents had attended mass before his father had passed away five years ago. His mother still wrote him every couple of weeks, and now and then he returned the favor. Did he miss his homeland? Sure! But what did it have to offer? He had become so busy with his career here in the states and had moved up the ladder so rapidly he had no time for a personal life. Now living on the outskirts of Washington DC among so many people, he still felt alone. Maybe someday he could retire and move back to the land of his ancestors.

Chapter 8

It had been two weeks since Abdur had met with the ERAMS software team in Atlantic City. Even before Scotty had notified him of the approval of his contact, Abdur had already started finalizing the software patch for testing. He knew the FAA had no other choice. The agency had already spent millions of dollars on worthless patches. This, thought Abdur, was his ticket to success. Not only was it going to give him the capital he needed to get his company off the ground, it would also give him the recognition necessary to land other big projects.

It was Friday morning when a courier arrived with a package having a return address of 800 Independence Avenue. Trying to hold back his excitement, Abdur ripped open the envelope and pulled out a twenty-page document, which laid out all the stipulations of the agreement he had discussed with Mr. O'Leary. Leafing through the first couple of pages, it finally caught his eye. There on page three, halfway down, it stated, "Compensation for the completion of the contract to satisfaction of the FAA will be in the amount of $1,000,000.00."

"Wow!" was all that Abdur could say. His mother would be so proud of such an agreement. Looking at this number caused a tinge of doubt to creep into his mind. *What if I am wrong? What if this doesn't work as I expect? I could lose everything I have worked for, especially my reputation.*

He knew what he needed to do next. He would not let any of his family know what was going on until it was complete. He would call upon a couple of his old friends, ones he could trust to help him finalize and test the program. It was noon before Abdur was able to reach his old college friends and fellow countrymen. Late Friday afternoon, both Samir and Khurram arrived at Abdur's small uptown Manhattan apartment. After swearing both of them to secrecy, Abdur showed the men the contract. He could see by the expression in their faces when they read the million-dollar figure they were absolutely speechless.

Khurram was the first to speak, "Can it be done?" Samir, who had spent many years in software development, was quick to respond, "It can be done. I have no doubt. What I am concerned about is the time. Can we get it done soon enough?"

Over the next two hours Abdur briefed his friends on the status of the program. He explained how he had been working on this for over three months.

"It wasn't until just three weeks ago I found the common denominator that led me to the problem with this extensive software. Working day and night, I developed a patch that would override the demand ERAMS software puts on the system. Now, my brothers, I want you to assist in the finishing touches and travel with me down to Atlantic City for the testing. We have one week to present this to the FAA's software development team. It is my desire to have a beta test ready for demonstration immediately following the meeting."

Scratching his short, straggly beard while deep in thought, Khurram finally responded. "I will clear up my calendar for three weeks, but it will cost you."

"I knew that was coming, my brother." Abdur laughed. "Never miss a chance to make an easy dollar. Fifty-thousand dollars for three weeks' work for you?"

"I'm in!" Samir quickly chimed in.

"Well, that makes two of us." Khurram responded. "When do we start?"

Standing up Abdur walked over to his friends, kissed them on the cheek, and whispered, "Right now, yes, right now."

Abdur and his team worked day and night for the next week putting the finishing touches on what seemed like an endless process. Each time they completed a task, another challenge would come up. On Thursday morning, just twenty-four hours before they were to be in Atlantic City, the analysis came back without any errors. Even while they were congratulating each other with high fives, they knew the real test was still ahead. How would it work when mated to the master ERAMS program? This question would be answered soon enough. It was time to get their presentation ready for the meeting of a lifetime.

Abdur couldn't sleep that night. The excitement of the next day would not let him rest. He had worked so hard for this dream, and now it was so close to reality. Now he could help his family move to the United States, as had been their desire for so many years. Finally they would be out from under the fear of terrorism. It was well past midnight when Abdur finally drifted off to sleep with questions of the future still occupying his thoughts.

Entering the conference room Friday morning Abdur and his team were surprised to see the long table completely surrounded by distinguished-looking individuals. He immediately recognized Sean O'Leary from their previous meeting. Sean arose and offered Abdur a seat next to his as he introduced him to the rest of the people seated at the table.

"Abdur, this is Hank Voltz, he is our COO, next to him my boss and the FAA administrator, Randy Culton."

Abdur's mind became a blur as Sean continued around the room. *These are not just software engineers,* he thought, *they are executives heading up the Federal Aviation Administration.*

Beads of sweat started to form on Abdur's forehead as he realized the seriousness of what he was about to show such a group of men and women.

It did not take long before a technician had the presentation up on the overhead screen. Abdur stood up and addressed the room.

"Ladies and Gentlemen, it is very obvious that you are intrigued by what we have to show you. I am humbled by your presence as we were expecting only to be presenting this to the program leads. Administrator Culton and COO Voltz, we are honored to have you here for this presentation. I pray that you will not be disappointed. First, let's review the background to the challenge. After the completion of ERAMS, it was brought here for testing. Everything worked out as expected. You had a couple of bugs that were quickly fixed, and it was sent on to Salt Lake for live testing.

"Once installed at Salt Lake, the program would run for twenty minutes and shut down. This, as you know, is the challenge we were presented with. Just before I contacted you, I read in the news that ERAMS had been pushed back three months. Now the media has been led to believe it is hardware installation delays not the software challenges we know previously existed. I say previously because, as of today, we have the fix you have all been so patiently waiting on. It is my understanding that all the adjacent centers have completed the installation of the ERAMS hardware. Is that correct?"

Acknowledging the nods around the room Abdur continued.

"I will not bore you with software language in describing what we have accomplished. I am sure you will comprehend the way we reached this goal. First of all, the software, as written by the ERAMS contractor, has absolutely nothing wrong with it other than the failed ability to communicate with the outdated HOST computers located at the other facilities. Therefore, all we will be changing in the ERAMS software is the removal of the communication patch. What we have done is build a new program that will be installed at all the other centers. This program will allow the local ERAMS program to communicate with the HOST computer until ERAMS is brought online."

"Novel concept," Hank spoke up, "but how do you know it will work?"

"That will be determined when we test it." Abdur replied. He was starting to feel his oats and knew the moment of truth was rapidly approaching. "We have brought the program with us and will be installing it in the Tech center's ERAMS lab as soon as this meeting is over."

"But the other test worked here and not at the facility," Mr. Culton interjected. "Why is this different?"

"Your other test was completed using a program designed to work with the operating ERAMS. This one works at a facility which has installed the hardware but is still using HOST. By bringing ERAMS online in Salt Lake with the Tech center as an adjacent facility, we will be able to test the communication process to the old HOST computers you have here."

By now Sean was sitting back with his hands grasping the back of head. He could just tell this Abdur guy knew what he was talking about. Why hadn't his people figured this out? There would not be any bonus money this year for the software team, you could count on that. He only had one lingering question before they moved on to the lab.

"Why did the program shut down consistently after twenty minutes?" He asked.

Abdur slowly paced back and forth what seemed like forever then spoke gently, "It seems that someone back in the original software design installed a safety switch. This switch looked at all kinds of perimeters to determine if there was a breach in security. When the adjacent facilities failed to respond properly to ERAMS, this safety switch activated. It was never discovered due to the nature of the test runs and the ability it had to reset when the system shut down. This is a hindrance to the program and you really should consider removing the switch."

Leaning on the back of his chair, he looked around the room at the men and women still in a state of disgust and shock. "The lab is ready for the demonstration. Shall we proceed?"

The demonstration went off without a hitch and the ecstatic team was on the five o'clock train back to New York rehashing the day's events. The work that lay ahead was complicated but doable. Security had required the team put an ironclad firewall into the program to resist any form of virus that may make its way into the software. The team was still busy hashing through the security process when the train rolled into Penn station. They stopped by Keen's Steakhouse for dinner and to celebrate the program's success. It was after midnight when Abdur finally arrived at his apartment. Exhausted, he flopped on his bed and immediately went to sleep.

Chapter 9

Abdur awoke to the sound of someone knocking on his door. Rolling out of bed, he looked at his watch. 1:00 p.m.! He had never slept this long. Must have been the long hard week he had just been through.

"I'm coming!" he hollered as he pulled on his pants and grabbed a shirt.

A courier greeted him as he opened the door.

"Mr. Abdur Rahman?" the courier asked as he handed him a package.

"Yeah! What you have here?" he responded.

"Don't know, I'm just the delivery boy." The courier smiled, tipped his hat, and headed back down the stairs.

Abdur had just shut the door when the package started ringing. *It sure sounds like a phone*, thought Abdur as he ripped open the package pulling out a thin line cell phone.

Opening up the phone he heard a distinctive Arabic male voice, "Hello Abdur! How is your day so far?"

"Who is this?" Abdur asked cautiously.

"It doesn't matter who I am. All you need to know is that we know who you are, and we know what you are doing." The voice continued, "We need your help, Abdur. Our organization has been badly damaged by the war the infidels have been waging against Almighty Allah."

"I no longer subscribe to terror," Abdur explained, not wanting to get involved.

"We are not asking you to. We are demanding you assist us in this great jihad against the infidels."

"How do you plan on that? If you know what I'm doing you know the security we are under."

"That's right, my brother. And they are watching you closely. Look out your window. See the blue sedan north of the intersection? They are following you. Everywhere you go, they are watching. They are listening to your phone. That is why we sent you this cell phone."

"Why would I help you? What is it you want me to do?"

"You will help by installing a program in the security section of the ERAMS software."

"What? No, I will do nothing to degrade ERAMS. They have trusted me, and I will not be bought. I am now a citizen of this country and will do my best to be a good one, at that!"

"Oh, my brother, you just don't get it. We have soldiers everywhere fighting for the cause of Allah and you want to be a hero. Did I tell you how beautiful your mother is? And did I explain how I know when your father goes to work, and how easy it would be for an accident to happen in the oil fields where he works? How lonely your mother is when your father is away, and what could happen to someone all alone in the house? You know the neighbors are a long way away and would never hear the screams."

Trying to sound strong yet knowing the dangers of these radical individuals, Abdur tried to disregard the stranger's threats.

"How do I know you're for real? Anyone could have come up with this information."

"Abdur, as a child you used to wake up at night crying, and your mother would come into your room and sing lullabies to you. Your favorite was "Doha ya Doha." Does that ring a bell? No one would know that but your lovely mother. Are you convinced?"

"You beast!" Abdur screamed. "If you lay a finger on them I will hunt you down and kill you myself!"

"That is not necessary, my friend. All you have to do is follow our instructions. No one will know. You will still get the credit for solving the infidels' problems and someday my organization will get the credit for airplanes falling out of the sky."

Now the soft voice deepened to a point Abdur could hardly hear.

"There is a CD in the box with the phone. Place it in your computer and follow the instructions. Good-bye, my brother, and praise be to Allah."

With shaky hands Abdur dug deeper into the box. Finding the CD, he slid it into his computer. It didn't take long before a video of the planes flying into the World Trade Center came into focus. Under the video was a caption reading, "Tip of the Iceberg."

"Tip of the Iceberg?" Abdur asked himself as he clicked on the icon moving the presentation to a well-designed menu. *Someone sure took a lot of time to put this together. Doesn't look like a fly-by-night operation.*

With a little half-hearted chuckle, he added, "No pun intended."

Following the instructions, the presentation took him through the process of installing the virus into ERAMS system. It explained in great detail how it would never show up as a virus or even be connected to Abdur's work.

At the end of the presentation was a video clip of someone Abdur had never seen, but the surroundings were very familiar. It was the backyard where he had grown up, where his aging parents still lived.

"Abdur, we know you are now a citizen of another country and it is your desire to be a good citizen in your new home. We also know where your roots are and where home really is. We have decided that if you follow through with this mission, we will give you the same amount the despicable infidels are giving you. That my friend, will double your money, and we will leave you and your family alone forever."

Abdur was just about to shut down the video when another clip started. This time it was his parents sitting at their worn kitchen table laughing with the narrator.

Turning to the camera, his father spoke, "Son, we have been told about your great work in America. We are so proud of you. Come home and visit us soon, son. We do greatly miss you. Do what this man asks of you. He is very wise."

At these words, his mother seemed to grimace and started to say something when the screen went blank. Abdur knew his mother disapproved, but because women of their culture were not allowed to speak their mind, she was quickly cut off.

After Abdur shut down the video, a window popped up with the following message. "Be at the corner of 32nd and Wall Street on Valentine's Day at 11 p.m. sharp for the first installment of $250,000.00 and further instructions. There will be a crate covered with an old blanket. Pick up the crate and blanket and walk away. Do not look in it or open the package until you're safely at home. Remember they are watching you, so use every caution to evade the snoops. Also, because you have yet to receive the funds from the FAA on your contract, do not spend the money other than small amounts for essential needs. Overindulgence will get their attention, which neither of us desires. We will be watching for confirmation that the program is installed. You may be asking how. A reporting mechanism has been placed in the program. Don't try looking for it. You will never be able to find it, even as intelligent as you are. Thanks again, my brother, and praise be to Allah." With that the presentation ended and the screen faded to black.

The next morning before Khurram and Samir arrived, Abdur transferred the Trojan horse over to his thumb drive just as he had been instructed, then he destroyed the CD. Now the only trace was in the miniature storage device he wore around his neck. The following week, they would be traveling to Los Angeles, Denver, and Oakland to install their new program, and unbeknown to the others, the Trojan horse. It took the team only three days to write and test the security software.

"Welcome to Los Angeles Center," Barney greeted Abdur as the software team arrived in the Palmdale, California air traffic control facility. "At the chief's request, I am to be your host during your stay. So whatever you need I am your man."

Abdur looked over at Barney with confidence and determination.

"Barney, all we need from you is to escort us to the Host computer room and then go get us a cup of coffee. We will be done by noon, and then you can buy us lunch."

Frowning, Barney looked like a puppy that had just been whipped. "Okay, but the chief won't be happy if I don't stay with you."

"So the chief is concerned about the three software engineers who saved the ERAMS program? What are we going to do, sabotage it? I guess if it is a problem I can call Mr. Culton. I'm sure your chief would love to explain to him why she doesn't trust us."

"No! That's okay! You want cream or sugar?"

It didn't take long before the team, each at separate terminals, rapidly installed the interim program. Khurram installed the basic program and Samir the security program. Abdur had hooked up his laptop to the mainframe and monitored the progress. As with the other facilities, as soon as Samir was finished with the security software, Abdur pulled the thumb drive out of his pocket slid it into the USB port and watched the flickering as line after line of the Trojan horse transferred into the security program.

Looking over at Barney sitting there reading an aviation magazine, he wondered why the FAA would retain such an incompetent employee. He didn't seem to do anything constructive, but he sure did a lot of talking. Abdur had first met Barney in a bar in Atlantic City when he had overheard Barney spilling the beans about the ERAMS problem. As a software engineer, he had made it a point to eavesdrop on the conversation. Later that night, he introduced himself to the FAA manager, and they spent the next two hours discussing what Barney knew about the air traffic control system and ERAMS in general.

Two days later, Abdur had met with Barney at the FAA tech center and had gone through the complete ERAMS documentation. It was there that Abdur realized how moronic Barney really was, but he also knew that he could use this contact to fulfill his dream. They had spent a couple of days together, and, finally, Abdur had convinced Barney to give him access to the software. It took a few days for Barney to get the approval to gain access. Finally it arrived at Abdur's apartment.

It didn't take long going line by line through the program to find the security switch. It had been a burst of energy finding the reason for the shutdown.

His next problem was to locate what caused the switch to activate. Following the shutdown switch, he found the communication break in a very obscure location. All he could do was to stare in disbelief at the layout of the whole program. Why would someone try to hide this function? Was it by accident, or was it just a screwup by someone not taking pride in his or her work? Abdur knew he had discovered a gold mine and immediately went to work on solving the problem and contacting the FAA. His old motor-mouth friend, Barney, had made the contacts and set up the meeting with the ERAMS program office. "I guess he was good for something," Abdur said to himself as a soft beep sounded, signaling the end of the Trojan horse transfer.

An hour after their arrival, the team packed up their equipment and headed out the door.

"You're done already?" Barney asked as he put down the magazine he was reading. "That sure was quick. You sure made a lot of money for no more work than you do."

Barney was starting to irritate Abdur, who wanted to just slit Barney's throat and let him choke in his own blood.

A man in his mid-thirties with sandy-brown hair and wearing dark sunglasses opened the door.

"Howdy, Barney, get any work done today? Or was this a normal day?"

"Shut up, Charlie. You know that's not how to treat managers," Barney shot back.

"You're right, that's not how to treat managers. I will remember that if I find one. Who are your friends?" Charlie asked, turning to the software team.

"These are the guys who fixed the ERAMS program. They happen to be the best software programmers in the country," Barney answered, kissing up to Abdur and his team.

"Good to meet you, gentlemen. Thanks for the great work you've done. It is always appreciated to see someone doing something good in the administration these days. It doesn't happen too often."

Barney was still grumbling about controllers and their total lack of respect when he dropped the team off at the airport after lunch.

Chapter 10

A fault line was running right down the middle of the air traffic control workforce at Los Angeles Center. The union had recently settled an agreement with the agency on the facility's upgrade. Now the older controllers were finally getting their just reward for the years of working higher-level traffic. The problem was with the younger controllers who had entered the FAA under the old contract and then were taken by the agency with the implementation of the imposed work rules. The young controllers, some of whom had come from the military and others from low-level towers, were losing their patience, feeling that their cause had been overlooked by the union they belonged to. This played into the agency's hands in destroying unity within the workforce.

Training for ERAMS had been pushed back again-this time due to the lack of controllers to keep the sectors open during training. Eventually Salt Lake finished up their training, and, to everyone's surprise, it actually worked. ERAMS up and working laid the foundation for the remainder of NextGen to fall into place. Numbers of employees had been dropping off, and there was a retirement party just about every weekend. Charlie had moved from the mid-teens to third in seniority. *How much longer can I tolerate this stuff?* he would question on the way to work, which consisted of six days a week again. It was on one of these overtime days that he heard the moan.

It had started out as an ordinary Thursday day shift. Traffic had continued to build at the high-altitude sector

68

northeast of Las Vegas. Charlie had been on position for over ninety minutes and started his ritual of complaining to the controller sitting next to him about the lack of quality supervision. The screen showed they had thirty-eight aircraft coming at them over the next thirty minutes, and he really wasn't thrilled about working another rush before his shift ended. It was a United pilot who first heard the sound. "Center, did you hear that moan?"

"Moan? Negative, United 22! Let me know if you hear it again."

"Roger, Center, we just heard it again."

Charlie turned to his assistant, "Didn't think I was keyed up." That was when they heard it. It sounded like someone in pain letting out a drawn out moan. "Heard it that time, United 22. Sounds like someone in distress."

"Affirmative, Center! We've been picking it up for about ten minutes."

By the time the supervisor got over to them they had heard it a few more times. Charlie's brain was racing for a solution to this weird phenomenon. How could he communicate with this moaner? Was it a downed aircraft? Was it an airborne incapacitated pilot that needed assistance? You never knew what you were going to get when an emergency happened.

"Individual moaning! This is Los Angeles Center. If you need assistance let out two consecutive sounds." It was silent for what seemed like forever, then loud and clear over the airwaves they heard two distinctive moans. It was as if the individual had gathered up all their strength for this request.

Charlie jumped into action. "Is anyone working a C-130? I need them to head towards our airspace. Next, get Langley on the line, we need the Civil Air Patrol airborne now. We're pretty sure we have a downed aircraft and CAP may be able to help. Ted! We need to close this sector. Look at the possibilities of either getting me a different frequency or moving this one to Sector 33."

"Why's that?" was all Ted could ask.

"You idiot!" Charlie burst back. "Don't you get it? If I can't get this individual to switch to emergency frequency, then we have no other choice but isolate this one."

"Stop the name calling," Ted admonished. "Why do you need to isolate the frequency?"

Oh, how Charlie wished they made all controllers be pilots. It would be so much easier. "Individual in distress, if you are able, turn your radio to 121.5 the Emergency Frequency."

They heard another moaning sound, this time lighter than the rest.

"Individual in distress, if able push your ident button on the transponder." Charlie thought just maybe the aircraft was either airborne or in a place that radar may pick it up.

All three of the controllers scanned the scope hoping to see the three dash marks representing an aircraft's response. *Nothing! Darn! Hoped maybe that would work.*

"It's going to take a couple of minutes, but we're moving you down to Sector 5."

Ted the supervisor was back behind them. "Charlie, when you move it down, put everybody on 118.02. You will stay here and work the emergency."

"That's fine with me, but where is my C-130?"

"Just thirty miles south of Las Vegas, north bound," his assistant, the D-side answered. "I'm all over it. I just got a call from Salt Lake. Seems they have a CAP aircraft working up in their airspace. They have turned south now to join the search."

Charlie handed off all his aircraft to Sector 5 and waited for the C-130 to arrive. "Individual in distress, we have isolated this frequency and have help on the way. I would like for you to save your energy and wait for us to call you. At that time, we will need you to transmit so as to locate your position." He heard a soft moan as if the statement gave the distressed person a small glimmer of hope.

"Los Angeles Center, Zapper One One checking on at flight level two-four-zero."

"Welcome aboard, Zapper One One. I gather you've been informed of our situation?"

"Affirmative, Center, we've had the directional finder toned to your frequency for the last ten minutes and would like to take up a heading of zero-five-zero if you don't mind."

"The sky is yours, Zapper one-one. Let me know when you want lower. It is available anytime."

"Charlie, Sector 7 called. They just got the handoff on CAP437," his D-side interrupted, "and they want to know what you would like them to do."

"Have them come up on this frequency. It will make it easier. Also make sure they continue to monitor the aircraft; we don't want anyone to get in the way. Let them know Zapper will be descending once he gets closer to the location of the transmission."

"LA Center, CAP437 checking on VFR at nine thousand five hundred on a heading of one-three-zero."

"Roger, CAP437, you are radar contact. Have you got a hit on any of the transmissions?"

"Affirmative, Center, a couple then it went dead. We are heading in that direction now."

Charlie did the triangulation, and it looked like the C-130 Hercules would be the first to arrive.

"Individual in distress, the search aircraft are in the area and will be there shortly. Start transmitting now." It took a couple of seconds before they heard the now-familiar moan.

"Zapper One One, pilot's discretion descend and maintain one three thousand. That will be as low as I can get you IFR. If you want to go lower you will have to cancel."

"Roger, Center! Descending to one three thousand and we will cancel out of eighteen. How far out do you estimate the target?"

"Looks like seven minutes, Zapper! You're right at twenty-eight miles, according to our estimate."

It was the Civil Air Patrol that spoke up next. "Center, what's our ETA over the target?"

"CAP437, you are still fifteen minutes out on your present heading."

"Roger, Center, how low can we go and still keep in radar contact?"

"Can't go any lower or I will lose you," Charlie responded.

"Roger, Center. We will wait until we get closer to start down. We would like to get down to one thousand AGL as soon as possible."

"Copy that, CAP437. Report the Hercules in sight. He is currently at two-o'clock and fifty miles. I'll call it once you get closer." Charlie heard the double click of the mic indicating the Cessna 182 acknowledged his transmission.

"Zapper One One is out of eighteen, canceling IFR."

"Roger, Zapper One One, maintain your present squawk. I show you fifteen miles from target."

"Roger, Center, where's the CAP flight?"

"Your traffic is at ten o'clock and two-zero miles nine thousand five hundred. He will be descending once he has you in sight, Zapper One One."

"Thanks, Center, we will be descending to two thousand AGL so as not to create any additional emergencies."

In between transmissions they could still hear the moaning, and the Zapper pilot could definitely hear it getting louder. Crossing over the estimated target point, they still could not see any downed aircraft. They circled back around and by that time the CAP flight was only ten miles out.

"Zapper One One, this is CAP437. I have you in sight. Start another run and I will call you over the target."

"Roger, CAP437, we are on line now. Tell us when we get there."

Thirty seconds later, the CAP437 pilot advised the Hercules he was over the target and a lat/long was established. Starting a grid work the two aircraft worked back and forth for the next fifteen minutes before they spotted the little red and white aircraft in a valley that faced northwest towards Cedar City.

"Center, Zapper One One, we have the target in sight. It's a downed red and white aircraft. Looks like the wings are really messed up, but the fuselage is still intact."

"Roger, Zapper One One, we have a rescue chopper on their way out there. They will be there in fifteen minutes."

"Center, CAP437 is close on fuel, we need to head for Cedar City."

"Roger, CAP437, thanks for your help. Zapper One One, how is your fuel?"

"Not a problem, center. We have five hours of fuel. We will be happy to stick around until help arrives." Circling overhead, the C-130 crew watched as the rescue helicopter arrived, slowly flying up the valley to the crash site, and lowered the rescuers to the aircraft. They continued to watch as one by one the winch lifted three people from the downed aircraft. After the last of the rescuers returned to the chopper, it turned around and headed back down the valley, leaving a twisted pile of metal lying there as witness to either a lack of good judgment by the pilot or a mechanical malfunction. This would be determined sometime in the future by the National Transportation Safety Board, the NTSB. For now, thanks to the crew of the C-130, the Civil Air Patrol, a United Airlines pilot, and a couple of controllers, the three people on that downed aircraft were given another chance.

Charlie opened up Sector 32 and brought the sector back to normal operations. He quickly briefed his relief and put his headset away. Hands still shaking and his head pounding, he walked up to the Operation Manager's desk knowing that a statement needed to be filled out before he could go home.

Chapter 11

The deadline for all IFR aircraft to be equipped with ADS-B had just passed as the controllers started arriving at WCATS (Western Center for Air Traffic Services) better known as West CATS. It was mid-spring, and mostly younger controllers chose to make the move first. They seemed more energetic to embrace the new systems, even at a godforsaken place like Ely. Training was going nonstop as the young controllers familiarized themselves with the new setup. Twenty-four hours a day they were monitoring ERAMS, which was now being fed, not by radar, but by each individual aircraft transmitting a burst of information on a real-time basis. That alone was amazing to the controllers who had been used to five times a minute.

They had been briefed a year earlier about the system and told that radar was an ancient horse and the ADS-B was a new sports car. Now they were living in the future as the FAA was finally catching up with technology. It was cool to watch as an aircraft sitting at the end of the runway in Laughlin, Nevada turned on his ADS-B and, simultaneously, the controller working Sector 6 observed the call sign of the aircraft, along with his heading, speed, and altitude. What thrilled the younger controllers even more was the fact that any other aircraft in the area could also see that aircraft on their display as well.

The older controllers were not so sold on such technology. For many years they had been in control of the sky.

It had been the controller who advised the pilots where their traffic was and what to do to avoid close calls and even disasters. First TCAS arrived, which advised the flight crew when they were on a collision course. Now this! What a mess. Sure, it will be nice for the flight crews to be aware of their surroundings, but this is too much. Pilots will complain, was their argument, every time we turn them instead of the other guy.

Management tried to act empathetic to the aging controllers but didn't do a very good job. It wasn't long before controllers were being told the day was coming when displays would go away and NextGen would process the flight path of the aircraft, determine the conflictions, and adjust the aircrafts speed, heading, or altitude appropriately. Then the only thing the humans would be doing is monitoring the system.

Certification training was completed for fifty percent of the controllers by early September, and the big day came for the transfer of control. It was going to happen at 6:00 a.m. just before the morning departure rush. All the controllers at Ely were excited to finally see this day arrive. It went off without a hitch, and by eight thirty the sky was alive with aircraft.

"West CATS Sector 6, Los Angeles Sector 6 on the one line." Charlie was still in Palmdale monitoring the sector.

The place was looking like a ghost town with just a skeleton crew. Charlie remembered when they had moved into this control room back at the turn of the century. First, all the controllers had completed training. Then they would just use the new equipment for a couple of hours a day, but it didn't take long before the controllers balked at going back to the old consoles. That was a dozen years earlier. They were so quick in adapting even after complaining about change. Was this going to be any different? Charlie and his family were not looking at all forward to moving to Ely. The only thing positive he could say about the place was the lack of state income tax.

Other than that, it would only be a stopping place before a future move.

"Go ahead, LA Sector 6." It was his old friend Jim up at West CATS answering his call.

"How's it going up there?" Charlie questioned, "From here, it looks like you're keeping them apart."

"This place sure is different. Everything is sterile up here," Jim responded. "I know you'll take care of that when you get here."

"Let he who is without sin cast the first stone." Charlie laughed. "We are scheduled to be up there in two weeks unless your fancy equipment decides to go south. What's sterile about that place, anyway?"

"It's new, and our chief wants it to stay that way. Said we can't have anything to eat in here except our toenails. Guess pizza on the mid-shift is out of question. Sups behind me, Charlie, guess I should let you get back to your high paying monitoring job. Miss you guys! See you in a couple of weeks."

"Roger that, Jim, tell Sandy and the kids we miss them too." Hanging up, Charlie went back to his monotonous job of watching Jim control aircraft 480 miles away. In only another week, the ERAMS at Los Angeles and all the other centers located throughout the lower forty-eight would be shut down.

Chapter 12

Charlie and Carrie packed up their car and watched as the movers loaded up all their earthly possessions. Carrie walked up beside Charlie, taking a hold of his arm.

"I knew this time would someday arrive. Just thought maybe we would be heading to Georgia instead of the barren desert of Nevada. Guess they didn't think we were unhappy enough here." Charlie looked over at his best friend and saw a tear run down her cheek. He took her in his arms, and holding her tight, whispered in her ear. "Don't give up my darling. The day will come when we will no longer live under the bondage of the FAA and will be free to live wherever we desire."

"That won't come soon enough for me!" Carrie said wiping her eyes.

Mitzy came out of the house, her suitcase in tow. "I'm ready when you are." She sure had grown into a spunky eight-year-old.

"Not so fast, Mitzy," Charlie grabbed her and swung her around. "Aren't you going to miss this place?"

"You mean the pits of hell?" Mitzy asked.

That caught Carrie's attention, "What did you say, young lady?" she sternly asked.

"That's what Daddy calls it." Mitzy whimpered.

"Well, just because Daddy says it doesn't mean we have to repeat it. And young man," turning to Charlie, who had a big grin on his face, "you need to watch your mouth."

It was late afternoon before the house was empty and the car was loaded and turning out of 33rd Place East in Palmdale. They hoped to never see the place again.

The moving trucks seemed to arrive nonstop in the little town of Ely, Nevada as West CATS was completing the final stages of its certification. Half of the controller work force had arrived earlier in the year. Controllers from Seattle, Oakland, Salt Lake, Denver and Los Angeles would all be working side by side in controlling the entire western third of the United States. In all, over fifteen hundred families were moving into this small town of fifteen thousand.

A new housing development had sprung up just south of the center between McGill and Ely along Highway 93 in anticipation of the influx of new residences. A school, park, and new shopping center were also built within the subdivision to accommodate all the controllers and their families. It was in this subdivision that Charlie and Carrie had purchased a home just across the street from their friends Jim and Sandy. The two-story home had three bedrooms and a two-car garage, typical of the tract home they had left in southern California. A clay tile roof accented the tan stucco siding. Carrie was happy to see that the landscaper had put sod in the back yard as well as the front. At least Mitzy would have a place to play when it wasn't too hot.

They spent their first three nights at the Best Western Park Vue Motel in Ely waiting for the moving truck to arrive. Charlie was constantly on the phone trying to find out where the truck was.

Carrie overheard him ripping into some poor dispatcher. "What could happen? It's not like luggage that could get on the wrong plane. We've been here for over two days and we did not drive fast." After a pause, he ranted on, "Well, it had better be getting here. I'm tired of this hotel. No! I don't care who's paying for it. I just want my stuff."

"Charlie!" Carrie interrupted, pointing towards her cell phone, "You can hang up now. The movers are at the house waiting for you to unlock it." Charlie didn't even tell the dispatcher good-bye. He just hung up and headed out the door with his family close on his heels.

By the end of the day, they were in their new home, but things were still a mess as the unpacking was in full swing. That didn't stop Jim and Sandy from stopping by to lend their support. By the time they left, it had been decided dinner over at the Gallaghers' place was in order for the evening. There on the back patio, as the sun was setting, the smell of grilled hamburgers seemed to attract the whole neighborhood. It wasn't long before a half dozen of Charlie and Jim's coworkers and their wives stopped by to welcome their new neighbors. It was rapidly approaching midnight when Charlie and Carrie said their good-byes and headed back across the street.

"I don't know if I'm going to like this subdivision," Charlie told Carrie, as they were getting ready for bed.

"Why's that?" she asked.

"Well, in Palmdale we didn't associate with my coworkers," Charlie responded, "for a good reason. I work with these people all day long, and to tell you the truth, other than a couple, I really don't like them. Did you see the amount of alcohol they drank tonight?"

Carrie smiled, "Yeah! And boy did they sound stupid."

On Monday afternoon, Charlie was finally going back to work. The center was located five miles north of the new subdivision up Highway 93. It was early October, and at an elevation of six thousand four hundred feet, it had cooled down to a brisk forty-seven degrees. The wind was blowing out of the north, and he wasn't sure it was his kind of climate. They said it wouldn't snow much here but he questioned that tidbit of information. Approaching the gate to the new facility, he encountered a couple of uniformed professional-looking guards.

Unlike the old facility, this one was guarded by the Transportation Security Agency.

One agent who reminded Charlie of Barney Fife approached the car, "How can I help you?"

Wonder if he even has a bullet in that toy gun he's wearing, Charlie thought. *Guess I'd better not push my luck on my first day.*

"I'm Charlie Beckler from the Los Angeles Center Area Delta looking for a place to work. Seen any controllers around here recently?"

"Well, Charlie, you're not in Los Angeles anymore. We take security serious here, so you can drop the I'm-better-than-you-are attitude and watch your step because we are watching your every move. We don't care who you think you are. It is not our job to protect you. It is our job to protect this building and everything in it." The guard pointed to the side of the drive, "Pull over there and get out. You need an ID, so bring your license and registration and proof of insurance. And, yes, if I want to, I'll check your colon. Now get on with it."

Charlie knew things were going to be different at this new state-of-the-art facility, but he didn't know they would go this far. The identification badges were the newest technology. Chips implanted in the badge were active up to ten feet. As the controller would drive up to the gate, his or her picture would appear on a big monitor set so both the controller and the guards could see it.

"What happens when we carpool?" Charlie asked the now somewhat-relaxed guard.

"Oh! This thing is cool," he responded. "It recognizes that more than one person is in the car, and it brings up both pictures in a split screen. And don't ever try to bring a stranger in. If they don't have the ID card, it flashes 'Unknown Intruder' and the gate goes down."

Charlie was amazed to see a parking garage. They finally got it right! It was a three-story structure with

81

connecting causeways to the main building. Charlie noticed that every spot had electric hookups. "Great, they've even gone green," he muttered as he walked to the causeway marked "Main Lobby." Just inside the door, he found himself on the second floor in a spacious lobby decorated southwestern style with northern Nevada wild life paintings adorning the walls. There were a number of sitting areas bordered with live plants common to the local area. The animals spaced throughout the lobby got his attention.

The taxidermists sure have been busy around here. Wonder if any of these are now extinct? Charlie asked himself. *I suppose they will have a stuffed controller with a headset out here before long. This looks more like a hotel lobby then a control center.* High on the wall above the lobby, a banner read "Western Center for Air Traffic Services – Where the future is today." Charlie walked past what looked like a gift shop with all kinds of sundries. At the far end of the lobby, a small human resource sign hung over what looked more like a candy shop than an office. Opening the door, Charlie called, "Mom! I'm home!"

A middle-aged lady came out of the back room, and her face lit up when she saw Charlie standing like a lost kid. "About time my favorite grumpy old controller got here. Have a good trip up?"

"The best you can with the moving company you people hired," Charlie responded with a smile. "What do I do now? This place gives me the creeps."

Linda had been at Los Angeles Center for the last twenty years. She still had ten more years to go before she could retire and was one of the first to arrive at Ely when the place opened last spring. Known by all the controllers as "the specialist," she knew her business; she had become a favorite. Pulling out a map of the facility, she started showing Charlie where he was supposed to go.

"You know I can't follow instructions. Why don't you just give me a tour?"

"You haven't changed at all," Linda sighed. "Okay! But I only have a few minutes. We have a group of ten arriving from Seattle at two, and I need to be here for that."

Walking along the north side of the lobby, they came to some steps leading down into an enclave about twenty feet across. Glass stretched all across the far end of the room. Walking up to the glass, Charlie caught his first glimpse of the new control room. Immediately below him was a circle in the middle of which appeared to be the Operations Manager's desk. Currently, a complete stranger to Charlie was manning this position. There were multiple spokes coming out from the ops desk. These spokes were lined with controllers bellied up to their scopes. At the end of each spoke, a map on the wall showed the area in which that aisle controlled. Charlie recognized the map of his area and the ASD (aircraft situation display) screens located underneath it.

"How do you get down to the control room?" Charlie quizzed.

"For that you have to take the elevator. And if you don't have your badge, you can forget about it. The elevator will only stop at the control room floor if you've been cleared to be there."

"If that's the case, I might as well go home," Charlie joked.

"Oh, right! You will want to see the cafeteria first, it's first class."

"Right," Charlie chided as they headed towards the elevator. "They must have hired some new cooks."

Taking the elevator to the third floor, they headed north down the corridor to double glass doors at the end. The white opaque sign on the door read "Cloud Nine Café – Fine Dining." Pushing through the door, Charlie was greeted by a top-notch cafeteria. The décor and food choices topped that of many downtown delicatessens. Behind the counter, a middle-aged chef in his smock and chef's hat was busy preparing a dinner whose aroma would make anyone decide it was lunch time. Walking through the dining room, they came to a glass wall with multiple glass doors leading to a large patio dotted with tables, each adorned with an umbrella. Along the sides of the patio, water fountains and plants created a tropical atmosphere.

"It doesn't feel much like the tropics out here today," Charlie commented as the now-cold north wind blew across the patio. Back inside, Linda led Charlie into the corridor and then to the first door on the right.

"This is your favorite room," she said as Charlie read the "Break Room" sign on the door.

"Yeah, I sure got a lot of sleep in the one at L.A. Center." Charlie yawned as a sign it was time to start the trend here.

"You may not want to do that here. They have cameras and are pretty serious about sleeping on the job," Linda advised.

The frown on Charlie's face showed his disgust. "Great! Next thing you know they will time your restroom breaks." The break room was quite large and arranged like a theater. It had over thirty recliners with reading lights. On the far end a huge high-definition television was playing a baseball game.

"This is one of three break rooms here in this facility," Linda told Charlie as they left and headed across the hall to the gym. The gym was contracted out to a national chain, and it showed. All the equipment was new, and a trainer was busy working with one of the controllers. "You need to be a member to work out here," Linda explained. "It's very reasonable, and the location is great."

Moving on to the south end of the building, they came to the training wing. They walked past numerous classrooms filled with trainees. The simulator room was humming with processors. They were busy running simulated scenarios, with instructors looking over the shoulder of nervous trainees.

"Do these kids know they are the last generation of controllers?" Charlie asked Linda as they watched the circus of confusion in the youngsters' faces as they tried to make sense of their new endeavor.

"You really think the dream of NextGen will happen?" Linda quizzed as they turned to leave.

"Linda, times are changing. We used to separate aircraft using altitude and time. We then went to radar, which revolutionized our job. The pilot no longer had to tell us where he was. We had technology showing us where the airplane was and the direction he was going. We moved on to the mode C transponders, which gave us the aircrafts' altitude. You would think it would get easier. It didn't, though; all that happened was air traffic increased. Now the aircraft are equipped to tell us where they are. We have to trust the equipment, not always an easy thing to do. The changes, while painful, are necessary to keep up with progress. And yes, we are only a generation away from automated separation. These kids will train their replacements only how to monitor a system. The art of air traffic control will die forever."

Across from the simulator room was another large room with rows of short tables with dividers between each one. "This is where we debrief trainees, both in simulated problems and live on-the-job training," Linda explained. "Notice the computer monitors along the side of each table. It is an incredible system. Each instructor is given a blue tooth equipped electronic tablet prior to training. During the day, they keep notes on this device. At the end of the training day, the instructor and student meet here where the information is transferred to the local area network. Then they are able to go back over the day's events prior to filing the training report. The program does a great job in tracking the trainee and recommending areas the individual needs to work on. Oh, and another thing, when you sign on to the debrief station, the program brings up the sector where you trained that day so you can replay any segment desired."

Charlie just shook his head in amazement. "Why don't we just let the computer train these kids? Obviously that's where they're headed."

"When are they expecting me on the floor?" Charlie quizzed as they headed back to the elevator.

"You're heading there now. I have to get back to my desk, but I'm sure you can find your area. Good luck, Charlie! I am sure glad to see you. This place needs some good old boy common sense."

"Would like to say I'm glad to be here," Charlie smiled, "but that would be lying. So let's just say I'm glad to see you too." He gave his favorite personnel specialist a big hug as the elevator door opened and he stepped out into a new control room.

Charlie noticed that very little had actually changed in the personnel arena as he entered the spoke clearly marked "Area Delta." The familiar faces, some of whom he had not seen in three months, greeted him with an it's-about-time attitude.

"What are you looking at, Allan?" he chided. Allan had always been one of Charlie's friends ever since they had met back at LA Center soon after the turn of the century.

"I am looking at my new trainee," Allan responded, "and he doesn't look too promising. Get your headset, lowlife, let's get started."

Allan spent the rest of the day going over the new equipment and the minimal procedure changes. As expected, it didn't take long for Charlie to settle into this new environment and, just before Thanksgiving, receive his certification at the new facility.

Chapter 13

The morning finally arrived that Data Communications had been working up to for the last fifteen years. Today as the aircraft departed, they would be using satellite-based communications. SBC had been a dream child of the previous administration and probably one of the few positive legacies they left in the field of aviation. The system, which operates like a satellite cell phone, gives each aircraft its own address. Delays caused by the *Columbia* disaster pushed back the launch of the satellites by six years. Then, after 9/11, a majority of the budget had been transferred to Homeland Security. At times, the project was put on hold. Now with twenty-four satellites set in orbit and all commercial aircraft equipped with satellite transceivers, today would be the real test.

United Flight 1511 departing Las Vegas for San Francisco was the first aircraft airborne. Once Allan, who was working Sector 16, took the handoff he saw the call sign flash one time on his communications display and then go steady green. "Do you really think he's there?" he asked Holly, who was working Sector 6 beside him.

"Reckon he had better be," she replied, "or somebody's going to be unhappy. They said we could verify if we questioned the system," she added.

The computer program received data from the sector that a handoff had taken place. Once it had received approval from the previous controller, it transferred the aircraft's SBC address to the new sector. This system had been sold as a way to reduce pilot and controller workload. Now with SBC, losing communications with aircraft would be a thing of the past. The added and most important feature of the SBC was the upcoming data link capabilities it encompassed. In just a matter of a couple of years, this feature would be added to practically eliminate voice communications.

Once the call sign had stopped flashing, Allan decided to try the system. "United 1511 climb and maintain Flight Level three-four-zero."

Almost immediately United 1511 responded with "United 1511 climbing to Flight Level three four zero."

"That is incredible!" Allan burst out as simultaneously his thoughts took him back to the beginning of his lustrous career controlling airplanes.

His mother had raised Allan in the Bronx. Allan had never met his father. He had been told his dad was serving life in prison for shooting a rival gang member when he was only 19. When Allan was twelve, he spent the summer in Johnstown, Pennsylvania with his uncle and aunt. It was here that he was introduced to aviation. On a Saturday morning, his uncle had taken him and his cousins to the Johnstown County Airport where the Experimental Aircraft Association was giving free rides to children. Allan was so excited by the flight that he declared that someday he would be a pilot and fly those big jets he saw descending over their apartment located under the approach path to JFK. At the age of eighteen, and not knowing where else to go, Allan enlisted in the air force, where they squashed his plans of flying but did convince him to be an air traffic controller.

After training, Allan was shipped off to Iraq. He, along with the rest of his squadron, controlled the airspace around the Baghdad airport within days after it was taken over by American forces. Many nights, while the squadron was eating in the mess hall, the sirens would go off and they would take cover only to hear the thud of mortars going off close by. Once his time was up, Allan did not reenlist but signed on with a contractor and headed over to Afghanistan, where he worked in a tower for the next eighteen months. Shortly after returning to the states, Allan received his acceptance letter from the FAA. He had been all over the world but finally felt his travel days were over, and he settled down in Palmdale. That had lasted only a few years before they moved him to this deserted place in Nevada.

Another handoff started flashing just north of the LIDAT intersection. Allan took the handoff and watched as the call sign N711NV appeared on his communication display and flashed a couple of times before turning to a solid green. "November Seven One One November Victor LA Center," Allan broadcast.

"November Seven One One November Victor with you, center," the pilot replied.

"Just checking out our new communication system, November Victor, thanks for the help," Allan explained. This was going to reduce workload considerably. Allan thought about all the airports within the jurisdiction of center's airspace where they were unable to communicate with the aircraft on the ground. This would solve that problem. Now with direct communications and the recently adapted ADS-B, they would greatly be able to increase the number of airplanes departing and arriving at the smaller fields around the country. Allan thought this was a good thing since he had just heard the twenty thousandth VLJ (very light jet) had recently been ordered.

At the turn of the century, the air traffic control system saw a major shift in traffic as the airlines moved towards smaller regional jets. The fuel-efficient aircraft created a challenge for the system as they occupied the same airspace and had considerably less passenger load. It wasn't long before the FAA noticed record traffic numbers with little increase in revenue. Controller pay was based on traffic count so the agency did what they felt was the right thing by rewriting the pay structure so as to lock in the controllers' salary. The controllers felt they had again been let down by the administration. It fell on their shoulders to handle the added traffic with no additional compensation.

Now the controllers faced the onslaught of thousands of very light jets that held only four to six passengers. While these would be flown at lower altitudes, they were still traffic and, as taxpaying citizens, desired professional service just the same. Allan was asking himself where the burden would fall with this onslaught when Holly interrupted his train of thought.

"This is cool. I just talked to a Cessna on the ground at Bull Head airport!" She bubbled with excitement. "This will really change the way we do business."

"Yes, and not a minute too soon," Allan replied, "not a minute too soon."

Chapter 14

As forecasted, data link was only two years behind SBC. Data Link was night and day compared to the first try with CPDLC (controller pilot data link communications) at Miami Center soon after the turn of the twenty-first century. The earlier version, while designed with the help of controllers, was still awkward and time consuming. It was before the use of multi colored screens, and programming was too complicated to ease the workload. The aging understaffed workforce at the Miami facility did not help. They would rather key up and speak directly to the pilots than to use the data link. It was shelved after only a year in service lacking the participation of airlines after 9/11. Technology had changed over the last fourteen years, and now the data link would use SBC to deliver the clearances, and the uses would no longer be restricted to communication changes which were no longer necessary.

Early in the spring, Charlie and his coworkers started training for this revolutionary communications program. It had been over thirty years since the concept had been conceived. Now on the threshold of national implementation, the wait appeared worth it. The controller/pilot interaction would be reduced to text messages generated by computer inputs. For the younger controllers it was easy. They lived with instant messaging, and this was only an extension of this technology. For the more senior controllers, data link was always something they talked about during the slow times. It was just a theory they never expected to happen in their career. Now it was for real, and they had to accept it. The only thing that saved the program was the ability to keep the voice override active. Anytime the controller found it necessary, they could key up and talk to the pilots.

Late August training had been completed, and data link start up was scheduled for Thursday. Charlie and Jim were working the mid-shift when the system came online. With doubt, Charlie typed in his first clearance. It was for a UPS flight coming in from Louisville, Kentucky, for Ontario, California. It wasn't really a necessary clearance as the aircraft was already filed over the Boulder VOR, but he just had to see it work. Bringing up the flight planning on the URET screen he entered the routing for direct Hector VOR and hit enter. The UPS data block turned to yellow for what seemed like forever then turned back to a solid green indicating the captain had received and accepted the clearance.

Eight months later, in early March, Charlie had started his collateral duties testing of 4DT (four-dimensional trajectory). This would be the meat and potatoes of the NextGen program. Once 4DT was turned on, in theory, it would automate the maintaining of standard separation between aircraft. The basic program had been completed, and testing was in full swing. The first phase of 4DT called TALC (terminal automated-landing control) would take over the job of sequencing and separating arriving, and departing aircraft. The second phase, encompassing the air traffic control centers, concerned Charlie the most as it was his area of specialty. The three air traffic control centers controlled the majority of the airspace covering millions of square miles and tens of thousands of flights every day.

The snow had melted and flowers were pushing their way up though the moist soil along the highway between the Western Center for Air Traffic Services and the Beckler's home. Charlie had picked up his travel orders today and would be leaving for Atlantic City, New Jersey tomorrow. He had known the collateral job would take him back east for six months. The need for controllers at the testing facility was a necessity, and he was willing to make the sacrifice.

Not being thrilled about leaving his family, they had decided Carrie and Mitzy would fly out once school was over in May. Spending the evening together with last-minute packing, Charlie reassured his family that he would be all right and would call them every day. Early the next morning, Carrie and Mitzy took Charlie to the Ely airport to catch the early flight to Atlanta.

Waiting in Atlanta for his flight to Atlantic City, Charlie sat in the terminal watching all the passengers come and go. He always enjoyed people watching in airports. Each one had a story, and they were all so different. There was a businessman on his way to an important meeting, a child on the way to his grandma's house, families going on vacation. A young pregnant girl sat there with sadness in her eyes. Where was she going? Most likely to see her parents, but Charlie would never know. She painfully got up from the rocking chair, which had been slowly rocking back and forth. Moving down the jet way she disappeared. *So much of our lives seem to go that* way, Charlie thought shaking his head. *There we painfully sit in our comfort zone. What is growing inside us is constantly driving us forward. Where are we going? Why are we going there?* These questions continued to occupy his mind as the loudspeaker called out his flight, and he, too, took the walk down the jetway, a symbolic walk that way too often was changing his life.

That afternoon, Charlie checked into the Residence Inn southeast of the Tech Center in Atlantic City and finally opened his NextGen 4DT manual and started reading. The manual consisted of over twelve hundred pages of mostly boring technical stuff. It was one of Charlie's jobs to pick apart the program looking for anything that would compromise safety.

Charlie, while up to the challenge, sometimes felt the weight of the flying public was on his shoulders. He would be working with the ITT staff and, of all people, his counterpart Barney. Barney had been involved in the NextGen program since its conception and wanted to see it through to the end. This did not make Charlie happy at all considering all the conflicts they had experienced in the past. *Oh well,* thought Charlie. *I guess it takes a village, even if half of them are idiots.*

The introduction was simple yet it slammed Charlie in the face. In bold letters he read, "4DT - Four dimensional trajectory program, designed to replace the high cost of human air traffic controllers."

"Wow!" Charlie gasped. "And they want me to assist in this slaughter of my coworkers' careers?" Knowing it was inevitable, he continued on page by page, word by word, dissecting the meaning and projecting the outcome. Finally the long day got to him, and he fell asleep with his head on the book.

Charlie's dreams took him back to the origin of ATC, an era so long forgotten. It was 1929 in a field in Saint Louis. Archie League, the original air traffic controller, was there in the field with his wheelbarrow and flags. As the aircraft lined up for takeoff, Archie would wave the red flag for hold and the checkered flag for go. In 1930, Cleveland Municipal Airport established radio communications, and over the next five years about twenty cities did the same. In December 1935, an airline consortium opened the first Airways Traffic Control Services, keeping aircraft separated between the airports. They had no direct communications with the pilots, but rather would get the position of the aircraft from airline dispatchers, airway radio operators, and airport traffic controllers. These individuals would relay instructions back to the pilots. During the early years of World War II the number of centers jumped from fifteen to twenty-seven to handle the added demand and still relied primarily on indirect communications and mental calculations.

It wasn't until the mid-1950s that radar was introduced to air traffic control centers. The controllers would move pieces of plastic called "shrimp boats" indicating aircraft movement, much as similar markers had earlier been used on maps. In 1961, the FAA began plans for new technology that would use data from ground radar and from airborne radar beacons. In 1967, IBM installed the first prototype computer into the Jacksonville Air Route Traffic Control Center. Technology advanced rapidly from those early days to the turn of the twenty-first century…nine decades of continually striving to enhance the ability of air traffic controllers through technology. Now it had come to the apex-- technology had now become the air traffic controller.

The phone rang, waking Charlie. Without even looking at his phone, he knew the caller.

"Sorry, darling! I fell asleep reading and forgot to call."

Charlie left the Residence Inn Tuesday morning and drove to the tech center. One roundabout after another finally got him to the right road leading to the airport. Pulling into the parking lot of the huge complex, Charlie was a little overwhelmed at the size of the place. It took him awhile to find what he assumed was the right entrance. It was marked 4DT with the *D* tucked in under the four and the *T* looking more like a jet taking off then a *T*. The parking lot was almost full, which told Charlie that either a lot was getting done or a lot of employees were wasting taxpayers' money. This complex had been built eight years earlier to house the contractors participating in NextGen development and testing. Now, with over twenty companies employing over twenty-five hundred technicians and scientists, the place was a buzz of activity. Charlie realized that the security division was doing their job when he tried to get through the door. He had thought the security at West CATS was ridiculous. Here at the mecca of

NextGen the thought of a rectal scan crossed his mind as he waited for approval to enter the sanctuary of humming processors and blinking lights.

Once through the torturous security check, and with a brand new ID card in hand, he followed the directions given him by a receptionist with a Jersey accent to the third floor, where he found rows of cubicles. Inside each was a white shirted geek typing away at what Charlie guessed was program code. Finally, two-thirds of the way down the hall on the right, Charlie found the glassed-in conference room he was looking for. Opening the door, he was greeted by Sean O'Leary, who welcomed Charlie and motioned him to take a seat.

Charlie was taken back when he noticed Barney seated at the far end of the table. *What the heck is he doing here?* were the words he mumbled under his breath. *Hasn't he done enough to destroy the world?* His thoughts were interrupted when Sean cleared his throat and brought the room to attention.

"We have come to a crossroad with NextGen. The hardware is in place and the software is completed. The manuals you have been given have been edited, corrected and edited again. We are confident that we have a viable product ready for scrutiny and testing by the user. That is why you are here. Each of you represents a different type of facility. We've also brought in your managers to assist in the testing. I am very aware of the friction between controllers and management, but for the sake of this program, put those differences aside for the moment."

Easy for you to do, thought Charlie. *You don't have to work with the lame brain I'm stuck with.*

Sean continued, "Over the next three months we will be running scenarios in which you will be at work stations much like you use back home. The scenarios use your airspace, so they will be familiar. Now let's go around the room and introduce ourselves so we know with whom we're working. As I told most of you earlier, I'm Sean O'Leary, current VP of

NextGen's 4DT program. I will be spending most of my time in Washington but will be here when you need me. This phase of the program is so extremely critical to its success that I personally will oversee it."

Barney was quick to jump in. "You all know me! I'm Barney Williams and am also an integral part of the program from West CATS. I have been with the FAA for thirty-five years and was a manager at Los Angeles Center before the consolidation. It was my keen awareness that led the agency to find the solution to the ERAMS challenge a few years ago."

It was all that Charlie could do not to speak up about the less-than-truthful statement. He decided to keep quiet and let Barney crash and burn on his own.

Next at the table was a chiseled-faced gentleman who leaned forward and looked around the table like he was making sure everyone was listening to him. "I'm Sam Reidel, a supervisor at Las Vegas Approach Control. My people run a lot of airplanes in and out of one of the top ten airports in the country."

Oh, this is great! Charlie thought. *It's another egotistical maniac from the management school of morons.*

Sam continued, "I am here to lend my expertise since I have twenty-five years of air traffic control experience at five different towers and three approach controls."

Wow! Charlie smirked to himself looking down at his fingernails to hide the smile. *I bet there are seven happy facilities out there.*

The next and last of the management types was the Las Vegas Tower supervisor who was fidgeting with his papers and manuals as if his intro was in there. "I'm Bill Brown. I have been a supervisor at Las Vegas Tower for three years. I am here because my boss thinks I can make a difference with the automation program. I really am not sold on it, so I will be your Doubting Thomas until it proves itself."

They continued around the table as Virginia Fisher from Las Vegas Approach and Tanya Jenkins introduced themselves. Finally it came time for Charlie to speak up, and as much as he had the right to remain silent, he did not have the ability.

"Hi! I'm Charlie Beckler of the Western Center for Air Traffic Services and unlike Barney here I do control airplanes. And thank you, Sam, for educating us on the traffic level of the Las Vegas airport which, if I remember right, was number six last year here in the states, two down from LAX, which we also control at number four. Nevertheless, you have a great facility, thanks to the hard work of the controllers. I know I'm not only speaking for myself, but also for my two friends here, that work traffic day in and day out. We are here to make a broken system work. I have read over half this manual, which I'm sure none of you managers have done. And, team, we have work to do. This thing is dangerous. I will not get into it right now, but in time it will come out." Charlie stopped long enough to get his senses and turned to Sean. "Sorry, Boss, you seem like a straight shooter and I am pleased to work with you. As for some others on this team, I question their sincerity."

Sean, looking around the room at the scowling managers, cut out a big grin. "Charlie, welcome to the team. I understand your opinion of this team, but it's the best cross section we could get; if you let it, it just may work. You three controllers will have equal input into the testing. Each of you will have my personal email address, and I look forward to reading your reports. Now let's take a break and meet in the laboratory at ten fifteen."

Sean looked over at Charlie, "Stick around, I need to talk to you privately."

The rest of the team filed out of the room and headed for the cafeteria for a cup of much-needed coffee.

Sean got up and shut the door. Returning to his chair he sat down and leaned back with his hands behind his head. To Charlie it seemed like forever before Sean spoke. "Charlie, I don't even know where to start. I have never controlled an airplane in my life. That is why we need you. It is your type that will either make or break this complete program. Sure, we can build it, install it, and demand that you use it. The problem with that kind of strong-arming is the probability of failure, and people would get hurt. One thing I have learned about an authentic air traffic controller is that they will do whatever is necessary to get their customers to their intended destination safely. In doing so, they have disagreements with those who manage them, especially individuals such as myself. I cannot do your job, Charlie. All I can do is empathize with you when it comes to working with the less-than-creative types. You have a whole file full of letters of commendation, time-off awards and other awards that make my career pale in comparison. What are your requirements to make this phase successful?"

Charlie liked the guy already, and this added to his instincts.

"What am I requiring?" Charlie raised his eyebrows in question.

"Yes. You are an intelligent man and have done your research. That is obvious. You know what we're getting into here, and I am sure you have dug up concerns that need to be met. What do you need from me to get this thing moving?"

Charlie knew he was now in the driver's seat. "Once we see the demo, have a couple of days to play with it, and read the rest of the manual, I will have a better idea."

"Very good!" Sean stood up as if to tell Charlie the meeting was over. "Let's get down to the lab."

Chapter 15

The lab consisted of four scopes, two for centers and two for approach control. At the far end was a tower simulator with 270-degree projection. Elevated along the one side were three rows of theater-style chairs for observers to witness what was transpiring with the testing. Above each scope was a large LCD monitor reflecting what was seen on the scope. The seven team members were joined by a handful of technicians anxious to see the new scenarios play out. One of the program specialists directed Charlie and Virginia to their scopes and Tanya to her position in the tower simulator. With some basic instructions, they started the simulated scenario.

One by one, aircraft arrived on the scope and Charlie watched as the computer-generated commands were displayed on the 4DT window and then sent to the aircraft. Somewhere in another room "ghost" pilots were busy receiving these commands and acting on them. It didn't take Charlie long to notice a hesitation in the system. He made a mental note to ask about it later. As if in slow motion, the aircraft moved through his airspace. Ten minutes into the test, the first conflict showed up as an arrival from Palm Springs and one from Burbank were tied over the arrival gate into Las Vegas. Charlie watched as 4DT took note of the confliction ten minutes prior to POC (point-of-conflict). The first command went out to the faster aircraft to increase speed twenty knots and to the slower aircraft to reduce speed twenty knots. Charlie did the math--forty knots, ten minutes that makes just over six miles in a perfect world. This is not a perfect world and the aircraft will not speed up and slow down instantly. Sure enough five minutes later the program recalculated and slowed the trailing aircraft back an additional twenty knots.

Virginia watched intently for the first aircraft to appear on her scope, and it didn't take long. For her scenario, it was mainly aircraft coming from Charlie's scope and a few added in from the other arrival gates to make it more realistic. Eventually they showed up and their speeds and altitudes were automatically sent to the pilots, and the responses were timely. A couple of small aircraft departing off of the satellite airports did create a distraction and a couple of questionable moves. In the end, it looked pretty good as the aircraft lined up on downwind and turned on final into the slots set up for them.

Tanya standing there all alone in her faux tower was happy to get message of inbound aircraft. Looking at her display she counted ten aircraft over the next ten minutes. "Cool!" She patted the display. "Let's land this metal." One by one, a minute apart, the aircraft appeared in the distance, wheels and flaps down and greased onto the runway. Tanya noticed the taxi commands were ones she had issued many times since she had arrived at McCarran five years ago. Finally the last of the aircraft were down and off the runway without one clearance from Tanya.

The scenario complete, the group met back in the conference room and discussed different issues each observed. Most of them appeared to be impressed by the precision of the program. Charlie kept quiet the entire time, jotting down notes on a legal pad.

"What is your take so far?" Sean asked Charlie.

"Let you know tomorrow," Charlie responded turning back to his notes. "I need time to analyze some data before I am willing to sell the farm."

"Fair enough, you all can take the rest of the morning to study up on your manuals, and we will run another scenario this afternoon. It will include a number of arrival aircraft as well as departures. And for you, Charlie, there will be numerous aircraft flying through your sky. You should enjoy it."

As soon as they were dismissed, Charlie took off to the software development department. He had questions that only the software designers could answer. Soon he found himself wandering down hallways of cubicles with computer programmers wearing short-sleeved white shirt and pocket protectors playing solitaire and minesweeper. He questioned them individually and each time was sent to someone else. It was a long, slow road finding someone who had his answers. Finally he met Walter Simons. Walter, or Bud as he liked to be called, had been with the FAA for over forty years and had seen a lot of programs from conception to operational.

After introducing himself, Bud invited Charlie to sit down. "I don't remember the last time I met a real live controller. What brings you here?"

"4DT. We're here doing run-down testing, and I am looking for some answers."

"Bet you are, Charlie. Most of us are still looking for answers to 4DT. It is working, but we have our concerns. Matter of fact, once this thing goes into operation, I'm only going to drive and take the train. No more flying for me."

That brought a grin to Charlie's face. "Well, at least I know I'm dealing with someone who understands his work. Really, what I am looking for are the logic files and preference commands for 4DT. Is that possible?"

Bud turned back to his computer and typed away for a couple of minutes, all the time humming some tune that sounded like "Somewhere over the Rainbow." Finally, he spun back around and tossed a CD to Charlie. "It's all on there. If you can figure out how to read computer language you should think about a job here. We need programmers who know what controlling airplanes is all about. It's kind of hard for them to understand what you guys go through."

Getting up, Charlie held out his hand, "Thanks Bud, but I think I'll stick with controlling for now. As for the computer language, we'll see when I open this baby. If I can crack this, I owe you lunch."

The afternoon scenario was much like the first, and again Charlie noted the hesitations on a couple of clearance commands. This time he took notes as to the situation when it happened. As the scenario was winding down he noticed his newfound friend Bud sitting in the observation seats.

"What do think, Bud, can we make it work?"

"Don't quit your day job, Charlie, we still need you."

"What a relief! The way this thing is running, it's just a matter of time."

As they were leaving, Bud stuck a thumb drive in Charlie's hand and whispered, "Don't lose this or let anyone know where you got it." With that, Bud turned and walked through the door. Quickly, Charlie stuck the thumb drive into his pocket, almost like he was doing something wrong.

Charlie stopped by the gym for a quick workout on the way back to the Residence Inn. He knew that with the work that lay ahead that night, he needed the exercise, but he was also anxious to open up the CD Bud had given him. He knew that if he could understand the logic behind the program, he would understand the reason for the commands it produced. *And what's with this thumb drive?* Charlie couldn't help but wonder about the mystery behind Bud's comment as he slid it into his hand. *Is there an underlying problem with NextGen?* The sun was setting as he pulled into the hotel. To most the workday was over, but for Charlie it had just begun.

Charlie quickly opened the logic files, and line by line he worked his way down the list. He was happy he had paid attention in the one computer programming class he had taken back in college. At least it wasn't all Greek. Taking notes, he made a list of what-if and if-then situations. It was after midnight when he was finally ready to shut down the computer.

Then he remembered the thumb drive. He slid it into the USB port and opened the only file that came up. The first page looked official with the FAA logo, but the title was one you would not expect: "The Dangers of NextGen." The author was none other than Charlie's new friend, Bud.

The next page was an insert that Bud had written to Charlie.

"Charlie, I didn't give this to you earlier because I have been told by my boss that if this ever gets out, I will lose my job. With the help of other software engineers here at the tech center, I wrote the following report. Please guard it with your life, as there are people in Washington who would have no problem with terminating you or me if we get in the way."

Charlie moved to the first page of the report and started reading. By the third paragraph he was shaking, but he did not know if it was from fear or anger. *What are they thinking?* was all he could ask. *How can they do this to the people they serve?*

At two thirty in the morning, Charlie finally shut off the light and tried to get some sleep. Sleep did not come easy as he kept thinking about what Bud had written and how he had to get to the bottom of it all and reveal the truth to a nation in danger. Was this his calling? Could he do it? Was his family now in danger? The alarm rang all too early.

Chapter 16

Charlie walked into Mr. O'Leary's office at eight thirty and plopped down in the overstuffed chair pushed back against the wall in front of Sean's desk. "Good morning, Boss! Had your coffee?"

Sean looked up from the paper he was reading, "On the third cup now. What's on your mind?"

"I need unlimited access to all the NextGen programs and a week. With that I can give you an honest controller's perspective as to the beast we are building."

Sean was kind of taken back. "Why so long? And why do you need access to all the programs?"

"Don't know for sure yet," Charlie replied, "but I smell a rat and need this access to find it. Sure you don't have to give it to me, but you asked for my help."

Now Sean had more than a puzzled expression. "Are you saying there is a cover-up going on here?"

Charlie knew he was again pressing this manager a little far but had to find out if he was involved. "Yes, I do believe so, but I will not be able to reveal it until I find the source."

Sean was now looking intently into Charlie's eyes. "Do you know who all is involved?"

This put Charlie on the spot. Would his life be in danger if Sean was involved?

"Sir, all I can tell you at this time is that if this program goes forward as it now stands, I will not fly again. Anything else I tell you will only be speculation, and that I do not like to do. Controllers don't take chances, they only take calculated risk."

"Well, great! What am I suppose to do?" Sean now had his head in his hands, shaking it back and forth. "We have a meeting with the administrator in thirty minutes. What am I suppose to tell him?"

This caught Charlie by surprise, and his eyes got as wide as silver dollars. "Don't tell him anything. Let's just go with the planned program, and we will open the can of worms once we find the answers. Let's go get another cup of coffee. We're going to need it."

Thirty minutes later, Sean and Charlie found themselves seated in the conference room with the FAA administrator going over the scenarios of the prior day and the plans for the next six weeks. After they had covered the plans for the team, Randy brought up the reason for his visit. "I got an email from Barney yesterday and he wasn't happy. He said that he was left out of meetings between you two, and he felt as if protocol was not followed. When I called him, he was belligerent about Charlie going over his head. Said he had no regard for authority and wanted him sent home. He claimed he was endangering the program."

"That was my call," Sean quickly responded. "I need to have unimpeded controller input, and Mr. Williams was acting like a road block on the highway of success."

"Did you discuss your challenge with him before you made the move to bypass him?"

"Absolutely not. I brought this team together to get individual perspectives. Not to hear some whiner complain about protocol."

Randy stood up and started pacing back and forth, "We have a lot at stake here. The NextGen program is now hanging on the ability of getting 4DT activated in the next two years. Barney has been part of the decision-making process since its conception. He may be a bit overbearing to work with, but we are required to keep him on. Don't ask me why! I can't tell you."

Charlie tried not to act too surprised. He had suspected and now it was confirmed that the administrator was at least somewhat aware of the discrepancies hidden deep within the program. Now he had to take precaution with every step. Charlie guessed he should not be surprised to find blackmail within the confines of the United States government. Who would believe him if he did bring it all to the surface? For now he decided he would play it cool and do his research and then figure out the path to take. It all started making sense why Barney had been such a difficult character to deal with over the last few years. He knew he could do as he pleased and always have a job.

Just how much did Barney cash in on? Charlie wondered. He intended to find out, but he knew he was going to need some help on this one.

"Sir!" Charlie said, standing up as if he was in command. "I will make every attempt to keep peace with Mr. Williams and include him in all phases of the testing. What I will not do is compromise the safety of the flying public. Like you, I took an oath to protect the citizens of this country, and that I intend to do." It was like a laser beam being directed right into the heart of the problem.

Charlie was relieved when Randy smiled and said, "For that I am grateful. Now let's go meet the rest of the team. Then you guys can show me some technology at work."

Late that night back in his room, Charlie was busy scanning page after page of documents and looking for clues for anything that could cripple the system. Finally, out of frustration, he called Jim. "I need your help, my friend."

"What's up?"

"I'm not sure I can tell you, but I will give it my best. First, do you remember anything from programming classes you took in college?"

"Not a lot! Things have changed over the years."

"Sure they have, but the basics are the same."

"Sure, Charlie, I'll do anything for you," Jim chided. "Even if you have skipped out on us here at the center."

"This is serious, pay attention."

"Talk to me, Grumpy."

"There is a serious flaw in the 4DT program, and I am having major challenges locating the source. I will overnight you a package that has all the info for you to look over. You need to be looking for code inserted into logic that would cause a hesitation in the program. This happens when decisions are made during climbing and descending commands."

"Are you sure it's an anomaly and not how the program was designed?"

"Oh, it's the way it was designed, but not intentionally."

"Explain."

"This is what I have found out: when they started preliminary testing on the new software, the only command that was ever given to converging aircraft was to descend one of them. The software programmers have never seen this as a problem. They had been told that aircraft have a service ceiling. Now if that were correct, then when a confliction arose, why not just descend the logical aircraft, which would be based on the following parameters? First, distance from destination; second, aircraft performance; and lastly, aircraft priority such as lifeguard or any other aircraft requiring special handling as stated in the ATC manuals."

"It sounds logical to me. Where is the problem?"

"Think about it, Jim! What happens when they are at the minimum IFR altitude?"

"I didn't think about that."

"Well, neither did the software engineers until they were questioned by one of the specialists who happened to be a pilot."

"So, is that the problem?"

"Not really. That's just the background. It gets juicier. They built a patch that now looks at the minimum IFR altitudes and takes the higher performance aircraft up a thousand feet."

"So, why the hesitation?"

"That is what we are looking for, Jim. My newfound software friend who turned me on to this advised that he had been in the company of none other than Barney Williams and had overheard a phone conversation he was having."

"Eavesdropping! You have great friends, Charlie."

"No wait! He heard him make a couple of pretty damning remarks about the glitches in the patch and that they were going forward anyhow. Barney stated that none of us would still be alive when it failed anyhow."

"So you're going off a comment that a software engineer heard an idiot make? That's real smart, Charlie. Now you're willing to waste my time?"

"Jim, the report I am sending you tells exactly what is going on. It's just that Bud can't get anyone to listen to him, let alone the authorization to research it any further. It's up to us, Jim. We have to find it."

"You're sounding pretty desperate, Charlie. I think you need to come home for a couple of days and we will dissect the thing."

"Not a bad idea, Jim. I'm missing my girls anyhow."

Chapter 17

After discussing his plans for a four-day working weekend, Sean approved Charlie's absence until Tuesday morning. "Better have an answer when you get back so we can move forward."

"Not a problem, Chief! Just tell Barney I'm missing my family and had to go home for the weekend. You do that and I'll have a story for you on Tuesday."

"Get out of here," Sean waved his hand indicating Charlie to leave. "You have your hands full. I will handle the personnel problem."

Charlie found himself chasing the sun west on Thursday night, passing through the Phoenix Sky Harbor airport on his way back home to Ely. During his layover, he had had numerous conversations with Jim, who had converted one of his computers into a virtual laboratory. It was now set up so the two of them could run test problems. It had been Jim's idea and, sure enough, once the software was installed, it allowed limited situations to be tested.

"Hope to have some answers when you get here, Charlie. Is Carrie picking you up?"

"What kind of question is that? Of course she's picking me up. Mitzy's at a slumber party and so we're going to have one of our own. Don't expect to see anything out of me until noon tomorrow."

"You horn dog! Don't you know work comes before pleasure?"

110

"Only people who don't know pleasure say that. And by the way, I won't be answering my phone either. So have a good night, Jim. See you tomorrow."

Saturday afternoon, Jim and Charlie were busy running airplanes at each other on Jim's recently created ATC simulator. They had run just about every type of aircraft they could think of at every angle. The hesitation was just as Charlie had described it earlier in the week.

"It may not be perfect, but it makes one heck of a game. Think we should market it, Charlie?"

"What, and get fired? You know how many billions they have spent on this thing?"

"My guess is somewhat more than budgeted."

It wasn't until late evening that it happened. They had two Boeing 737s at minimum altitude head on when there was a longer than normal hesitation. Simultaneously, the commands were given to climb both aircraft.

"Whoa!" shouted Jim, "look at this!"

"That, my friend, is what we have been looking for," Charlie had a half grin half scared-to-death look on his face. "That is exactly what Bud said in his report could happen."

"Has it happened in the laboratory out there?"

"No, here's the deal. This is like an electrical discharge. A little bit of static does no harm, but if you let it continue to build, all of a sudden it becomes a lightning bolt that can destroy."

"Please explain, Charlie. You're scaring me."

"Jim, your computer has only the fraction of the capacity that the tech center has. What we have been able to do here is accelerate the process to a point that it could no longer make the correct decision, and therefore it crapped."

"So what you're saying is that some time in the future, this could happen in real life?"

"Exactly!"

"What are you going to do?"

"Don't know yet. I really don't know!"

Sunday morning, Charlie and the girls attended church, giving Charlie the peace he needed to move forward. Afterward, they met Jim and Sandy for lunch.

Charlie and Jim excused themselves and headed over to Jim's to wrap up their work. After replaying the crash scenario a few more times, Jim transferred it over to his portable hard drive.

"All you need to do is start the program. As far as the analysis, that will have to be done by someone much brighter than us. They may be able to dissect this hard drive and find the answers. Good luck, my friend. Remember when you get a big fat cash award who it was that helped you."

Laughing, Charlie gave his friend a hug. "This is the FAA not AIG. I will stay in touch."

On Tuesday, while the rest were eating lunch, Charlie ran upstairs to find Bud, who greeted him warmly. "What's up Charlie? I heard you were out of town over the weekend."

"You got someone keeping an eye on me?"

"Nope! Just ran into Barney, and he was pissed! Said they had to postpone two days of running test problems because one of the team got lonely for his family. I figured it would be you."

Charlie grinned, "Let's just keep him thinking that way. I have something to show you. We discovered it over the weekend, and it needs to be analyzed."

Charlie pulled the hard drive out of his brief case and plugged it into Bud's computer. Twenty minutes later, Bud was speechless just shaking his head.

"What do you think, Bud? Is this something you can dissect? Can you show what's causing the logic to melt down?"

Bud scratched his head, "I know I can only answer one question at a time. Let's start with what I think. This is a visual representation to the concern in my report. Second, I will put one of my software engineers on breaking down what happened. It's a guy I trust from school, name is Joey White. And last, once we find the code, we can show the logic."

"Thanks, my friend, and please keep this private until we get our ducks in a row. There will be hell to pay, and we need to know what we are talking about."

Charlie emailed Sean later that afternoon that he needed two weeks of running advanced scenarios to make a final determination. Sean was not too happy with the time frame, but it was making progress nevertheless. At least running the test problems would get the others involved, and maybe something good would come out of it.

Barney started sending the whole team emails about the importance of meeting deadlines and that no excuses would be accepted. The rest of the team just rolled their eyes and kept quiet. Charlie did not reveal his concerns to the others.

For the next few days, Charlie made sure that each problem set up multiple opportunities to reveal the glitch. Nothing happened, and it started to bother him. Was this just his imagination? Was he opening a can of worms that did not exist? The hesitations were still there. Some were more pronounced than others.

On Wednesday of the second week, he got a call from Bud. "Call me when you finish up today."

"You got something?"

"Yes, but let's discuss it over dinner. I know a great place."

At six thirty, Charlie met Bud and Joey at the Island Grill Seafood and Steak house. Over one of their famous ostrich steaks with mushrooms and crabmeat, Joey explained the find.

"Your hard drive showed symptoms of loose data being saved in sectors and tracks. When the program logic reads a conflict, it uses massive amounts of data to arrive at a decision.

In most cases it then discards the now useless data, clearing the way for additional processing. When the patch was installed, it started saving certain amounts of data related to the minimum altitude resolutions. The data itself is not the problem. The problem is there is active code within the data that, like yeast, multiplies itself. Now, if you have enough hard drive space it could go on forever."

Bud interjected, "We never would have found it on the main frame, it's just too big."

Charlie had stopped eating by now. "So why didn't they fix it?"

"That we don't know," Bud continued. "It is my speculation that they are only aware of the symptoms, not the results."

"Are you telling me that the designers are ignorant to the solution?"

"Exactly. What they did was add code that hid the symptom. That is why when you see an altitude confliction, it hesitates."

"How can we make this public knowledge in order to clean it up?" Charlie asked.

"Don't expect any help from management. They are aware of the cover-up and will deny it even exists."

"Sean?"

"No, I don't think so. It seems they don't trust him."

Charlie was adamant, "Well I do! I have given him the preliminary briefing and will follow up with him tomorrow. One more thing. Can you manipulate the laboratory main frame to duplicate what happened in Ely?"

Bud had to think about that one. "Yes, I think so. All we need to do is put a capacity block on the mainframe to eliminate additional storage space. If it works, I can have it done before you run tomorrow."

"Great! Let's get out of here. I need my sleep." Charlie picked up the tab and headed for the door.

Charlie sent Sean an email asking for a ten-minute private meeting before the team met for their morning briefing.

"What you got?" Sean asked as Charlie walked into his office.

"A runaway freight train."

"Enough with the metaphors. Give me something I can work with."

"Sure, we have confirmed my hunches. And unless you're lying to me, you have been left out of this cover-up because you have integrity."

"Seriously, Charlie, I have not been lying to you, and you're starting to piss me off just questioning my integrity."

"I apologize if I have offended you, but this is serious." Charlie went on to explain what they had found out. "I think they have let it slide just to meet deadlines. As you know, all studies show that within the next two years air traffic will be at its maximum capacity without this program. I'm sure they knew that it would take years to rewrite the program, so they made the decision to hide the discrepancies. What they did not know was the outcome."

Now Sean was disturbed. "And you say Randy knows what's going on?"

"I'm pretty sure, but it's not for me to say. Now let's go see what happens today."

At their briefing Charlie explained that today's test problems would be brought to capacity. "You mean we're running 100 percent problems all day?" Virginia groaned.

"No, we will start with 100 percent, then after lunch move up to 120 percent of designed capacity. Don't worry, you can handle it. Remember the NextGen is doing the work, you're just watching the show."

"Yes, but it seems so real when we get into it."

"That's right! Just keep your head and we'll have fun."

"I noticed you changed the flight altitudes," Barney spoke up.

"Yes, that I did. Is that a challenge for you?" Charlie knew he should leave it alone, but he just couldn't help it.

"Well, you moved all the aircraft to the minimum altitude and that's not realistic."

"You wouldn't know realistic if it jumped up and bit you in the butt!" Charlie smiled.

"This is for a test only, and we need to see what will happen in all instances, not just your idea of realism."

"Wait a minute, guys," Sean interjected, "I need you to get along today. I just received word that we have VIPs here today from Washington. It seems that the aviation subcommittee will be represented today along with members of the media."

Charlie knew this was exactly what was needed. He hoped this whole thing would crash today.

Chapter 18

Charlie was happy to see Bud and the rest of his team in the observation seats. Also sitting there was a group of suits. Charlie made his way over to Bud and asked, "Is everything in place?"

Bud smiled and gave him thumbs up. Looking down at the suits he said, "Yep! It looks like timing is everything."

"Let the chips fall where they may," Charlie whispered and glanced around. "Just keep your eye on Barney. It may not be just airplanes that crash today."

Moving on down to the VIPs, Charlie introduced himself to the visiting senators. Then Charlie grabbed Virginia and Tanya and pulled them aside.

"Okay, we're going to get our butt kicked today. There is a problem with the program that I haven't shared with you. Just keep your eyes open and enjoy the ride."

"What do you mean by that?" Tanya asked.

"Don't worry, it should happen somewhere just outside of Virginia's airspace. Keep your eyes on the monitors. Let's go!"

The problem started out like all the others. Airplanes started coming in from every direction. The only difference was that they were all at minimum altitude. As the first conflict was recognized, Charlie held his breath. The hesitation came and then sure enough, the command came out to climb the higher performance aircraft. One after another, the conflicts were resolved and Charlie could see the guests leaning up in their seats, watching the monitors. This was the taxpayers' money at work. This would look good with the voters when it reduced delays, which had become so common.

Charlie was getting nervous now. He started focusing on each conflict and noticed that with each one the hesitation was longer. *Would it happen during this problem? What would the guests do? Man! Barney is going to go postal.* He looked over at Sean who was intently watching Charlie's monitor.

Looking up, Sean raised his eyebrows as if to ask, "Where's the air show?"

It was Southwest Flight 765 inbound to Las Vegas and American Flight 777 departing the same airport. Both leveled at eleven thousand feet. At thirty miles out the commands should have been given. It became obvious to Charlie that this was the one. The command generator hesitated, started to give a command, and then retracted it. Two seconds later two identical commands were sent to both aircraft.

As it appeared on his LCD Charlie read, "American 777, climb and maintain one-two thousand." Then the next command popped up. "Southwest 765 climb and maintain one-two thousand."

"Bingo!" Charlie sighed leaning back in his chair. Both aircraft climbed straight at each other with a closure rate of twelve miles a minute to twelve thousand feet. The targets merged. One thing Charlie did notice-no conflict alert! Guess they figured the computer knew there was no need to tell the controller.

Looking around he saw Sean trying to hide his big Irish grin. Bud was giving his engineers high fives. Barney was just sitting there as if nothing happened. *I guess he wouldn't know a midair if that bit him in the butt either,* Charlie thought to himself. The senators just seemed to be scratching their heads. Two minutes later, another midair transpired, and Charlie keyed up his mic and terminated the test run.

Speaking into his mic, Charlie turned around as if speaking directly to the VIPs. "What you witnessed needs to be explained. It would be my pleasure to have you join us in the briefing room in twenty minutes. Thank you."

The briefing room was packed when Sean and Charlie entered twenty minutes later. The senators were sitting around the table listening to Barney run off his mouth about all his accomplishments. Virginia and Tanya were sitting along the wall next to Sam Reidel and Bill Brown. The other side of the room was Bud and Joey, along with a couple of their software friends. The press occupied two other seats along that wall.

Sean addressed the media first. "Gentlemen, I need you to agree only to release what you hear in this meeting with the consent of the aviation subcommittee. Can you agree to that?" Both men nodded, so he continued. "What happened today is a program failure. As you witnessed, twice the program ran aircraft into each other. This is not normal. We have run over two hundred scenarios without a glitch. Today can be explained and for that I am going to ask Mr. Beckler to take the floor."

Charlie moved to the far end of the table. "Senator Benton and Senator Wells, thank you for sticking around. What I am going to show you may cause me to lose my job. That is a risk I am willing to take to protect the flying public, which I have taken an oath to do." Looking around the table, it was quite obvious that he had the attention in the room. Barney was fidgeting like a school boy who had gotten caught. Bud was smiling from ear to ear knowing that today he was getting vindicated. "Before I explain, let's watch what happened."

Charlie turned on the sixty-inch LCD at the front of the room and a replay of the morning scenario started. Fast forwarding it to the first hesitation he stopped the tape. "First, please notice the hesitation. It may be something that is hardly noticeable to some of you. To us who are controllers it is very apparent that something is amiss." Charlie watched Virginia and Tanya. He felt they would most likely notice the hiccup, and, sure enough, their faces showed it. "Now let's move on to the midair."

"What do you mean midair?" Barney almost yelled. His face was red with anger. "Don't you think you're a little out of place here?"

Knowing he was getting the upper hand, Charlie kept his cool. "Mr. Williams, that will be determined in time. And yes, we did have what is called an operational error in the real world of air traffic control. While operational errors do not always lead to midair collisions, they can. If you had any air traffic control experience you would know this. Now please watch."

Running the problem at normal speed he used his laser pointer to point out the two aircraft head on at the same altitude. Step by step he took them through the commands and the merging targets, stopping the replay right before the targets merged. "When a controller makes this kind of error he or she is immediately removed from the position and goes through considerable rehab and retraining to be able to work traffic again. An error of this magnitude is unacceptable, let alone two within minutes of each other."

The senators just sat there staring at the screen. Neither one wanted to believe what he had just witnessed. Finally it was Senator Benton from Wisconsin who spoke up. "Do we know what caused these errors?"

"Yes, we do. Do you want the technical explanation or the simplified version?"

"Let's keep it to a level we will understand. Thank you."

"The bottom line is," Charlie hesitated in order to heighten the impact of the statement he was about to make, "this program is flawed. Shortcuts were taken in its design and we have discovered the weakest link. These shortcuts were hidden with expectations that it would not be discovered prior to an updated program being installed. While this in itself may seem logical, in our world we don't take this kind of risk."

Now Senator Wells spoke up. "We have put a lot of money in NextGen. Should we shut the program down?"

"That is not my call," Charlie replied. "I am an air traffic controller asked to do a job, and that is what I have done. As far as the details of what has transpired in covering this up, you need to ask Barney, he is part of that underhanded operation."

"You don't know that!" screamed Barney jumping up from his chair pointing his finger at Charlie. "I will have you fired. You are an inconsiderate brat!"
Charlie didn't say a word, just pulled out his chair and sat down. Sean got up and moved over to the door.

Barney continued his rage. "Don't believe anything he says! I knew nothing about this problem, and this insubordinate controller can't prove otherwise!"

By now, Sean had opened the door and motioned outside. Two security guards came in and grabbed Barney. "What are you doing? Let me go." It looked like he was going to have a stroke. "Don't you want to hear my side of the story?"

By now both Senators had seen enough. Senator Wells responded, "We will be holding a congressional hearing into this matter and you will get your chance. Take him away, guys."
The room quieted down once Barney was gone. The senators returned to asking Charlie questions, but Charlie quickly turned the technical questions over to Bud. Bud was thrilled to answer each and every one. In the end, it was decided that they would remove the main frame capacity block and proceed with normal testing. This could be done without jeopardizing NextGen. Senator Wells and Senator Benton felt that it was Sean's responsibility to meet with the Administrator and the Secretary of Transportation as soon as possible to brief them on what had transpired. Sean was not too keen on the idea but knew that it had to be done.

"What about the President?" Sean asked.

They agreed that the Secretary of Transportation would need to address that. "A press release will go out in a week. Is that time enough for the administration to get its ducks in a row?" Senator Benton asked.

All Sean could do was smile and shake his head. "Fair enough, thank you!"

Chapter 19

Testing continued the following week. Barney had been removed from the NextGen program team and sent back to Ely. Sean had not been seen since the meltdown. Charlie assumed he was in Washington meeting with his boss and the transportation secretary. With the block removed they went back to the preplanned problems, which performed normally with the ever-present hesitation. Three weeks later, Charlie and Bud each received a subpoena to appear before Congress.

Loaded down with documents and Jim's hard drive, they boarded the train for the two hour ride from Atlantic City, NJ to Washington. They spent three days explaining to Congress what had transpired. The questions were tough, but Charlie concentrated on answering truthfully and without malice. It was hard not to input a couple of jabs at Barney, who was in the room the whole time. On the third day they were dismissed after lunch and decided not to wait for Barney to testify.

"He's just going to fill the room with lies and deception anyway," Charlie told Bud as they boarded the train for the return to the tech center in Atlantic City.

It took just two weeks of hearings for Congress to make their recommendations on the NextGen debacle. It was decided that the Transportation Secretary and the Administrator were not aware of the severity of using the faulty patch. Barney had told them that, while it was faulty, it would be transparent to the user. It appeared as if Barney and two contract managers were

123

the only ones aware of what could happen, and even they were ignorant to the havoc it could cause.

Barney was permanently removed from the program and was told he would spend the rest of his FAA days as an administrative assistant. The two contract managers were fired and advised that they would no longer be able to hold a security clearance. Sean was found innocent of any wrongdoing and given authorization to spend what was necessary to fix the patch and move forward with NextGen. Sean, in turn, promoted Bud to manage the software redevelopment.

Charlie received an urgent email from Sean the following morning requesting a meeting over lunch.

"Charlie, I've got a proposition for you. Thanks to you there is an excitement around this place that I have not seen in the last ten years. You have given those working here a sense of pride and a feeling that they can make a difference. Now they have a mission to solve the challenges that have been inflicting NextGen."

"That sounds all mushy, but I didn't hear a proposition in all that," Charlie grinned.

"Well! I would like you to consider staying here. You would be my eyes and ears here at the tech center. I have a lot of fish to fry in Washington and need to spend a lot of time down there."

"Don't think that will be possible, Sean. I need to control airplanes. You take me away from that and I will be just a worthless shell of a man."

"Can you at least stay on until I get this thing ready for live testing?"

"Let me make a phone call." Charlie knew Carrie had to be brought into this decision.

It was a long phone call that evening and it was decided that Charlie would take the position. Sean was on the phone the next morning as Charlie stepped into his office. Motioning for

Charlie to take a seat, Sean quickly finished up his conversation and hung up.

"That was the administrator on the phone. He's having trouble coming to grips with the cover up. He will be announcing his resignation this afternoon."

"Wow! What a bummer. Now I'm starting to feel bad."

"Charlie, it is not your fault. You may have discovered the discrepancy, but you did what was right. No one has asked Randy to leave, it is his choice. What's your answer?"

"Let me be frank. I don't want the job, but I do enjoy working with you. So if you agree to do the live testing at West CATS I am willing to stay. My other stipulation is that the FAA moves my family over here and gives us housing for the duration. I am not willing to leave my family for the eighteen months needed to do complete the job."

"Well, Congress gave me the authority to do what I need, and I consider this is what I need. Welcome aboard, Charlie, we have a deal."

At the end of May Charlie picked up Carrie and Mitzy at the Philadelphia airport and drove them out to their temporary home just north of Vineland, New Jersey. A coworker had located this furnished two-story home situated on two acres. The owner had moved to Hawaii and left her furniture at the home waiting for it to sell. Massive oak trees covered the property, creating a sense of seclusion. The circle drive led the way past the split rail fence up to the front porch. In the back yard was a huge in-ground pool. On the far side of the pool, shrubs and other greenery were intermingled among the rocks leading up a hill to the waterfall. The soft blue light behind the eight-foot waterfall created a calming atmosphere. Charlie could just picture himself at night sitting in the hot tub with the cares of this world melting off his shoulders as his wife and daughter enjoyed the crystal clear water. It was perfect for the three of them.

Charlie had been working nonstop all spring and took a couple of days off to help his family settle in to their new home. Saturday morning they loaded up the car and headed down to Cape May for lunch. What a great town for those who love the Victorian architecture! After spending all morning walking up one street and down another, Mitzy finally had enough. "Dad, I'm getting hungry."

"What you got in mind, Sweetheart, are you buying lunch?" Charlie grinned at his little girl.

"Sure, Dad, with your credit card."

They stopped at a cool looking restaurant called the Mad Batter that was advertised in the local flyer. The large Victorian hotel, Carroll Villa, housed the restaurant. Carrie requested that they get a table on the porch where they could look up and down the street at all the great homes. Charlie was quick to order the Blackened Grouper sandwich. It was the Cajun spices with lettuce, tomato and Remoulade sauce that tempted his taste buds. Carrie ordered the Vegetarian sandwich, which consisted of eggplant, basil pesto, portabella, roasted pepper, spinach, and fresh mozzarella on a Panini with a side salad. Mitzy had trouble deciding on this incredible menu and settled on the Maryland crab cake sandwich.

They spent the afternoon walking along the beach looking for seashells. It was an enjoyable day, and as the sun descended over Delaware Bay, Charlie sat there on the sea wall with Carrie tucked into his arms and Mitzy snuggled against his side. *What more could a man ask fo?* he thought. "Thank you, God," he whispered as the sun dropped below the horizon and the flickering lights of Dover appeared in the distance.

Chapter 20

It was Friday morning, October 20th, and Charlie was looking forward to a weekend with the family. The last seven months had taken a toll on his life. Mitzy was not happy in New Jersey. The culture was not what she was used to, and the kids in the neighborhood treated her differently. Carrie had no desire to get involved with the local community and spent all her time homeschooling Mitzy. The family made a couple of trips down to Georgia to visit grandparents and one trip back home to check on things in Ely. Summer was over. The oasis in the back yard had been shut down for the winter, and leaves from the oak trees had started falling, completely covering the ground in red and orange.

Charlie was working at his desk looking over the status reports on the software redesign. Bud and his team had been working six-day weeks since April. Bud had told him it looked like about three more months until this thing would be ready for testing.

"Sean, how're things in Washington?" Charlie answered his phone.

"Charlie, I got a problem. Need your help."

"Wait a minute. The last time I heard that statement I got sucked into working here."

"Not this time. Want to hear what I need from you?"

"Fire away, you old dog. What you got?"

"Ever hear of the National Business Aviation Association?"

"Sure! Don't they have a convention going on in Las Vegas this week?"

"Exactly, that's what I need. You see, I was supposed to be there as a guest speaker tonight presenting NextGen 4DT and I can't go."

"What happened?"

"It's my kidneys, Charlie. Think I may have had too many pints when I was younger, and they're giving me a fit. The thing is, they are expecting to hear about 4DT tonight, and I can't think of anyone else who could do a better job than yourself."

"How in the heck am I going to get to Las Vegas by tonight and what am I suppose to tell them? This brings up another question. How many of them are there?"

This got Sean laughing. "Charlie, the venue holds about nineteen thousand and they said it was sold out. People are excited to hear what's transpiring with 4DT."

"Nineteen thousand people!" Charlie almost screamed the number. "That is a lot of people. Man! I think you should just get better and go."

"Listen, Charlie! I can't go, and I need you to do this. You'll figure out what to say. You were able to bend the ear of Congress, the President knows your name, and you solved the mysteries of the hesitation. Charlie, you know what you're doing."

"I'm still not convinced, Sean. What about getting there?"

"That is the cool part, Charlie. I got approval from the administrator for you to use the Gulfstream. It will be at the Atlantic City airport at 4:30. You will need to be wheels up before five."

Charlie was stunned. They never used the Gulfstream for travel. That was the administrator's ride. He decided it was a chance of a lifetime so why not. "I'll do it if I can take my family."

"Sure, go ahead. There's plenty of room in the plane. Just be back by Sunday night with the jet. The boss needs it on Monday."

"I'm having trouble following you. Slow down," Carrie explained to Charlie as his excitement translated into blabbering. "Why are we going to Las Vegas tonight?"

Charlie took a deep breath and shared the weekend plans in a way only Carrie could understand. Once she comprehended what lay ahead, she was almost as excited as he was to be taking the trip. "At least I don't have to be speaking to almost forty thousand eyeballs," she giggled. "We will meet you at the airport at 4:30 with your suitcase."

Charlie headed over to Bud's office to get the latest update on the program and ask his advice on what to tell the throng of pilots and aircraft owners on the upcoming live startup of 4DT. "Just speak from your heart, Charlie. Speak the truth. They're not used to that."

"Thank goodness I have a five hour flight to write this speech."

"Enjoy the plane ride. Wish you the best, my friend."

Carrie and Mitzy were already on board the G4 as the driver dropped Charlie off at the FAA hanger. The Captain was busy loading the flight plan into the flight management system. The First Officer greeted Charlie as he approached the stairs. "Am I to assume you are Mr. Beckler?"

"Correct, but please call me Charlie."

"Great, Charlie, I'm First Officer Jerry Nelson and along with Captain Todd Lincoln, we will be your pilots tonight. We have already heard quite a bit about you from that darling daughter of yours. She thinks you're the greatest. Must be, considering the trip you're about to take."

"What do you mean?"

"Normally our passengers are either the DOT Secretary or the FAA Administrator. You must be a VIP."

"Nope! I'm just the wrong person at the right time," Charlie replied.

"Welcome aboard, Charlie. The weather is looking good across the country. We have one cold front to cross, but at flight level four-five-zero we should clear anything out there."

After greeting his wife and daughter, Charlie took a seat on the left side of the airplane right in front of the wing. Sitting back in the big leather seat he fastened his seat belt and smiled as he heard the engines whine while spooling up. Taxiing out, they headed up taxiway B for a runway one three departure.

Charlie looked out the window as the sun was setting behind the tip of the winglets. "This has always been my dream," he said to no one in general.

It was almost five o'clock and they were just about to take off for the other side of the country where he would speak in front of thousands of waiting pilots and peers. *What have I become?* he asked himself as the jet bumped along on the taxiway. *All I ever wanted to do was control airplanes. That's what I do.* He allowed himself to smile. Was it a smile of apprehension? Maybe it was a smile of determination. Even he had no idea what would be communicated to the audience that night.

The jet rolled onto the runway and the scream of the Rolls Royce jets with a combined thrust of over thirty thousand pounds caused the jet to rapidly accelerate down the runway and climb into the darkening skies over New Jersey. The lights of the boardwalk quickly disappeared from view as they turned west. Again Charlie was chasing the sun to the West Coast. This time though it was in luxury, but what a price he had had to pay.

Twenty minutes later they leveled off at altitude, and the pilot called back for Charlie to join them up front. "You must be on a mission, Mr. Beckler. ATC just gave us direct Las

Vegas. That hasn't happened in a long time. Not out here on the east coast anyhow. What's going on?"

Charlie really didn't know how much he wanted to share, but figured the captain had been flying long enough to understand the need for change. "Tonight I am supposed to give hope of a better way of doing business. One even I approach with extreme skepticism. Captain, things are changing. Years ago, flying required a person to have skill and guts. You would take off in a machine that would spit oil and fly at an altitude where the weather would ensnare you. Instruments were basic, and you had to picture where you were based on what you interpreted from those instruments. They often failed, and you had to be efficient at partial panel flying or you would never grow old. I would bet that you know what I am talking about. You have most likely flown a lot of hours in those conditions."

The Captain nodded his head, and Charlie continued. "Today we depend on high-speed processors to calculate everything for us. There is no such thing as pilotage anymore. The GPS tracks our every move and situational awareness is the name of the game. You have absolutely no need to touch that yoke until we are ready to land. Is that flying?"

"You're right, Charlie. I miss the old days when the excitement came from you questioning your own sanity late at night with lightning flashing all around your airplane. The exhilaration of seeing the runway lights as they appear out of the darkness on a rainy night. That was flying."

"That's the same thing we are dealing with in air traffic control. In the old days, we had limited information, but we were the eyes on the ground. We would help a flight get to its destination safely and took pride in doing so. We are losing these skills. Today controllers depend on computers which alert them of pending conflicts. They never acquire the gut feeling or get the picture. The system goes down and they panic. So tonight I am to plant the seed of confidence that the next generation of air traffic control will be safe. It is not an easy thing to do when I myself am not sure." Charlie excused himself and returned to his seat.

Sitting there in his wide leather seat, Charlie pulled out his laptop and started writing. All kinds of things came to his mind. This was his chance to tell the world, or at least his world, what was going on in the aviation industry. After thirty minutes of typing and deleting one paragraph after another, Charlie hit a brick wall. "What is my problem?" he asked out loud. "I am an experienced controller, I fly airplanes, and I know this program. So why can't I express myself?"

Leaning back in his seat, he shut his eyes and groaned to God. *Where are you?* That's when it dawned on him that maybe this was bigger than he. For too long he had been the one in control and had pretty much pushed God out of his life. Too much to do, he had kept telling Carrie.

So here at forty-five thousand feet inside an aircraft Charlie had only dreamed of someday flying, he stopped his struggle and prayed. "God, this is not what I asked to do. For some reason you have put me into this situation. Your book says that I should not worry about what to say, that you will put the words in my mouth. God, I am going to leave it up to you. Please give me the strength to speak the truth yet the compassion to do it without malice." Charlie continued talking to God until he drifted off to sleep.

Charlie woke up when he felt a hand wrap around his arm. Carrie had crawled into the seat beside him and laid her head on his shoulder. "Get your speech written?" she asked.

"Not going to write one. It just wouldn't be me."

"What you going to say?"

"That is yet to be determined, my dear. Only God knows. Are you and Mitzy going to the arena?"

"I wouldn't miss it, my man," Carrie smiled up at Charlie with a big grin. "You are a celebrity tonight. Just don't forget who's taking you home."

"Never, my dear, but please wait until after the dance to determine the celebrity status."

"You will do a great job," Carrie mumbled as she drifted off to sleep.

Charlie got up and made his way back up to the flight deck. "One hour to go, Boss," the captain explained, pointing down to the FMS.

"Boss! Captain, I think maybe that would be your job. I am just a passenger on an incredible airplane."

The captain turned around and put his hand on Charlie's shoulder. "Charlie, I know where you're coming from, but let me explain. You and I work for the citizens of this great country. In doing so, we are given responsibilities. We are responsible to provide our customers with the best service possible. I want my passengers to walk off this airplane with an unforgettable experience. So while you're on this ship, you're the boss."

"Thank you, Captain, I commend you on your service and outlook. I never really looked at it that way. We need more controllers with that attitude. We get so wrapped up in all the things wrong with the system that we kind of forget who's working for whom."

"Charlie, I have flown a lot of hours and talked to a lot of controllers over the years, some good ones and some bad ones. Overall you guys do a great job under extremely stressful conditions. Don't be too hard on 'em."

The alarm sounded with an inbound message. Pressing the accept button the first officer read, "On frequency with West Coast Sector 33. This is your airspace, Charlie, do you want to talk to 'em?"

"They know we're priority handling, but do they know I'm the one on board?"

"Not unless you spilled the beans. I don't think the news has even hit Las Vegas. They're still expecting your boss."

"Gulfstream Zero Three Golf Alpha, West Coast Center, with you flight level four-five-zero." Jerry had keyed up his mic verbally communication with the center.

"Gulfstream Zero Three Golf Alpha, West Coast, roger. Are you ready to start down?"

"Anytime, Center! We got one of your friends on board. Don't want to make his nose bleed."

"Dang! Are you giving Charlie a free ride? He gets all the breaks."

The Captain had to join in on the fun now, "Careful, Center, he just may be your next chief."

By the time the bell chimed with the descent clearance, Charlie recognized the voice. It was Mike Johnson, one of the more pragmatic controllers. "N03GA, make sure you tell Charlie we miss him. The new janitor isn't nearly as good as he was." This brought laughter to flight deck as the Captain reduced the throttles and the aircraft started its slow descent into the desert city.

November Zero Three Golf Alpha taxied up to the ramp at Signature Aviation and as the jets spooled down, Charlie thanked the flight crew. He advised them of their plans to fly on up to Ely later that night if that was all right.

"We would love to, Charlie. Our orders are to serve you this weekend. And that means wherever and whenever."

"You mean we could go anywhere we want this weekend?"

"That's right! But now don't forget we need to get some sleep if you're going to go gallivanting all around the country."

"That's cool, Captain. We just want to go home to Ely tonight."

"Great, I will get a flight plan filed and be here waiting when you get back. And now don't you worry, Charlie, we will be watching you on the television in the pilots' lounge."

"Thanks, I need all the encouragement I can get right now." Charlie stepped out of the airplane to find a limo with Carrie and Mitzy already inside waiting to whisk him off to the Mack Center. "The two mile ride seems like it's taking forever," Charlie muttered as he looked at his watch. "I go on in ten minutes."

Carrie couldn't help but laugh. "Don't worry, lover boy. They will wait for you. Remember, you are the keynote speaker."

"Yeah, guess so. Just hate to make anyone wait." The limo pulled past the security guard and into a tunnel at the back of the arena. As they came to a stop, two men in black suits with badges and radios opened their doors and ushered the three of them into a golf cart.

"You're just in time, Mr. Beckler. The band is on their last song and the M.C. said he would only be spending five minutes on your introduction."

"Five minutes on an intro?" Charlie couldn't believe it. "I could do it in five seconds. This guy must be a politician."

"Coincidently, Mr. Beckler he is Senator Rister of Nevada. Supposedly he met you in Washington during some investigation."

"Great!" responded Charlie quietly, "not only am I speaking to all these pilots, but to the Aviation Subcommittee also."

They stopped at a door marked "Do not enter" where Charlie said goodbye to his family. He and his escort walked through the door and down a hallway made of black cloth curtains. Charlie could hear the senator explaining to the crowd why Mr. O'Leary was not able to attend. When the senator told the crowd of the stand-in keynote speaker, the whole arena

135

exploded in applause. It rapidly became obvious to Charlie that the word had leaked out about his arrival and there were great expectations in what he would be sharing with them this evening.

As they approached the stairs to the stage, Charlie stopped his escort. "Sir, there is something I must do before I can go up there."

"Oh, sorry, Mr. Beckler, the lavatory is back by the entrance."

Charlie grinned, "Thanks, but that's been dealt with. What I need is some quiet time with God. If you're a praying man I would appreciate any help I can get." Charlie's escort led him over to a curtained off area where he was alone. Charlie spent the next couple of minutes asking God to speak through him as he shared from his heart words of wisdom to a changing world.

Chapter 21

"It's time, Mr. Beckler," his escort whispered.

As they reached the foot of the steps, Charlie heard the senator's voice echoing throughout the arena. "Flown here tonight from Vineland, New Jersey, the man most of you have talked to on the radio over the last twenty-one years. This is the man who will guide you into the next generation of air traffic. Please welcome Charlie Beckler."

The applause was deafening as Charlie climbed the eight steps and walked across stage. At the podium he was greeted by one of the senators who had just a few months earlier hammered him with questions. Graciously Charlie shook Senator Rister's hand as they exchanged greetings. The applause died off as Charlie positioned himself in front of the microphone and looked out over the audience. *Now is not the time to freeze he told himself. You have controlled hundreds of thousands of airplanes. Unknowingly you have communicated with each of these pilots over the years. Show them some love.*

"To all of you pilots out there who have heard my acknowledgement, 'Los Angeles Center, roger' and more recently with the consolidation of air traffic, 'West CATS' I am humbled by the opportunity to be here. It has been an honor to serve you over the last two decades and, if the good Lord is willing, I hope to continue this endeavor another five years. I bring you salutations from Mr. Sean O'Leary who regretfully could not be here this evening. Tonight I have been tasked with bringing you the latest from NextGen. I will fulfill this obligation but first let me tell you a story of long ago.

"It was early June of 1921 when Robert Schnitzel climbed into the seat of his 1917 Jenny JN-4. As the OX-5 power plant came to life the adrenalin started flowing through his veins. Looking over the side of this fragile aircraft he taxied to the end of the recently mowed grass field. The sun was directly overhead as he turned west into the wind and started his takeoff run. Within a few feet the tail came off the ground and shortly thereafter the aircraft lifted off the ground and took to the skies. Robert stayed close to the treetops as he headed west, leaving upstate New York behind him. Over the next three months, he moved from town to town and from state to state. All he needed was a pasture and a county fair to make a living in his flying machine. He sold hundreds of rides to first time passengers. Robert enjoyed the screams of delight as passengers were able to pick out their homes from the air. He continued moving westward, ever dancing with the clouds.

"October of 1921, Robert settled down in a little town in central California where he started a flying school. Over the next twenty years, his love for flying was ingrained into the hearts of many young men and women. Storm clouds were building over the mountains that day in 1941 when a man showed up at the airport. He requested Robert fly him to Carson City, Nevada for a meeting. Robert advised the man that the weather didn't look good and he would rather wait until the next morning. The man continued to insist and finally offered him a large sum of money to make the trip. After making a call to his wife, Robert loaded up the Stinson AT-19 and flew the businessman to Carson. Why he attempted to fly home that night would never be known. Robert never arrived back at the airfield and his aircraft was never found. It was

assumed that he met his fate that night high in the Sierra
Mountain range.

"Why do I tell you this story with such an ending? It is
the birth of aviation. Do not mourn for Robert. He lived and
died doing what he loved to do. He danced around the clouds.
He was there when the sun rose in the east and he witnessed the
sunset from the sky. He felt the wind in his face as he turned
onto final, deeply inhaled the smell of grass as the wheels of his
flying machine reached out to grab those very blades, and
shared the joy with others as he helped them break the bonds of
earth.

"We move forward another forty years or so to our
generation. A young man only eighteen years old started
spending time at the airport watching as airplanes took off and
landed. He got the fever to learn to fly. He started taking
lessons and day after day he and his instructor took the Piper
Warrior out flying. Then one day the instructor got out of the
airplane and told him to do three takeoffs and landings. As I'm
sure you recall your first solo flight, I remember that day so
vividly. As the wheels left the pavement, I was alone. No one,
no one was there in the airplane to gently pull back on the yoke
or to advise me to increase power. As I made my way around
the pattern looking off to the left, the end of the runway moved
beneath the wing. Landing checklist, reduce power, lower nose,
so much to do. From all the times around the airport traffic
pattern, things started falling into place. Lower flaps, report
final, watch the speed; the centerline came into view. The first
landing was not perfect, but as the saying goes, 'If you can walk
away from it, it's a good landing.'

Where in years past it took something special, today we,
as a society, have decided that anyone can learn to fly. We used
to sit down over a map, plot out our flight, and plan each leg of
every trip. We would know to look for the water tower or the
railroad track. We watched the time, knowing that, at this
heading, for this amount of time, it would take us to our

destination. We would listen to the engine and keep a diligent eye on the instruments. On a dark night over unpopulated regions of this great country, we would suck up the seat of our pants any time the engine missed a beat. Remember the feeling of relief we felt after a long flight when the airport beacon flashed on the horizon? That is why we bravely fought the law of gravity and learned to fly.

"Today we no longer share those characteristics of flight. Flying is easy! That's right, flying is easy. Today, navigation is moving maps using GPS. Today, computers monitor every detail of your flight and every hiccup of your aircraft. Today, ADS-B broadcast the details of your aircraft identification and what you are doing. It does this not only to ATC but also to every aircraft around you. The love of flying may still exist, but the excitement has been taken away by technology. We look back almost a century ago to the early years of the airlines. Varney Speed Lines started service between El Paso and Pueblo, later to become Continental Airlines. Another one is American Airlines, which grew up under C.R. Smith bringing the DC-3 into commercial service. During these early years flying was a thing of romance and excitement. You would go out to the airport just to watch your friends and family depart. You would go to the gate, and, after many good-byes, hugs, and kisses, they would walk out and board the airplane. A lot of airports had observation decks where you could just watch the airplanes take off and land. Today we drop our friends and family off at the curb. We can't even go to the gate. The observation decks have disappeared. Security and familiarity have reduced flying from a thing of romance to an everyday necessity. The airlines today are more interested in how many passengers they can pack into an aircraft than the comfort of those passengers. Airline food that at one time was as elaborate as a seven-course meal has been reduced to a box lunch or a bag of peanuts. Where passengers used to dress professionally to fly, they now arrive at the airport in shorts and sandals. Times have changed and so has the technology that goes along with it.

Over the last ten years you have witnessed changes in aviation. You have adapted. You have conformed to NextGen by installing the necessary equipment. First ADS-B replaced the radar. Next, SBC replaced ground-based communications. Finally, you, as pilots, are able to see what the controllers have been watching all along. You are able to see all the other aircraft around you. This technology is a double-edged sword. On one hand, it provides the safety of the individual flight crews assisting the controller. On the other hand, it reveals the controller's plan, which is not always appreciated by the pilots. Soon you realized the benefits outweighed the aggravation, not to mention the savings were significant.

"Tomorrow! Tomorrow is here, my friends. What you will be witnessing over the next seven years will take you from the dark smoke filled control rooms, with grouchy controllers barking out control instructions, to a sterile environment with computers humming and monitors covering the walls. No longer will you hear that friendly voice on the radio. What will you hear? Nothing! Nothing at all! You will sit in your cockpit, no longer listening for the controller to call your name. You will watch your displays waiting for the clearance to be transmitted to your autopilot. What? What are you thinking? Is this the way you want to fly your aircraft? Is this what you signed up for? It may not be, but the future is here. We are not alone in the sky. It has been determined that we no longer have the ability, as humans, to provide a safe environment in these skies.

"Over the last eight months I have had the privilege of testing the next big thing. The four-dimensional trajectory is the next step in the puzzle we call NextGen. We have run hundreds of scenarios and solved scores of issues. Now, as I speak, the software engineers are putting the final touches on the program which will put the controllers in the back seat and take over the stressful job of controlling the skies. Are you apprehensive?"

The roaring acknowledgement told Charlie that they had their doubts. He continued, "Let me explain in common language what 4DT is designed to do. In your cockpit you watch your ADS-B display, which gives you situational awareness. 4DT processes your position, both geographical and altitude, your direction of flight and speed. All the time it is processing all the other aircraft in the system the same way. When 4DT recognizes a potential conflict, it transfers the data to another macro that looks at the variables. The first variable is the type of aircraft, particularly to the capabilities of the aircraft. Next, it looks at the logic of turning one of the two aircraft. What is the logic? Time! It looks at the delay caused by vectoring versus the cost of an altitude change. We have laboriously compiled data on all known aircraft and company procedures. So you should not be asked to perform beyond either the manufacturer's specifications or your company's guidelines. The third calculation the macro performs is distance from departure airport and destination.

"Once all the data have been calculated, the macro will issue the proper clearance that is directed to the aircraft. All aircraft flying in controlled airspace will be required to be NextGen equipped. The SBC has the ability to either direct these commands to the autopilot or display it on your LCD. Manual mode requires the pilot's acknowledgement and compliance.

"As a controller and a pilot it is my advice you approach 4DT with cautious optimism. Maintain control of your aircraft, captains! The welfare of your passengers and crew are and will always be your responsibility. In theory, our program will safely take you from runway to runway. But as with anything mechanical, it is susceptible to failure. I have witnessed the testing and am confident with moving forward with live testing, which will be starting right here in Las Vegas next spring."

Charlie didn't know if the applause was one of approval
of the program or the location. "In seven years, NextGen is
scheduled for completion. At that time the National Airspace
System will be under its control. As for the technical details of
the program it is available on the FAA's website. Please read
this information and become familiar with its contents.

"One hundred and six years ago, a pilot in a Wright
Model EX took 84 days to go from coast to coast. Seventy-nine
years later, a couple of pilots in an SR-71 Blackbird crossed the
West Coast at a speed over 2000 miles an hour and sixty-four
minutes later crossed the East Coast. That is progress! Where
will it end? Or will it ever end?

"We pilots have been given some reprieve to this
insanity of technology. A few years back the FAA created the
sport pilot. This gave us the ability to go out and dance through
and around the clouds in uncontrolled airspace. We are able to
leave technology behind and once again experience the joy of
flying in its simplest form. To watch the sunset from a
thousand feet as the last glimmer of light is rapidly fading into
darkness. We are blessed to witness the lights of our city flicker
to life. Reducing the throttle we glide our flying machine
around the pattern and gently return it to earth.

"My fellow pilots, be not concerned with the drastic
changes facing us as a community of aviators, but rather
embrace the future while retaining the past. Never give up that
first love of flying. May God bless you and this great country!
Goodnight!"

Charlie felt as if the applause would never end as he
waved to the audience. The arena vibrated from the noise and
his head started spinning. Thankfully Senator Rister arrived at
his side and took the microphone from his hand.

"Thank you, Senator," Charlie softly whispered as he
felt the strength drain from his body.

Chapter 22

Charlie's escort was waiting at the bottom of the steps. "They want me to take you to the green room. There are a handful of VIPs waiting for you."

"VIPs can wait! Where are my wife and daughter?" Charlie asked very pointedly.

"Don't worry, Mr. Beckler, they are in route to the car." On the way to the green room, the escort's radio blared that someone was inquiring about the media wishing to speak with Mr. Beckler.

Charlie shook his head, "No way am I talking to the media tonight. Tell them to go to the FAA website."

Arriving at the green room, Charlie found it occupied by about twenty people, all dressed in suits. They all wanted to meet Charlie and shake his hand. One by one, he made his way around the room and tried to remember who they were. From the General Electric CEO to the president of Cessna, all of them were great leaders in their fields, and Charlie felt honored even to have a chance to meet them, let alone receive congratulations from these industry giants.

The one thing he remembered in all the conversations was from the president of Boeing. "Mr. Beckler, as much as I would love to have you join our company, we really need you right where you are. This country needs more people like you. You could be a politician if you weren't so honest."

After making his rounds, Charlie motioned to his escort that it was time to leave.

"Are you in a hurry?" the guard grinned as they headed for the car.

"You bet! I can't handle too much of this stuff. I'm afraid it might wear off on me, and I can't have that happen."

"I would like to know how you feel, Mr. Beckler, but it's hard not to put you in that category."

"What do you mean?"

"Come on, Mr. Beckler, you flew in here tonight in a G4 and were driven over here in a stretch limousine."

Charlie smiled at the guard, "I see what you're saying, but trust me, I'm just like you. We both have a job to do, and thanks so much for doing yours." Charlie shook his new friend's hand and crawled into the limo.

No sooner had the limo left the arena than Charlie's cell phone started buzzing.

"Sean, how are you feeling?" Charlie asked as he answered his phone.

"Charlie, you did it! I just wanted to commend you on a job well done."

"Who have you been talking to, Sean?" Charlie asked.

"Nobody, I watched it live. They had it on three different networks. Whether you like it or not, Charlie, you are now a celebrity."

"Guess the real question, Boss, is if I still have a job."

"Don't worry about the job," Sean answered. "You just go enjoy the weekend and we'll talk about your job on Monday. Heard you're going on up to Ely tonight."

"Yeah, I thought we should, considering we're so close."

"Don't forget, Charlie. Everything is close when you have a jet. Just bring it back in one piece. Thanks again for stepping in."

146

"Mr. Beckler!" Captain Todd Lincoln called from the cockpit as Charlie entered the G4.

"Everything okay, Captain?"

"Don't know about everything, but that speech of yours sure brought back memories of my younger days back in Ohio where I learned to fly. Sure do miss those times."

Charlie smiled, "Don't ever lose those memories. Sure you fly around in this multimillion dollar Gulfstream, but when you get the time, go fly a little puddle jumper around the countryside a couple of times, it will do your heart good."

"Thanks, Charlie. The controllers pulled some strings with Nellis and got us clearance through their airspace. It will save us ten minutes or so. We can depart anytime you're ready."

"Light 'em up, Captain. Take us home."

"November Zero Three Golf Alpha, winds three-five zero at six knots, cleared for takeoff." This time Charlie was sitting back with Carrie and Mitzy in the club seating area of the aircraft. No longer was he stressed about the future. Mission accomplished, it was time to enjoy the reward.

"Guess what?" Charlie grabbed Carries hand.

"What?" she mocked.

"No, really! I have an idea I think you will like."

"Really? Does it have to do with moving back to Georgia or sex?"

"Oh, nice! Don't talk like that in front of your daughter."

"Oh, Charlie, don't be a fuddy-duddy," she drawled as she leaned over and kissed him as the jet screamed off the runway and into the night sky. "Sorry, darling, I shouldn't make fun of you. I love you tremendously, and we would not be here if it weren't for you. What are you thinking?"

Charlie gave Carrie the pouting look and squeezed her hand. "Don't know if you deserve it now. I was thinking we should fly up to Seattle or over to San Francisco tomorrow night with Jim and Sandy. He was an integral part to solving the 4DT problem. Why not give him something back?"

"We can do that?" Carrie grinned from ear to ear.

"Sure! You and Sandy talk it over and we'll make it a date."

Thirty-three minutes after taking off from McCarron International airport they were on the ground in Ely. Charlie looked at his watch. He had gotten up this morning at five thirty, worked all day, flown to Las Vegas, given a thirty-minute speech, flown on to Ely and it was still only ten fifteen. The airport shuttle was waiting at the ramp. Charlie said goodnight to the flight crew and crawled into the van. All of a sudden, he felt very tired. The next thing he remembered was Carrie waking him up. "We're home, darling."

Chapter 23

It was after ten when Charlie's phone rang. "Get up you old fart!" Jim hollered. "What time did you get in?"

"We got in too late for this phone call. What are you up to?"

"Got us an eleven thirty tee time at White Pine. Are you up to it?"

"You bet, my friend. Give me fifteen minutes." Charlie jumped out of bed and into the shower. It sure felt good to be home. It would be a great day.

They were only on the third hole when Carrie called. "We decided to go to Aspen. Can we do that?"

Charlie yelled over to Jim, "Want to go to Aspen in the G4 tonight?"

"Oh, no," Jim groaned, "I was hoping for downtown Ely, but if they insist."

Charlie laughed and turned back to Carrie. "It's a done deal. I'll call you back with the departure time in a few minutes." Charlie hung up and dialed the phone number Captain Lincoln had given him the night before.

"Good morning, Charlie. What's up for the day?" Charlie explained what they wanted to do and advised the G4 driver that they would like to arrive in Aspen around seven in the evening.

"That's great, Charlie. We will plan a six o'clock departure and be ready when you get there. How many passengers will be on this trip?"

Charlie waved the foursome behind them through. "It's just four of us this evening, Captain."

"We'll be ready, Charlie, and if you don't mind, make it formal. The women will like it."

"Like clean jeans and a new t-shirt?" Charlie quipped back.

"You know what I mean. Business dress! You do that and we'll make it worth it for you. Not only that, I know a great restaurant in Aspen and will take care of reservations. That's if you don't mind. You like French cuisine?"

"You know it, Captain."

Soon Charlie was on the phone to his wife. "Carrie, you and Sandy need to get your hair done and dress formal. We will need to be at the airport before six."

"Formal?" Carrie questioned, "I know that wasn't your idea."

"Come on now, I am the romantic type. You know that."

"Yes, I know, dear, but somehow I feel you've had help on this one."

"Think whatever you want, but this is going to be the coolest date you've had in a while. I've got to go, babe, my turn to hit the ball."

"You need to call your wife," Charlie told Jim after he had hung up with Carrie. "Just tell her what I told Carrie."

"Dude, you are the greatest. This will be a night to remember," Jim fist-tapped Charlie.

"I'm going to owe you."

"Jim, this is only partial payment for all the time you spent on 4DT."

For the rest of the round of golf, all the guys could talk about was what the night would be like. They reminisced about all the corporate jets they had worked on their way to Aspen and Vail. So many times they would make the comment,

"Wonder who's on this Learjet?" Or, "Someday I'm going to be riding in the back of one of these Citation jets." They finished their game at four and quickly headed home to prepare for the time of their life.

The two couples arrived at the airport fifteen minutes before six. As they pulled into the parking lot, an airport truck with a follow me sign was waiting with lights flashing. It was obvious that the word had got out about what was going on. The parking lot was full and there were well over a hundred people crowding the fence. The truck led them through the gate out onto the tarmac. As they approach the G4, Charlie could only laugh. There had to be at least another twenty or thirty people around the Gulfstream. Coming to a stop next to the plane they could see that this group had lined each side of a red carpet leading to the steps of the aircraft. Charlie and Jim recognized most of the faces as coworkers.

"Dang, guys, you didn't have to come out here for me," Jim hollered as he got out of the car. Considering all the witnesses, the guys did the right thing and opened the doors for the girls, and together, arm in arm, just like a movie premier, they walked up the red carpet, stopping and shaking hands with their friends.

At the steps to the aircraft, they met Captain Lincoln, and he was all smiles, "Don't know what kind of workplace you have here, Charlie, but you do have a lot of friends. All I did was file a flight plan, and obviously someone noticed."

"Did anyone try to sneak onboard?"

"Oh! We had lots of volunteers."

As the two couples were making themselves comfortable in the back, Captain Lincoln was busy talking to ATC. "Just don't ask too many questions, Center. Yes, this is a VIP trip but we do *not*, I say again, we do *not* require special handling!"

"That's all right, November Zero Three Golf Alpha, we'll take care of you. ADS-B has a lock on at the ramp at Ely. What's your estimated time of departure?"

"We should be rolling in five minutes, Center."

"Roger that, November Zero Three Golf Alpha, your clearance is on the way now."

"Thanks, Center, you've been great." Todd hated the way data link had taken away the personal touch pilots used to have with controllers. He always enjoyed the two-way communications. Sometimes it would get testy, but most of the time it was just two professionals getting the job done.

The data link display flashed an incoming message. Sure enough there it was. *N03GA, cleared from the Ely airport via runway heading until reaching twelve-thousand, right turn direct Red Table. Expect flight level four-on- zero ten minutes after departure.* Jerry had finished up his work in the back and slid into the right seat. "Buttoned up and ready to go, Captain. You got our clearance?"

"Affirmative. Straight out runway three six. They are pulling strings again. Got us direct Red Table."

"You have to love flying this guy around. Wonder if he will ever be the administrator?"

"Not likely! Not the bureaucratic type."

"Reckon so. Spinning number one, Captain."

They taxied to the south end of the airport and turned on to the active runway. As with any VFR airport, Todd clicked the mic and broadcast on Unicom frequency. "November Zero Three Golf Alpha departing Runway three six Ely, straight out."

The data link bell sounded as they passed through eighty-five hundred feet. Todd pressed the receive button and read, *N03GA climb and maintain FL410.* Accepting the clearance he entered the altitude in the autopilot. "Up to four one oh," he said out loud as had been the procedure since he had started flying. He wondered if that would end once 4DT took over.

Two minutes later, Jerry called, "Out of twelve thousand and turning direct Red Table." The sleek jet climbed into the ever-darkening sky passing over the rugged mountains of the Humboldt National Forest.

Charlie sat in his favorite spot on the left side of the aircraft just in front of the wing. Carrie sat on his right. Jim and Sandy sat across from them facing back. "First time I've flown backwards," Jim commented.

"It's probably because the cattle haulers don't face backwards," Charlie laughed. "It's only an hour flight. If it bothers you I'm sure the captain will let you get up and stretch."

"Charlie, I don't think anything could bother me right now." He pulled up his footrest and lay back in the seat.

"Jim, while we are here enjoying life, tell me what is it you would like to accomplish? When the time comes to give up controlling airplanes, who and what do you want to be?"

"Heck of a question from someone I thought was my friend. Is this an Amway meeting?"

Charlie gave Jim a stop being funny look and responded, "Would it matter if it was? You are up here in the lap of luxury and you're questioning my motive. Jim, times are changing and we need to change with it or be left behind. I know you have studied the changes coming. The day will be here all too soon when we will no longer be relevant. Make your plans now on how you will transition."

"You think they're going to force us into retirement?"

"Most likely, but there will always be something to do if you are on top of your game and have prepared yourself for the future."

"What do you mean by top of my game?"

"Jim, the reason you're on this flight is the ingenuity you used in solving programming challenges. That same ingenuity will open all kinds of doors. Not only with aviation, but any field you step into."

153

Jim's frown told it all. "I don't know anything else. What am I supposed to do?"

"Dang it, Jim! You've got to stop being so pessimistic. We still have a job, and we have contacts. You are so far ahead in the game. Your confidence level should be about as high as this airplane. Let's map out a plan."

Captain Lincoln picked up the microphone and announced to his passengers that they were ten minutes out and to get ready for landing. For the last fifty miles they had been on a gradual descent towards the Red Table VOR.

Charlie headed up to the cockpit. "Is there any chance of riding up here on the approach, Captain?"

"Sure, Charlie, we will be over the initial approach fix in just a couple of minutes."

Charlie quickly strapped himself into the jump seat. Crossing over the VOR at fourteen thousand feet, the autopilot started the step-down approach to a missed approach altitude of ten thousand two hundred feet above sea level.

Charlie thought back to a cloudy March evening back in 2001. A GIII, inbound from Los Angeles, was on this same approach. Like this evening, a passenger was seated in the jump seat, and in the back of the airplane were seated thirteen of his friends, all excited about their weekend in Aspen. Something dreadfully wrong happened that night, and the airplane crashed short of the runway killing everyone on board. Charlie, while somewhat concerned, knew that this night was different. This aircraft had an infrared display, which greatly enhanced night vision. Looking out the windscreen, you could only see the glow of lights from the town. A black and white display showed the outline of the mountains, and one could even see the shape of the vehicles on Highway 82. Breaking out of the clouds well above the minimums, Captain Lincoln called the runway in sight. They made a descending right hand

154

turn followed by a left turn lining up with Runway One Five. Charlie would never get tired of this part of flying. The whole concept of transitioning from airborne to earthbound was by far the most exciting part of flying. The radar altimeter called out the altitudes as they descended onto a dark runway lined with brilliant lights. Captain Lincoln brought N03GA down to taxi speed and taxied back to the ramp.

As soon as the engines died down, a limo came out to the aircraft to pick up the four hungry travelers.

"Hope you don't mind," First Officer Nelson told Charlie. "I knew you'd need a ride to town. Don't worry about the cost. I was told to put it on our expense account."

"Do I mind? No way! But do the taxpayers know what they're paying for?"

Jerry shrugged his shoulders, "Just doing what I'm told. You need to quit worrying about the small things, Charlie. From my understanding they wouldn't care considering what you have done for the cause of aviation."

"Thank you, Jerry. You guys going to go eat with us?"

"Now, you know we can't do that. We are just the hired help. The captain and I will be heading up town for a quick dinner. Just give us a call thirty minutes before you folks want to take off. It'll give us time to get our flight plan filed."

Fifteen minutes later, the two couples were escorted to their window table at the famous Cache Cache Bistro. The candles flickered against the bone white china which adorned cotton white tables. Through the reflection in the window, the flames gave a warming effect to the snowflakes starting to fall outside the window. A sharply dressed elderly waiter immediately offered them a wine list from which Charlie ordered a Chardonnay from Italy called Via De Romans along with the foie gras terrine for appetizers. The duck arrived quickly along with the white wine. The guys decided they wanted the New York strip steak which was served with pommes frites, better known in English as French fries. This along with a Dijon-Peppercorn sauce completed their entree. Carrie chose the veal osso buco with marsala sauce and french lentils. Sandy was brave and went for the lamb. The Colorado Rack of Lamb came with potatoes au gratin and veal jus.

For two hours, they sat enjoying dinner as snow started to build on the tables outside. After a dessert of chocolate mousse parfait and coffee, they said goodnight to their waiter and walked out into the cold Rocky Mountain air. They walked down the streets of Aspen as a brisk breeze blew in off the mountains. At ten thirty, Charlie called the pilots and advised that they would be heading back to the airport in fifteen minutes.

Departing to the north, November Zero Three Golf Alpha leveled off at forty-thousand feet. In the back of the airplane, Charlie turned down the interior lights and put on some soft classical music. It was quiet in the airplane as the two couples pondered the experience of the evening. It was not every day that you could fly over four hundred miles, eat an incredible dinner in such a beautiful setting, and be home by midnight.

"Charlie, would you come up here?" asked Captain Lincoln on the speaker.

"What's up?" Charlie asked as he stuck his head in the cockpit.

"West CATS wants to know if we can accept holding. I think they're messing with us. Want to talk to the hillbillies?"

"Sure, it's got to be a joke." Picking up the hand mic, Charlie pressed the button. "West CATS, Gulfstream Zero Three Golf Alpha, how long can we expect to hold?"

"November Zero Three Golf Alpha, West CATS, we were just yanking your chain. Heard you were on board. It's all good, cleared direct Ely."

"Direct Ely November Zero Three Golf Alpha, Allan is that you?"

"Welcome home, Charlie. We need you man. When you coming home for good?"

"I haven't released that info my friend, but it should be before the snow melts in the spring."

"Great! Come by and visit before you head back east."

"Thanks, Allan, but we'll be flying out tomorrow right after church."

"You and church, you never change. Well, take care and look forward to seeing you back." Charlie gave the mic back to Captain Lincoln and headed back to his seat.

Carrie was sitting all alone in the club seating area as Charlie slid in beside her.

"Jim and Sandy got a little frisky so I pulled a Mitzy and told 'em to get a room. And they did. They headed back to the couch. Don't think you want to go back there."

"Great, how will I explain that one to my boss?" Carrie grabbed Charlie and kissed him hard on the lips. "What was that for?" Charlie asked as they came up for air.

"Just for being the best friend a woman could ask for," Carrie replied and kissed him again. Midnight found the FAA's prized airplane on final to Ely.

Sunday morning was like a homecoming for the Becklers. Their pastor, along with all their friends, welcomed them. The same question was asked over and over. "When are you coming home for good?" It felt great to be loved. Charlie and Carrie had met people in New Jersey, but it wasn't the same. The church they attended on the east coast welcomed them, but knowing the short duration of their stay, they subconsciously withdrew.

After all the goodbyes, they took the shuttle back to the airport. No fanfare or red carpet, just the three of them and their luggage.

157

"Greetings, Captain, did you get my message?"

"Sure did, Charlie. Have you told them?"

"Heck no! Otherwise it wouldn't be a surprise."

"Great! Then I will just shut up and let you guys get settled."

Carrie, overhearing the captain, squeezed Charlie's arm and through her teeth asked, "What surprise?"

"Oh, nothing much, you will see." As an afterthought Charlie added, "In time, darling."

"Oh, if I didn't love you so much I'd...." Carrie growled. Charlie ignored Carrie's comment and sat back in his favorite seat. It was the one that, just two days, ago he had first acquired.

Chapter 24

They were in the air headed east by one in the afternoon. Climbing through Flight Level three-six-zero, they passed through some high cirrus clouds. They had just a couple of bumps and it smoothed out again as they reached the upper levels of the atmosphere. "Daddy," Mitzy purred as she slid into the seat beside him.

"What, my little girl?"

"Mommy said you had a surprise, and you know how I like surprises."

"Yes, I do."

"So, what is it?"

"Not that easy, kiddo." Charlie picked up a magazine and started reading. Mitzy smacked him on the arm playfully and went back to her seat.

The sun was setting behind them as the aircraft started down. It had been a long weekend, and even though they had traveled a lot of miles none of them felt tired. It was different from riding coach on the airlines. No standing in lines. No hassling with gate agents. No elbows in your side in the narrow seats.

"I always want to travel this way," Carrie told Charlie. "This has to have been one of the best weekends of my life. I just don't want it to end."

Charlie reached over and grabbed her hand, "The clock hasn't struck midnight, Cinderella. You're still wearing the glass slippers."

"Yes, I know," Carrie replied, "but I just heard the landing gear go down, and the ground is growing bigger."

Charlie looked deep into Carrie's eyes. "Think not about what you see, but think about your dreams, my darling. What do you want more than anything else in this world?"

"I want to go home."

"Where is home? Is it California, Nevada, New Jersey? We have so many homes. Just where is home?"

Now tears were coming to Carrie's eyes. "Don't do this to me, Charlie. You know my home is in Georgia. I want to see my mom and dad."

The speaker blared as Captain Lincoln announced they were on final and for everyone to prepare for landing. Captain Lincoln taxied up to the ramp and shut down the engines.

"Sure going to miss that sound," Carrie commented as they gathered up their things.

"Wait just a minute, Carrie. I have a couple of friends that want to meet us here."

"Can't we meet them outside?"

"No, they want to check out the airplane. You know, sit in the seat and smell the luxury."

"Sure, my man! Why not? Let's just not be too long. You have to go to work tomorrow."

"Not a problem darling, we will get 'em out of here in a hurry."

First Officer Nelson lowered the air stair door and Carrie let out a scream and jumped up. "Mom! Dad! What are you guys doing in Atlantic City?"

"Welcome to Georgia, Carrie."

"You mean we're not in New Jersey?"

"Guess you got on the wrong flight. This one's in God's country."

Carrie turned around and gave Charlie a big hug. "You never cease to amaze me."

Charlie stopped by the pilots' lounge to cover their departure time for Atlantic City later that night and the family headed out to the farm. They spent the evening sitting around the fireplace eating popcorn and drinking apple cider. They shared stories of the weekend, and Will shared how his flying buddies had watched the telecast of Charlie's speech. It was decided that Mitzy would spend a few days with her grandparents and they would fly her up the next weekend.

"Now the Cirrus isn't as fancy as what you flew here in, but I'll let you fly," Grandpa Will told Mitzy, who smiled her agreement to the plan.

The Shoemakers dropped Charlie and Carrie off at the airport at ten forty-five. Charlie looked at his watch as the Gulfstream took them one last time to the skies. It was eleven fifteen.

"Is this really it?" Carrie asked.

"Yes, darling, this is the last flight. We are headed to Atlantic City. Are you ready for the weekend to be over?"

"No! I have one more thing I would like to do." She got up and headed back to the lavatory. "I'm going to freshen up. Meet me on the couch." As the plane started its descent into Atlantic City, Carrie ran her hands through Charlie's hair and said, "Now I am complete. Thank you for a great weekend. One more question."

"What's that, girlfriend?"

"How are you going to top this next weekend?"

Chapter 25

Charlie's notoriety became a challenge as the calls started coming in on Monday morning. He had roused the interest of the flying community, and they wanted his attention. Charlie instructed his secretary to turn down the offers for speaking engagements. He had too much work to do in the next three months to accommodate their request. The stress of Bud's software team taking so long to fix 4DT was getting to Charlie. Every day he would be briefed on the progress, which seemed to be moving forward at a snail's pace.

It was Sean who came to his rescue in early December. "Charlie, do you have plans today?"

"I don't have a thing to do. This waiting game is killing me, Boss. What's up?"

"Be at the hanger in an hour. I'll tell you about it when you get there."

Charlie arrived at the hanger as the Gulfstream was taxiing up to the ramp. "Good to see you again, Boss. How's life inside the beltway?"

"It sucks, my friend! That's why I decided we needed a road trip. Or should I say a sky trip."

"Where are we going?" Charlie asked.

"Oklahoma City, ever been there?"

"What the heck is in Oklahoma?"

"Tell you on the way. Let's go!"

Climbing on board he had to stick his head in the cockpit and greet his old friends. "Good to see you again,

162

Charlie." Captain Lincoln turned shaking his hand. "Is it just the two of you today?"

"Yep, the boss isn't all that bad, but I think I'd prefer the wife."

"You got that right, Charlie. Sure enjoyed that weekend out west. You guys make great passengers. When you strike it rich and buy one of these things, give me a call."

"I'll remember that!" Charlie laughed and headed back to his familiar seat.

"So, why are we going to Oklahoma?" Charlie again asked Sean as the G4 was climbing out westbound.

"Simulation," Sean responded.

"What do you mean by simulation?"

"Sure, we now have three full motion simulators at the Mike Monroney Aeronautical Center. They have been equipped with 4DT equipment and we get to fly 'em."

"What are we looking for?"

"Reality, Charlie! You have been working your tail off from the controller's perspective. We need you to see what is happening in the cockpit."

"Okay, but what about the new software? We don't have the patch completed."

"Don't worry, the problem is only ground-based."

Charlie raised his eyebrows, "So are you saying that if there was a problem the flight crew would be unaware?"

"I hadn't thought of it that way. That's why we have you. You have this uncanny ability to see the 'what ifs' in the scheme of things."

"Thanks, Boss! Don't know whether to take that as words of encouragement or condemnation."

"Anyhow you will get your chance to run it through the ringers today. Hope you know how to fly a 737."

"If it has a throttle and a yoke, it's all mine," Charlie shot back at his boss, who was rapidly becoming one of his best friends. They descended on the GPS approach to runway three five.

Crossing over the Canadian River, Charlie thought back to his first time here at the aeronautical center.

He had arrived here with his wife in September 1996 as a new trainee. He had only four years experience controlling airplanes around the world and at sea. Arriving here had been a new chapter in their life, moving into the civilian sector of air traffic control. His instructor told the class of twenty-six students that half of them would not make it through the screening program. Charlie sat there listening to each of his classmates introduce themselves and brag about their education. By the time it got back to Charlie, he was pretty sure he was under-educated in his classmate's eyes. Knowing what it took to be an air traffic controller, he stood up and looked around the room. His introduction was not one of description of his education but of his resolve. "My name is Charlie Beckler, recently resigned from the United States Navy, and I am not here to uphold your statistics, I am here to make new ones." With that he sat down. The silence had been awkward until the stunned instructor welcomed him and moved on the next student.

They had spent the next three months learning the air traffic control manual and the map of "Aero Center." Aero Center was the airspace the school used to run the simulated scenarios to determine the abilities of the students. This had been accomplished using flight plans printed on strips of paper calculated by time and altitude. By the end of the three months, the class of twenty-six had been reduced to seventeen and Charlie passed with a score of 83 percent, well above the 70 percent required. It had been the strength of his score that had sent him to Palmdale and Los Angeles Center. If he had just gotten a lower score, he could have ended up at a tower where he really wanted to go.

As the plane taxied up to the ramp, he recalled the meeting with the placement officer. The students had to fill out a dream sheet for where they wanted to work. When it was Charlie's turn, the officer noted that he had left the air traffic control centers blank and only filled in the tower positions. "That's because I have no desire to work in a center," he had responded. Charlie ended up with a choice of Oakland or Palmdale.

"What a choice!" he grumbled to himself eleven years later.

Charlie was buckled into the Boeing 737 simulator with First Officer Jerry Nelson at his side. In the Airbus 320 simulator, Captain Todd Lincoln was at the controls with Sean riding shotgun. The speaker crackled with the voice of the program controller. "Okay, gentlemen, we are setting you up at ten thousand feet on a collision course. For this first run all you have to do is fly straight and level and enjoy the ride."

The screens came alive, and Charlie found himself flying over the beach of southern California. He was caught up in the clarity of the visuals, even recognizing Santa Ana Airport sliding by his left side. If it weren't for Jerry calling his attention to the 4DT display he would have missed it all together.

"There they are! Think we can hit 'em?"

Charlie looked at the display, then out the window. Sure enough just there was the Airbus closing in on them from the east. An alert flashed on the 4DT screen and the incoming command appeared. "November Two Six Five Alpha, climb and maintain one one thousand."

"What do we do now, Charlie? Are we suppose to climb or is this thing linked with the autopilot?"

"Don't know! Let's see what happens." Sure enough the simulator throttles moved forward, and the aircraft climbed

165

a thousand feet. Leveling off at eleven thousand feet, Charlie watched as the Airbus passed underneath them and out to sea.

They spent the next two hours flying different scenarios. It really was an educational experience for Charlie to see 4DT from the pilot's eyes. It really got exciting when they added a dozen simulated aircraft into the program. The commands came quicker and more pronounced as the computer weaved the group of aircraft into a sequence for landing at LAX.

Crawling out of the simulator, the four men agreed that there was a future for NextGen and were anxious to put it into play in real life situations. It was four in the afternoon when the Gulfstream departed Will Rogers International Airport and turned east climbing to flight level four-five-zero. With the wind at their back, they had a ground speed of 550 knots. Charlie stared out the window with a million things on his mind. Why had he been so blessed? All he had done was to tell the truth and embrace the future. Was that what it took?

Sean interrupted his thoughts. "Charlie, I have been thinking. I would like for you to come to Washington."

"You want me in Washington tonight?" Charlie asked.

"No! I'm talking about you transferring to headquarters."

"Sorry, Boss! Washington is not on my to-do list. Why do you need me in Washington?"

"You are a man of integrity, and that is uncommon inside the beltway. The FAA has spent billions of taxpayers' dollars and needs a face on the money."

"Face on the money," Charlie laughed. "I thought that was for famous presidents."

"So now we have a comedian. What I'm talking about is a face on NextGen. You are now a celebrity among pilots and people trust you. If we could get you into the position of spokesperson for the FAA, it would improve our image."

"Sean, thank you for the thought, and I would be happy to play your game of spokesperson, but it has to be done from Ely. We are taking 4DT out west in two months, and I'm going with it."

Sean scratched his chin. "I hadn't thought about it that way. I will run it by the administrator and see what happens. He really wanted you at headquarters."

"Great! Now I've dissed the administrator. Give him my regards and apology but I need to go home."

"Understood! We will see what we can do with the idea of telecommuting from Nevada."

Turning back to the window he could see the sun was rapidly disappearing behind them as darkness engulfed the aircraft. *Was it only the administration that wanted him in Washington?* Charlie thought to himself. *Or was he running from God's plan?*

Chapter 26

It was February and the team was on the move west. Bud had assured Charlie that the fix worked and he should no longer notice even an inkling of hesitation. 4DT was installed into the ERAM system and ready for the first live testing. Charlie and his family had arrived in January so he could regain his currency. Now just the day before Valentine's Day he plugged into Sector 6 and called Las Vegas approach, "Granite Sector 6!"

"Go ahead, six."

"Is that you, Virginia?"

"Affirmative, Charlie! You ready?"

Charlie looked at his inbound list at N03GA coming in from Burbank. "You bet! The first bird will be in my sky in ten minutes."

"West CATS, this is Gulfstream Zero Three Golf Alpha descending to flight level two-four-zero."

"Gulfstream Zero Three Golf Alpha, West CATS, roger. You are cleared to descend via the Kepec seven arrival. Las Vegas altimeter is two-niner-niner zero. Switch over to 4DT crossing Kepec."

"Roger, Center, descending on the Kepec, two-niner niner zero. We're going to 4DT at Kepec. Gulfstream Zero Three Golf Alpha." Charlie was not sure about this test flight and had decided to verify contact with the pilot. Las Vegas was the first approach control and tower to go 4DT in conjunction with the center. This test had been well publicized thanks to

168

Charlie's collateral duty as the new face of the FAA. Once the aircraft switched to 4DT, NextGen would take over and send control instructions to the autopilot all the way through landing.

Charlie felt the presence of additional people behind him. Turning around, he recognized Barney, who was trying to explain what was going on to a couple of civilians with visitor badges. *Oh, that's just what we need,* Charlie thought, *IWH and the press.* It makes a moronic combination with tomorrow's newspapers.

"Charlie! Pay attention!" growled Ted, the supervisor who had been assigned to watch Charlie during the test. "This is for real. We need to watch what the Gulfstream does."

"Are you serious?" Charlie responded turning around looking at Barney. "If this was that critical then you would get the nonessential personnel out of here." Ted shot Charlie a 'please-don't-start' look as three other participating aircraft started flashing at the sector. As with the others, Charlie chose not to use data link to clear these aircraft to 4DT control.

"Sector 6, Vegas on the arrival line!" Virginia shouted over the arrival line to Sector 6 at the center.

"Go ahead, Vegas, this is Sector 6," Charlie answered.

"What is the status of November Zero Three Golf Alpha?" Virginia asked with apprehension in her voice.

"He's twenty miles outside of Clarr on the flash as we speak," Charlie replied in a much calmer voice.

"Thanks, you know this is real, right?" snapped Virginia.

"Yep," Charlie drawled, annoyed at Virginia being so on edge, "It's gotta make you proud. We're being replaced by a computer." Charlie signed off with his initials and punched off the line.

Virginia sat in silence as she watched the four aircraft start flashing from all four corners of her scope. She took the handoffs knowing that it didn't matter anyway. She was only going to be an observer this time as NextGen sent instantaneous messages to the aircraft.

Todd sat at the controls of the Gulfstream. As he dialed in the Kepec arrival and hit enter, he knew he was about to give up what he had worked his whole adult life in achieving. Todd had worked hard to become a pilot. As a young boy, he had run through the pastures of their Kansas farm with his arms straight out pretending to be an airplane. He had lain on his back in freshly cut grass looking at the contrails in the sky and small planes flying overhead, dreaming that someday he would be at the controls of a big jet. Those were the things that had caused Todd to move towards a career in flying.

He had spent many years at a small FBO in Pratt, Kansas, working his way through his ratings. Todd's goal was to someday fly a corporate jet. This goal was answered when he got picked up by an oil company to fly right seat in their citation jet. Three years later the company bought a second jet, and Todd was promoted to captain. *That was fifteen years ago,* Todd thought. *Look at me now, all I have become is a computer operator for the FAA. Now if I can remember to push the activate button over Mison we have it made. Someday it will do that for me too!*

"What do you think?' Virginia's supervisor, Sam, asked, breaking the silence.

"Not comfortable at all," she answered, "not used to giving up control."

"Keep a close eye on them. Oh! And, not to add pressure, but this is being shown live on all the major news channels. They got a feed from Central Flow. This is being heralded as the first ever hands off sequence and auto landing. Seems it's as important as when man stepped on the moon."

Virginia thanked her uncouth boss for his input and went back to the job of watching four aircraft moving rapidly

towards one runway. The computer display to her right showed
the sequence coming into play as the Gulfstream from over
Kepec was number one, followed by the Learjet coming in from
the northeast over Luxor. The number three was the Boeing
747 from the Orient arriving over Fuzzy from the northwest.
The final aircraft in the test was a Southwest airlines flight
coming in from the southeast over Kaddy. As the Gulfstream
crossed over Kepec, NextGen sent a speed and altitude
command to the aircraft. Virginia watched as the aircraft
started slowing and descending. Virginia keyed the mic,
"Gulfstream Zero Three Golf Alpha, Las Vegas approach."

"Go ahead, Vegas!"

"Just a little nervous here. Just making sure you're here
if we need you."

"We are here with our eyes wide open. Just say the
word, and we'll shut this thing off."

"Roger that!" Virginia quipped. She felt a little better
knowing there was a live person in that aircraft and not just a
bunch of bits and bytes. By now the other three aircraft were
crossing their fixes, and NextGen was calculating the sequence
over one thousand times a second and sending adjustments to
the aircrafts' autopilots. Virginia could only sit there and think
about the time it would take if she had to verbally issue all these
instructions and wait for each pilot's response. As much as she
hated to admit it, she knew that, once again, man had created a
system that could supersede his own ability in handling
complex situations. Virginia and the other controllers at Las
Vegas were the best there could be. They worked an average of
eighteen hundred flights a day. It was estimated that NextGen
could double that amount. It wasn't long before Virginia saw
the plan and watched NextGen line all four aircraft up on final;
speeds were slowly matching up and spacing was perfect.
Wow! She thought. *I could not have done that better myself.*

Virginia jumped as the speaker blared loudly,
"Approach! This is local! Where are the airplanes?"

171

"Are you nervous? Know what you mean, me, too! The first one is twelve miles out, you should see 'em anytime. The rest are three miles in trail. Might as well take a break, this thing knows what it's doing." Virginia hung up and continued watching as the four aircraft, one by one landed and dropped off her scope.

Up in the tower, Tanya watched as the first aircraft under NextGen control touched down on 25 Right. N03GA, the now famous Gulfstream that had flown Charlie in here just last fall, was off the runway as the Learjet crossed the threshold. Next the 747 landed, and to Tanya's amazement, TALC gave additional spacing behind the heavy for the Southwest 737, which was the last to land. Each aircraft called ground control for taxi instructions as it left the runway. It would not be long before that too would be NextGen's move. Tanya knew that once that happened, the job she did would lose the zeal it had held for controllers over the last nine decades.

Chapter 27

"Samir, you have to get over here!" Abdur growled into the phone.

"Why is that, my friend? What's going on?"

It had been over ten years since Abdur and his friends Samir and Khurram had solved the ERAMS problem. Abdur was the only one with knowledge of the Trojan horse, which he, as a result of coercion, had installed in the program. For all these years, he had been spending his spare time trying to determine the contents of this virus. Finally he had succeeded, but to his dismay. He had to tell someone and the only one he trusted was his friend and now partner of their software company. "I can't tell you on the phone. Just get over here."

"So what's this all about?" Samir inquired as he slid into a chair next to Abdur and turned to his old friend, who had a look of depression mixed with fear.

"Samir, I have always trusted you as a brother and a friend. I am most ashamed at what I am about to tell you." Abdur took Samir back to the meeting with the terrorist and the threats on his family. He told him of the Trojan horse and how he had installed it.

"That is an incredible drama, my friend. So why are you telling me this now?"

Abdur looked out the window as if someone were watching, and turned back to Samir with tears in his eyes. "Samir, I have never done anything to hurt anyone. If this Trojan horse is allowed to engage the program, it will take many lives."

"How do you know that? It may not even work."

"Oh, it will work. It has taken me ten years to break the code, but it is there. It will not only take over the airspace system, it will take over security, locking down all systems that go up against it."

Samir sat there stunned as Abdur brought up the code on his computer screen, showing him line by line how the Trojan horse would take command of NextGen.
Ten minutes into the review, Samir grabbed Abdur's hand. "Stop! Back up! There, look at that. It's worse than you thought."

"What are you talking about?" Abdur looked perplexedly at his friend.

"Look at this code right here. It is taking over the autopilots. This language here sends security commands to the aircraft that will lock out the disconnect switch for the autopilot." Samir scooted up closer to the screen. He was now getting into the program he had just been introduced to.

Abdur still did not quite understand. "How is it doing that? There is no direct connection between security and the autopilot."

"Simple, my friend! When the framers of NextGen developed the system, it was decided that all seven modules would be linked together. The security module would protect the complete package. Through that design is how the Trojan horse is able to move."

"What should we do now?" Abdur was beside himself pacing the floor as if his life was hanging by a thread.

"You need to contact the FAA. I know it will hurt, but it's not too late to do the right thing. It will save a lot of lives, and it just may keep this country out of another war."
Abdur and Samir laid out a plan on how they would get the information to the Federal Aviation Administration without revealing their identity. If they sent a message via snail mail, it could not be traced to their office. Once the Trojan horse was

found it would be scrubbed and all would be well. *What a perfect plan,* Abdur thought as he hugged his friend when they parted. He sat down at his computer and wrote a letter to the NextGen security division at the FAA.

Sarah Andrews looked back over the letter delivered to her desk that morning. It was written with eloquence and was obviously written by an individual with knowledge. It claimed a Trojan horse was in the system. It didn't explain how, it just said it was there. She was required to act on all threats, but this wasn't really a threat, it was already there. She would bring it up at the next security meeting. They security team would dissect the letter for authenticity. Setting it aside, she went on with more pressing matters on her agenda for the day.

A few days later the security team looked over Sarah's letter somewhat jovially at their weekly meeting. After making jokes about a big wooden horse rolling into the NextGen building, they decided to pass it on to the software development team. That is where the link was broken. Once it landed in the inbox of the software development department, it just made the pile of papers higher. Software engineers made lousy organizers, and an inbox was a thing for rainy days.

Abdur kept watching the NextGen blog sites waiting for something that would ensure that the Trojan horse had been discovered and removed. It had been three months since he had mailed the letter and still not a word. Not even a mention of anything wrong. The bloggers kept saying that the 4DT would be operational nation-wide by September 2020. That was less than eighteen months away. Surely someone would take him seriously. But who in the FAA could he trust without going to jail?

Abdur was reading an aviation periodical when he came across an article about a retired air traffic controller who had bought a farm in Indiana. He had cut a runway into the property, creating a haven for pilots. The thing that really impressed Abdur about this former ATC Specialist was his ingenuity and generosity. The airport was not the only thing on the property. They had built a Christian camp where families could come for help. Its purpose was to help people get their lives back together. It did not matter where you came from or who you were. When things were falling apart you could find a friend at this laid-back camp. *That is just what I need* thought Abdur. *This guy could help.* He picked up the phone and called Camp Cloud Nine.

"What do you mean I need to fly out there?" Charlie replied to his old friend Daniel Winster.

"Charlie, just get on a jet and fly into Indianapolis. I will have my brother pick you up there. You will be home by tomorrow morning."

"So why don't you come out here? You are the one retired."

"Can't do that! I have someone here at the camp you need to meet with. I'm sure you know him."

"Put him on the phone, it will save me a trip."

"No can do, Charlie! You never know who may be listening to this conversation. Come on, Charlie, it will not be a waste of time."

"I think you're crazy, Winster, but if you insist I'll be there. You said your brother would pick me up? Is he as crazy as you?"

"Worse! He's older and only flies with his seeing eye dog."

As Charlie entered the luggage area, a grizzly looking guy with a cardboard sign with Charlie's name scribbled on it met him.

"Charlie?"

"You Dan's brother?"

"Yep! Duane's the name. You got any luggage?"

"Only my carry on. How far is the camp?"

"About an hour flight in the Archer. You like small planes?"

"You could say that. Fly a little myself. Where's the dog?"

Duane laughed "That old codger. He tells everyone about the dog. I got rid of the dog a couple of years ago. Use Braille these days. You know, keep feeling for the runway till I find it."

They departed on runway three-two, climbing to twenty-five hundred feet and headed north.

"Heard you tell ATC our destination is Kokomo. How close is that to the camp?"

"Don't really matter, Charlie, not landing there anyhow. Don't want 'em to know where you're really going. It's better that way."

Charlie looked over at his pilot and shook his head in amazement. "I'm sure glad I trust your brother. You know I worked with him for ten years before he retired. He was my instructor on a couple of sectors at LA center. So where are we landing?"

"Watch and learn, ATC man!" As soon as they left Indianapolis airspace, Duane canceled flight following, shut off his transponder and descended to five hundred feet. Reaching up, he put in a new destination in the GPS. The aircraft turned five degrees to the right and the display showed seventy miles to destination.

Forty-five miles later, as they passed over a reservoir, Duane turned the Archer thirty degrees to the right to go around the Kokomo airport traffic area. Back on course, they crossed over the Wabash River. Three miles from their destination, Duane dropped the airplane down to three hundred feet, flying just above the trees.

177

"It scares the cows sometimes, but nobody out here seems to care." Duane answered Charlie's concern even before he asked. "They're kind of used to our shenanigans."

A mile to go and Charlie still could not pick out a landing site. But then again, he told himself, at this altitude, who could? Clearing a line of trees along a small stream, they dropped down to about fifty feet and headed toward another wooded area. Right before they got to the woods, Duane made a steep left turn, due north.

"There to your right, just past the lake," Duane pointed as he pulled back the throttle and clicked on a notch of flaps.

"Sure enough," Charlie replied. "The grass strip along the wooded area?"

"That's it, twenty-five hundred feet of green grass."

Passing over a well manicured lake, they turned onto a right base. Another right turn put them on final. Flying low over the country road Duane clicked on another notch of flaps before performing a perfect soft field landing.

Charlie took in the mowed runway and the woods off to the left. What really impressed him the most was the pristine lake on the right. He had heard rumors of this place and thought that someday he would bring his family here. It was 160 acres of well manicured property with cabins scattered throughout the western portion. In the middle of the property was a large lake surrounded by the owners' homes and a lodge. On the northern end was a campground set up for RVs and tents. Next to the runway just outside of the woods was a large hanger with a paved ramp. There had to be at least a dozen airplanes of various sizes parked on the ramp. Standing in his bib overalls, Dan was waiting for them as they taxied up to the hanger.

"So what is it that brings me halfway across the country?" Charlie asked as he and Dan walked over the lodge.

"Like I told you, we have a feller here by the name of Abdur. He has a story to tell you, but it ain't going to make you happy."

"Abdur? Don't recall the name. What does he do?"

"He said he's a software engineer. He had a contract with the FAA a few years ago." They reached the lodge and Dan showed Charlie to his room. "A meeting is set in one hour for you two to meet in the downstairs conference room. At the request of Abdur, I will be there."

Dan left and Charlie threw his overnight bag on the queen-size four-poster bed. The room was decorated in old farmhouse style, which reminded Charlie of his in-laws' home in Georgia. The bathroom was spacious, with marble tile and a walk-in shower. Charlie took a quick shower and dressed business casual, then sat down in the rocking chair. Picking up a country magazine, he thumbed through the pictures drawing the reader to the serenity of country living.

Walking into the conference room right on time, Charlie immediately recognized the man sitting at the sturdy oak table. "Mr. Rahman, it's a pleasure to meet you again," Charlie offered as he looked into the eyes of a man that looked distant and scared.

"Mr. Beckler! Have we met?"

"We met at the Los Angeles Center. Barney Williams introduced us as you were leaving."

"That was a long time ago, Mr. Beckler. You have a good memory."

"Yes, but age is taking its toll on that memory. Getting to the point, Mr. Rahman, what brings me here?"

"Charlie, I came here to the camp because I felt lost and afraid. I have made a very bad mistake. When I read about this place where faith and hope was restored in a person's life, and

179

that it was run by a retired air traffic controller and his wife, I knew I had to come here."

Abdur explained the story of the virus program and how he had been coerced into installing it. He explained to Charlie how he had tried to warn the FAA, how he continually read all the reports on NextGen, because he was hoping the software engineers would discover the Trojan horse and remove it. "Mr. Beckler, can you take the message back to the FAA? They will believe you."

"Thank you for revealing to us your true identity, Abdur. I have been privy to the letters you have written to the FAA. Our software engineers have scoured the NextGen programs with a fine-toothed comb and found nothing. Security has determined that your story was either a hoax or the Trojan horse has been deleted. I will have my friend Bud continue the search, but upper management will no longer fund the ticket."

Abdur looked crestfallen. "Mr. Beckler, do you believe me?"

"Sir, I don't even know you. I do know that your willingness to share this story with me reveals the conviction you have. If we cannot locate the Trojan horse, what do you recommend?"

Abdur sat up straight in his chair, beads of sweat appearing on his forehead. "You should create a backup plan. If, or I should say, when the Trojan horse activates, it will be disastrous."

"What do you mean by a backup plan?"

Abdur shook his head, "I really don't know. It will take the mind of a controller to devise a recovery plan to a NextGen failure. The administration may not be prepared but the controllers must be. Mr. Beckler, I am sorry, but there is nothing more I can do."

Charlie sat back and looked at the ceiling. After a couple of minutes, he looked back at Abdur. "Sir, you are right! You did screw up. Under duress, you committed a crime. We could have you thrown in jail for a long time. I know you are aware of these obvious things. I just have a couple of questions. Why did you reveal the hidden virus? Why didn't you just let it play out? No one would have traced it to you."

Abdur looked down at the floor. "Mr. Beckler, I have a conscience. I cannot let people be harmed because of me. When I agreed to plant the virus I did not know the outcome. All I wanted was to save my family. Now that I can see the dangers, I have to do something." With sadness in his eyes and his voice choking up, he looked up at Charlie. "What are you going to do to me?"

Charlie looked over at Dan, "What info has been leaked?"

"None, Charlie, no one other than the wife and I know why Abdur is here. The staff thinks he's just in need of some counseling and time to recover from some unfortunate event."

"Good! Let's keep it that way. Mr. Rahman! I would like for you to stay here for a couple of days. It will do you good. Is that okay?"

Abdur looked perplexed. "Sure, but why?"

Charlie was now standing as if the meeting was about over. "In two or three days, I will be back with some help. They will need some sort of verification this is a reality before they buy off on developing a plan. You will be the one that provides that verification. Over the next few days while I draw up a plan of action, you come up with a way to verify the virus. Gentlemen, I have to make some phone calls. See you at dinner."

Back in his room, Charlie sat back in the rocking chair and shut his eyes. His mind was moving quickly through all the things Abdur had told him. He asked himself to identify the worst-case scenario and the backup plan to a NextGen shutdown. Charlie's head hurt. So often he made the mistake of depending on his own keen ability to solve problems. But he knew this would be different. This was a problem that could not be found. He knew Bud and the software team had already searched the ERAMS program for the virus to no avail. Would they expend the resources in doing it again? He picked up his phone and called Sean.

"When you coming into town, Charlie?"

"If I can get a flight out of Indianapolis, I will be in Washington tomorrow morning," Charlie replied. "Sure sucks having to fly commercial."

"Hold on, Charlie, I'll call our flight department and call you back in a few minutes. What airport can I tell them?"

"If I only knew! I think it's close to Wabash."

"That's Indiana?"

"Think so! There's nothing but trees and corn fields, so I would suppose so."

Fifteen minutes later, Sean called back. "We have a King Air departing Oklahoma City in the morning. The pilot will call you with the ETA. Once you get to the airport, a car and driver will be waiting to bring you downtown."

"Thanks, Boss! See you tomorrow."

Chapter 28

Charlie woke up to the sound of a dinner bell ringing. Pulling on a clean pair of jeans and a fresh shirt, he headed down to the dining hall. There were close to a hundred people filing into the large hall. The smell of grilled steak, and chicken drifted through the kitchen door. The long dining tables were neatly decorated with checkered table clothes and flowers. Dinner rolls and salads were already in place waiting for the hungry guests. Charlie knew Abdur would be looking for him, but he really did not want to talk to him that night. He slipped into a seat next to an elderly couple and introduced himself. The dinner, consisting of steak or chicken, was complimented with baked potatoes and fresh green beans. Dessert was apple pie with a dip of vanilla ice cream.

After dinner, Charlie took a walk down a wood chip path to the lake. The moon was coming up over the trees and cast a reflecting light across the water. Sitting down on a bench, he looked up at the sky and talked to God.

"What is it that I am supposed to do? I am only a man and need your help. Open the doors I am supposed to enter and shut the ones I am not supposed to go through."

Feeling more at ease, Charlie took a walk around the lake. At the southwest side of the lake, a walkway led through the woods to a lighted miniature golf course. Charlie picked up a putter and started playing around the well-kept novelty. The

183

small windmills, ponds and waterfalls on the golf course brought some much needed mental relief to Charlie as he moved from hole to hole. The breeze picked up, bringing a scent of pig farm from the west. *Guess no place is perfect,* he said to himself as he finished.

Walking through the campground, he stopped and chatted with a couple sitting around a campfire. On the east end of the campground he came to a clearing that looked down the lighted runway. He stopped long enough to watch a small aircraft turn final and land. What a place for aviation enthusiasts to camp. He continued along the trail, walking by the small cabins, some with lights burning inside. Turning south, he crossed the main drive and walked down a walkway lined with solar powered lights illuminating the way. He arrived at the chapel with its lighted steeple and bell housing. He pulled on the large wooden doors, and they creaked open. The dim light through the windows cast a glow on the pews. Charlie walked up the center aisle, the floorboards sounding out each step. Sitting down on the front pew, he looked up at the stained glass above the podium. The artist had portrayed Christ with outstretched arms, inviting those who would, to come to him. Twenty minutes later, Charlie walked back to his room and immediately fell asleep.

"Good Morning, Mr. Beckler," called the King Air pilot early the next morning. "We will be at the Wabash airport at eight thirty." Charlie dressed and headed down to the dining hall, where he found the breakfast buffet waiting. Bypassing the heavy stuff, he settled on some fruit and cereal.

Dan showed up with news that Duane had the airplane ready for the trip to airport. Fifteen minutes later, they took off to the south and climbed straight out. Crossing the Wabash River three miles later, they set up for a right base for runway one-eight. Wabash Municipal Airport is a typical small town airport with little activity and lots of heart. Taxiing off the runway onto the ramp, Charlie noticed the normal airport junkies sitting around a picnic table. They all yelled at Duane when he got out of the plane.

"Are they friends of yours?" Charlie asked.

Duane gave Charlie an evil grin. "We're all friends in these parts, ATC man. You come around here enough, we will either make you our friend or our BBQ."

No sooner were they out of the airplane than they heard the King Air report twenty miles south west of the field, entering a right downwind.

Airborne and climbing out to the east, Charlie pulled his laptop out of his briefcase and started writing. He knew that the things he had been told would need to be documented. He also knew that a plan would be developed and all information leading to this plan would come from these notes. He had been writing for about an hour when the pilot announced they were starting their descent for Washington National.

A car was waiting for Charlie at the hanger, and twenty minutes later he was on his way up to Sean's office.

Charlie's phone buzzed as he stepped off the elevator. "Charlie, this is Sean. Where are you?"

"Trying to find the cubicle you call an office."

"Go all the way to the west end on the right. My little cubicle has glass doors and windows."

Charlie was impressed when he walked into his boss's corner office. The view to the west took in the Washington Monument and the National Mall all the way down to the Potomac River. To the northwest, you could see the White House and off to the right the Capital Building.

"You can see it all from here, Boss. How did you rate this pad?" Charlie asked.

"Some well-mannered ambitious employee made it happen with a couple of his shenanigans. Wouldn't know anything about that would you?"

Charlie smiled, knowing that Sean was talking about some of Charlie's activities over the last five years. "I really wouldn't have any idea, Boss. Speaking of shenanigans, I have a new one for you."

"Yeah, I got your email this morning and took the liberty to send for Bud. Thought he could be of assistance. He would have already been here if it weren't for those obnoxious controllers. He was delayed by ATC due to saturation. Ever hear of the like?"

"I have used it myself a time or two. Is anyone else in on this meeting?"

"Emailed the Administrator, but he will not be back in town until tomorrow. He did send his congratulations on the live test last month. I decided to keep it quiet beyond that."

"Good idea. We would hate for the media to get their hands on this one. It would be the death of NextGen."

"Greetings, my comrades," Bud's booming voice broke into their conversation. Standing in the door was the man who had moved from an obscure software manager to one of the most respected software experts in the FAA.

"Come on in, Bud, we've been waiting."

"Waiting? I am the one who's been waiting. We spent an hour on the ramp in Atlantic City waiting for those air-headed controllers to give us a slot here in Washington. You would think that I could at least garner enough respect to get some kind of priority."

That got both Charlie and Sean laughing. Sean looked over at Charlie with a question no one ever likes to hear from his superior. "How bad is it?"

"It's bad enough to redirect whatever assets necessary to scour the program. We need to find this thing and get it out of there." Charlie went on to explain Abdur's revelation.

"Do you think we should bring the FBI in?" Sean was fidgeting with his pen, jotting down some of the points of Charlie's conversation.

"That is a decision for you, Boss. I am only the messenger not the executioner. I feel you should give the man a chance to redeem himself. He could do this by finding the virus. Naturally that would be with the help of our own software specialist."

"Okay, I will take care of the legal end. You and Bud take care of Abdur and find this damn thing. Use whatever resources necessary, but I do want a daily report. Understand?"

Bud, who had been quiet during this time, got up and looked out the window at a Falcon jet on final to Reagan International Airport. "Boss, we need to do this in a hurry. We sure could use some faster transportation."

"If you're asking for a jet, you can forget it. That's the Administrator's, and he ain't about to give it to a geek. But, if you ask nicely, I will put the King Air at your disposal for this program. You had better make it worth it, or Congress and the GAO will have our butt. What is your plan, Charlie?"

"I'm flying home this afternoon. I have a family. As for Bud, he can take the King Air up to Atlantic City, put together his team and meet me in Indiana on Friday."

"Sounds like a plan to me," Bud chimed in now with a big grin. "Thanks for the wheels, or I should say wings, Boss. My guys will be stoked." Bud dismissed himself and called the airport to arrange for the flight home.

Sean stood up and grabbed his jacket. "Let's go for a walk, Charlie. There is something I want to show you. Anyway, you need lunch before you head home."

Walking across the street, they turned right and came to the steps of the Smithsonian National Air and Space Museum. "Always like to get lunch here. The food's not all that great, but the ambience is spectacular."

Once inside the welcome center, Charlie was like a kid in a candy store. High overhead, the Voyager hung suspended as if in flight. Charlie had watched on TV as this aircraft, piloted by Dick Rutan and Jeana Yeager, finished its round-the-world flight. From the 1903 Wright flyer to the modern day Predator, all kinds of flying machines begged for his attention, which he was more than willing to give.

On the way to the airport, Charlie called Carrie, "Interested in spending a few days in Indiana?"

"I can't think of any good reason unless you're going to be there."

After telling her about the camp, they decided instead of him coming home, she would fly out to Indiana and meet him there. "It will be a great getaway," he told Carrie. "I could use a couple of days of rest before the software team arrives on Friday."

"Just make sure you get the honeymoon suite," Carrie interjected.

Charlie laughed, "This is Indiana, not Maui. Do my best darling. See you tomorrow."

Charlie found a flight arriving into Indianapolis early in the evening. He had decided not to call the camp for a ride but to rent a car and drive up. It was seven in the evening when he left the airport, taking Interstate 465 north around the city. Reaching Wabash ninety minutes later, he headed out through the country. *Sure is dark out here,* he noticed as he got close to the camp. With no moon visible, the stars were brighter than normal. Charlie drove up and down a couple of narrow country roads, but still the camp seemed to evade him. It wasn't until he saw the lights of a small plane descend towards the runway that he found his target.

"Welcome back, Mr. Beckler," the receptionist greeted him at the front desk. "Gather you're going to be staying with us this evening? Your room is still available if that suits.

188

Charlie thanked the receptionist and made his way back to his second floor room.

It was the sound of a two-cycle engine that woke Charlie from a peaceful sleep. After breakfast, he made his way over to the hanger where he found Dan hunched over a map with Duane.

"Well, look what the cat brought in!" Dan quipped. "I heard you made it back. What's the plan?"

Charlie explained the schedule for the next few days, making sure the camp was able to handle the additional guests. "Not a problem, we will put 'em all in the girls dorm. Just kidding! We have five cabins empty this week. As for you and Carrie, we'll set you up in the Crow's Nest. She'll like that."

"Crow's Nest?" Charlie asked.

"Yep, I built it myself. Now naturally I didn't decorate it, otherwise it would look like a chicken coop. Did you want to use the Archer to go get your wife? That is, if you can fly the thing?"

Charlie took Dan up on flying the Archer down to Indianapolis to pick up Carrie, and by dinnertime they were back at the camp. When they stopped by the front desk to pick up the key to their room, the receptionist advised Charlie that Mr. Winster and his wife were expecting them for dinner in the main dining room at seven thirty.

At the top of the wide curved staircase they came to a door marked Crow's Nest. Opening the door only led to another stairway. The Crow's nest was beautiful. The first floor of this suite consisted of a bedroom decorated in an aviation theme. Wallpaper with vintage aircraft covered the walls. The inlaid carpet was designed to look like runways. The headboard was an old wing. The bathroom was no less glamorous, filled with marble and gold-plated fixtures. The huge whirlpool tub was surrounded by one-way glass looking to the west where the sun was sinking below the horizon.

"You haven't seen it all, darling," Charlie teased as he grabbed Carrie's hand and took her to a circle staircase. The second floor was incredible. It was a sitting area with glass from floor to ceiling on all four sides. There was a kitchenette in the center backed by a breakfast bar. Overstuffed leather chairs and a loveseat overlooked the runway.

"Wow! How long can we stay here?" Carrie asked wide-eyed.

"Trust me, darling, this place gets booked, but Dan said we have it through the weekend."

Chapter 29

Early Thursday morning, Charlie took a morning run on the trail surrounding the woods. He ended up at the bench by the lake. The sun finally made itself known by burning off the hazy morning fog that was drifting across the cornfield. It was so quiet. All Charlie could hear were the birds singing and the occasional rustling of leaves as the breeze blew through the forest. Sitting there, meditating on the task at hand, he did not hear Abdur walk up behind him. "Mr. Beckler, can we talk?"

Startled, Charlie turned and invited Abdur to sit down. "Abdur, please call me Charlie. What is on your mind?"

"I would prefer to address you formally, Mr. Beckler. Someday, when I have redeemed myself, I would be happy to be your friend, but for now I don't feel worthy. It's the seriousness of the mess that I have created."

Charlie said nothing. He knew Abdur was right. He had created a mess. He also knew it could end up putting this Middle East immigrant behind bars for many years.

Abdur continued, "I have been here for seven days now, Mr. Beckler, and have seen something that is missing in my life. So many of the people I have met here seem to be at peace. They are friendly and almost always smiling. Some seem a little rustic and old-fashioned but still happy. You don't see that in the city. I don't want to be rude, but they don't even appear to be highly educated people."

Charlie looked up at the sun reflecting off the lake. A frog jumped off the shoreline causing ripples to spread across the otherwise glassy water.

"Abdur, see the ripples? That frog jumping into the lake is an analogy of what you have done. Your actions caused a disruption, which in turn created a ripple effect throughout the program. You can't undo it, but in time things will go back to normal. As with the water in the lake, which once again reflects the sun, you, too, will be known for the positive things you have accomplished. Now let me tell you about these undereducated people."

"Please don't mistake humble for undereducated. These people live close to God. Their God is alive and very instrumental in the day-to-day workings of their lives. They believe, as I do, that God created everything around us. That He gave them all that they have and will provide all of their needs."

Abdur interrupted Charlie, "Who is this God, and where do you find him?"

"Abdur, he is the God of Abraham. He is the creator of all mankind. As far as where we find him, we can find him through his son, Jesus Christ."

"Maybe so, but considering what I have done, I need to fix that before any god would be interested in me."

Charlie stood up and stretched. "Let me tell you about forgiveness, Abdur. None of us is perfect. We have all sinned. It may be telling a lie, lusting after someone other than our spouse, or stealing something. Anything that would not please God is a sin. Fortunately, we can be forgiven."

"How can this forgiveness happen?" Abdur blurted out. "Doesn't sin have to be paid for?"

Before he could answer, the ringing of the dinner bell sounded out a call to breakfast. The two headed for the dining hall. "Come on over to the chapel on Sunday, Abdur. There you will learn the truth."

After breakfast, the morning's conversation weighed heavily on Abdur's mind. He decided to take a stroll down to the chapel just to think about some of the things Charlie had told him about forgiveness. How could God forgive him? It wasn't just the virus he had planted. It was all the other things in his life. He had never considered himself a bad person, but now he wasn't so sure. And anyway, Jesus was for the religious people. He had sworn off religion when he left his homeland.

As he approached the small chapel, he heard a voice coming from inside. He quietly made his way up to an open window and listened. A man was inside reading from the Bible. At least he thought it was the Bible. He continued to listen.

He is despised and rejected by men, a man of sorrows and acquainted with grief. And we hid, as it were, our faces from Him; He was despised, and we did not esteem Him. Surely He has borne our griefs and carried our sorrows; yet we esteemed Him stricken, smitten by God, and afflicted. But He was wounded for our iniquities; the chastisement for our peace was upon Him, and by His stripes we are healed. All we like sheep have gone astray; we have turned, every one, to his own way; and the LORD has laid on Him the iniquity of us all.

Abdur had heard enough. Entering the chapel he saw an elderly man sitting at the front of the sanctuary on an old rugged bench. As the door creaked behind him the man turned and smiled at him. "Looking for a place to pray?"

Abdur didn't know what to say. "I was just looking for someone," he apologized, "sorry to interrupt you."

The gentleman got up and turned around, "Oh, you didn't interrupt me. This morning I felt God tugging at my heart to come down here."

Immediately, Abdur liked this old man. He stretched out his hand, "I'm Abdur Rahman, a friend of Dan's."

The elderly man smiled and reached out for Abdur's hand. "Pleased to meet you, Abdur. I'm Dan's father, David. Have a seat. I just can't seem to stand much anymore."

"I...I just wondered who you were reading about?" Abdur stammered.

David picked up his Bible and turned to the fifty-third chapter of Isaiah and repeated what he had just read. "Abdur, this is the old prophet reading about the coming of the Messiah."

"So, you're telling me Isaiah was talking about Jesus?"

"Exactly, and Jesus did come into this world to save us. He became a sacrifice for our sins. You do realize you have sinned?"

"Oh! Mr. Beckler explained that to me this morning. That's why I decided to come down here. I'm still looking for answers."

"You know what happens to sinners?" Before Abdur could answer, David thumbed through his Bible and started reading "Romans 6:23: *For the wages of sin is death, but the gift of God is eternal life in Christ Jesus our Lord.*"

"Okay, I get the sin part, what do I need to do to make it right?" Abdur was still not getting it.

"Let me show you one more verse," David replied as he turned to Romans 10:9. He continued reading, "*That if thou shalt confess with thy mouth the Lord Jesus, and shalt believe in thine heart that God hath raised him from the dead, thou shalt be saved.*"

"So, that's it? Just confess Jesus is the Lord and that God raised Him from the dead, nothing else?"

David shut his Bible and smiled at Abdur. "You're starting to understand, my new friend." He got up and walked to the back of the sanctuary and took a Bible off the shelf. "Here, Abdur, you take this and read. Start with the book of John, and soon you will understand."

Friday morning, all participating individuals received a text message from Charlie advising of a ten o'clock meeting. Bud and his team of five software specialists had arrived from Atlantic City and were enjoying a good home-cooked breakfast in the dining hall.

Sharply at ten o'clock, Charlie, Abdur, Bud, and the five geeks were seated around the conference table. After brief introductions, the geeks were brought up to speed as to what had transpired. Abdur opened the files of the Trojan horse and projected it onto the screen at the end of the room. He took them line by line through the program, explaining the ramifications of the virus.

Bud sat there, taking it all in. "Mr. Rahman, I am stunned at even an attempt of a Trojan horse on NextGen. We have in place layer after layer of security on this software. Now that I have seen the code I am fairly certain our security has encapsulated the virus. I am stumped, because we haven't been able to find the virus or any traces of it even having been there. We are going to continue looking now that we have an idea of what to look for."

Abdur sighed with relief. "Thank you, Mr. Simons, I am sorry for the problems I have caused and will continue to be at your disposal."

Bud turned to Charlie. "We are going to take this information to all three facilities on a witch hunt for the virus. We will keep you informed as to the progress, but seriously I think our security software nixed it."

Bud and his team left for their first stop in Kansas and Duane flew Abdur down to Indianapolis to catch a flight to New York. There to see him off were Dan and Charlie. Both of them had noticed a change in Abdur.

Abdur grabbed Dan's hand and smiled. "I looked for your father today and couldn't find him. I talked to him in the chapel yesterday and he gave me a Bible. Just wanted him to know I have come to the realization that Jesus is for real and is now my Savior."

Dan gasped and struggled to maintain his composure, "That's great, Abdur! It's what this camp is all about. You're welcome back anytime you want. We had better get you to the airport."

After the Archer took off, Charlie turned to Dan. "What was that all about? He almost floored you with his meeting your dad."

Dan shook his head. "Charlie, that's impossible, Dad's been gone for years."

Chapter 30

As always with the FAA, 4DT had to be a big media event. After all, they had spent 3.4 billion dollars getting NextGen to this stage. Tuesday morning, August 3rd 2021, forty years to the day since the historic air traffic controller strike, all three consolidated en route facilities were ready to flip the switch bringing 4DT online. Normally this kind of change would have happened during the night when traffic was at its lightest. This time was different. It didn't matter how many aircraft were in the sky. Management was convinced. The controllers were not that certain. There were too many variables with over fifty thousand flights a day.

"Start it at night when things are slow and pick it up during the day," the union had argued. "Let our controllers monitor the situation as it builds. That way we will be ready to recover when the system crashes." The union's concerns were ignored and so the show was scheduled.

The transition took place at ten in the morning as the arrivals were flooding into the Las Vegas airport. To the pilot, it was transparent, because the data link clearances were identical to the ones issued by the controllers. It was a drastic change from the controllers' perspective. One minute they were busily analyzing the situation, mentally maintaining order, solving any conflicts; the next minute a "4DT" notation displayed at the top of their scope and the data link display started scrolling orders to the aircraft at a rapid rate of speed.

Charlie counted off fifteen clearances in a minute. "That's faster than I can do it," he commented.

The controllers sat dumbfounded as they watched the future unfold before them. That evening, the news highlighted the technological takeover. The FAA management gloated in their interviews about the demise of the esteemed job of the air traffic controller.

"From now on, we will not be looking for type A personalities. It is time to bring salaries down to that of an airline dispatcher or a traffic cop."

The FAA administrator went on record saying, "This is a big step towards freeing up more money for greater technological advances. Air traffic will continue to grow, and we will need more money to build runways and airport terminals. It is only time before service will be provided to every town with a municipal airport."

Charlie tried to calm the outrages of his coworkers as they exchanged stories the next day. "We need to look to the future ourselves. Yes, over the last ninety years, we have been an elite group, but we cannot stop progress. Even though it all seems so strange, in time we will accept it as the norm. Look back over history. In every facet of our lives, we see change. Did the lamplighters complain when electric lights first illuminated the cities? No, they went to work for the electric company. Did the livery owners complain when the automobile flooded the streets? No! They just opened a service station. When the airplane became the preferred choice of travel, many conductors found themselves unemployed. Times change, and we need to change with them."

Four months had passed since 4DT had taken over the separation responsibilities, and complacency was setting in with the bored controllers. It had become quite obvious that the next generation of controllers would be hired using different criteria. The type A personality would now be considered a detriment.

Charlie kept busy monitoring the program and researching the glitches that seemed to constantly bring concern to his fellow controllers. One of the more nagging problems which concerned Charlie was the return of the hesitation experienced in Atlantic City. It was nothing more than a hiccup, but it still drove a wedge of doubt in the controllers' fragile faith in the 4DT system.

He was on his way to work when Charlie heard the news on his radio. A midair crash had just happened over eastern Kansas. The newscaster announced, "An Airbus 320 and a Boeing 737 both, according to Flight Tracker, inbound to MCI had somehow come together eight miles northwest of the town of Ottawa, Kansas. No survivors expected. Calls have gone unanswered at the Central Center for Air Traffic Services. We will bring you more news as it becomes available."

Charlie was in shock. His brain was moving a thousand miles an hour as he sped up the drive towards the guard shack. Parking in his favorite parking spot, Charlie grabbed his phone to call Bud. He had two missed calls with voicemails to match. Charlie knew who they were from. He went ahead and called Bud first.

"I have no idea what happened," Bud responded to Charlie's call.

"We have had the tapes pulled, and they are being analyzed as we speak. We should have an answer within the next thirty minutes. Have you talked to Sean yet?"

"Not yet. He left me a message, but I called you first. Thought I should get some answers before the shooting starts. This is not good, Bud. We can only hope it was mechanical, but I have my doubts."

He could hear Bud sighing on the phone, "I have my doubts, too. I will call you when we find out."

Charlie hung up the phone and made another call. "Sean, this is Charlie, just got off the phone with Bud, they're still running the tapes. What have you got?"

"Just what the authorities are telling us from Kansas. Debris spread over about five miles, no survivors. Looks like 223 dead including crewmembers. The majority of the debris ended up just outside the little town of Centropolis. Fortunately no one on the ground was hurt."

"Have you talked to the folks at CCATS yet?" Charlie asked.

"Yes, they're not saying much, other than that their controllers are on the verge of panic. Charlie, I need to get you out there ASAP. How soon can you make it?"

"That depends on what form of transportation we're using these days. A train sounds pretty good right now."

"Dang it, Charlie! This is serious. Call dispatch and find an aircraft. I'll see you in Kansas City tonight. We will set up shop at CCATS and work from there."

"A King Air, is that all you can find me?" Charlie was on the phone with the FAA dispatcher. "That's a four hour flight. Do you have anything faster?"

"Sir, we could get you into a Hawker jet," the dispatcher replied, "but it would not be there until later tonight. We can have the King Air there in an hour."

"Guess that will work. We will be waiting at the terminal." Hanging up, Charlie headed back home.

"Charlie, where are you?" It was Jim answering the phone. "Things are a mess in here, and the controllers are seriously concerned with the integrity of the system."

"Jim, I won't be coming in. Furthermore I need you to get out of there. We're going to Kansas tonight. They need our help with the controllers at CCAT. Get home and get your bag packed, I will pick you up in forty minutes."

"Are we going by air?" Jim asked.

"Wish there was another way. Don't forget, it's cold in Kansas this time of year. The wind will blow right through you."

When he spoke to her, Carrie was not happy. "What do you mean, you're going to Kansas?"

"It will just be for a day or two, my darling. You know how much they need me," Charlie was really trying to smooth things over.

"We need you, too," Carrie complained. "I told you last week not to plan anything for this weekend. Mitzy has a Christmas program at school, and you need to be there. If not for me, at least be here for her."

Charlie took a deep breath, "I wish you would not always bring her into our discussions. She's seventeen now and doesn't need her dad at every function. All she needs is my credit card." He curtly added, "Furthermore, how do you expect me to schedule an accident?"

Carrie was somewhere between crying and screaming, "If you were half the controller you think you are, I'm sure you could arrange it."

This made Charlie laugh as he wrapped his arms around his wife. She hit him with her fist a couple of times before she stopped resisting and cried on his shoulder. "I will try to be home by Friday night. Seriously, I will try." Carrie pushed him away and went upstairs.

An hour later, Charlie and Jim were seated across from each other at twenty-one thousand feet. Even the constant roar of the PT6 turboprops beating the air outside the partially fogged-up windows couldn't drown out their heavy thoughts. Wiping the fog from the window, Charlie was mesmerized by the cloud formations over the eastern end of the Grand Canyon left by a recently passing cold front. Over sixty-five years ago

201

clouds like these were instrumental in bringing down two great airliners.

The morning of June 30th, 1956 at 9:01, TWA Flight 2 departed Los Angeles International Airport nonstop to Kansas City. Three minutes later, United Airlines Flight 718 departed for Chicago. The United flight plan took it over Needles and on to Durango at an altitude of 21,000 feet. Somewhere around Barstow, California, Captain Gandy flying the TWA Super Constellation requested 21,000 feet. The Los Angeles controller denied the request because of the United DC-7 already at that altitude. Shortly thereafter, Captain Gandy requested "one thousand on top," which canceled his IFR clearance and allowed him to climb to any altitude he desired, as long as he stayed a thousand feet above the clouds.

It was a fateful morning as the two large aircraft weaved back and forth around the building cumulus clouds that morning. At approximately 10:31 a.m., Captain Shirley and First Officer Robert Harms, rounding a cloud, found the Lockheed Super Constellation filling their windscreen. Making a hard right turn in an attempt to avoid collision, the DC-7's raised left wing clipped Connie's vertical stabilizer. An unfortunate chain of events killed 128 people that day.

"So we change the rules," Charlie sighed.

"What are you talking about?" Jim was looking at Charlie with a puzzled look. Charlie shared with Jim what he had been thinking.

"Charlie, you know as well as I do, the word is *reactionary* when it comes to the FAA."

"That may be true, but it was the CAA back then," Charlie mumbled.

"It's the same bird, different spots." Jim continued, "You think we're in for more reactionary changes in Kansas?"

"They will always change the rules to continue to protect the weakest link. I cannot fathom what that weakest link may be this time until we see the data, but we will see soon enough."

Chapter 31

It was coming up on eight in the evening when the King Air touched down on runway three six at Johnson County Industrial Airport. As the turbines wound down, Charlie could see the FAA Gulfstream sitting gallantly on the ramp. Sean met them in the lobby along with his entourage, which, Charlie was glad to see, included his friend, Bud.

"Welcome to Kansas, gentlemen. It's too late to go to the crash site tonight. We will schedule that tomorrow morning. What I would like to do tonight is get to CCATS and review the data."

"Are there any preliminaries yet?" Charlie asked as they loaded their bags in the white government van.

"Sounds like 4DT did something unusual, Charlie. I know that's not what we want to hear, but it doesn't look good. They do have the lab set up for us to run the scenarios."

"You're right. It's not what I wanted to hear. Should we shut down the system?" Charlie asked.

"I don't think so. Not yet, anyhow. We have been running for over four months without even a close call. Let's look at the data before we pull the plug."

The trip from the old naval air station through the town of Gardner was just a little over four miles. West of town, they turned off Main Street onto West Santa Fe, named after the old trail that used to come through the town. Arriving at the center, 204 located on the grounds of the municipal airport, they were quickly ushered through the guard gate. The well-lit center looked more like a large Midwest barn then an air traffic control center.

"Doesn't look like ours," Jim commented, staring up at the huge structure. "Is this thing secure?"

"Oh, it's secure," Sean replied. "Underneath the siding is nothing but reinforced concrete. This thing can take a direct hit from a tornado and stay operational. What you see above ground is only the administrative wings and training. Control room is subterrain."

"Well, it makes me homesick," Jim continued, "since I grew up on the farm."

"If you like this one, you would love ECATS." Sean replied, referring to the Eastern Center for Air Traffic Services located outside of Harpers Ferry, West Virginia. "It looks like a mansion straight out of the Colonial age."

"Have to get there someday," Charlie piped in. "I think maybe old John Brown may have been a kin of mine."

Meeting the team at the front door, a young lady introduced herself as a quality assurance specialist. "I've been asked to escort you folks to the executive board room. The chief is there with the National Transportation Safety Board."

It was a quiet walk through the lobby, carrying on the theme from the outside. It looked like huge, hewn-wood barn beams stretched across the ceiling. Americana décor gave way to commercial glass doors leading into offices. Their new acquaintance led them down a rather sterile hallway to the conference room.

"Greetings, gentlemen," welcomed a burly looking man with a two-day beard as he came across the room to greet them. "I'm Darrel Pence, the facility chief. Everything is ready. We will assist in any way you need." Looking around the room, as if taking inventory of who was there, Darrel added, "To tell you the truth, we have no idea what happened, and it scares me. I need to know if this can happen again."

"Well, glad to meet you, Mr. Pence," Charlie stuck his hand out. "I'm Charlie Beckler from West CATS."

"Oh, I know who you are," Darrel responded. "Our controllers need your reassurance that this is not going to happen again. I am glad to finally meet you. Wish it were under better circumstances though."

"Don't we all," was all that Charlie could say, feeling humbled by the burden the chief unknowingly placed upon his shoulders.

The room darkened to a soft glow as three large screens illuminated the wall. On the left was the high altitude sector controlling the airspace twenty-four thousand feet and above. The screen on the right was the low altitude with airspace started at twenty-three thousand feet down to the surface. The center screen was displaying the clearances being sent by 4DT to the aircraft under the sectors' control. They sat silently as the aircraft marched across the sky. Charlie recognized the two doomed aircraft. The Boeing 737, Southwest 2356, was descending out of flight level three-three-zero for flight level two-four-zero. The Airbus, USAir 223, was climbing to flight level two-three-zero. Both aircraft were on a converging path, but everything looked normal. It appeared as if USAir 223 would level off a thousand feet below the Southwest jet.

Charlie and Jim did not focus on the two doomed aircraft. Years of controlling airplanes had ingrained in them necessity to scan all available data. The aircraft were still fifty miles apart when Jim leaned over and whispered to Charlie, "Are you watching the speeds?"

Charlie just nodded and leaned forward in his chair. Twelve miles from impact, Southwest 2356 showed a speed of seventy-six knots, and 4DT cleared the Kansas City arrival for descent onto the arrival. "Center, this is Southwest 2356," blared a voice out of the speakers. "We have been cleared to ten thousand. We've got traffic. What's going on here?"

"Southwest 2356, maintain flight level two-four-zero. I repeat, Southwest 2356 maintain flight level two-four-zero. Do not descend!"

"Center, we are trying, but the autopilot will not disconnect."

Now you could hear panic in the controller's voice, "USAir 223 turn sixty degrees right immediately."

"Center, USAir 223, the autopilot has overridden us also. We are trying to disconnect now."

By now the aircraft were four miles apart and the Southwest altitude showed twenty-three thousand five hundred descending. Everyone held their breath as they watched the targets merge. Even though they knew the outcome, it was as if they could change the course of this disaster.

No one was prepared for the scream that followed, "Mayday, mayday, mayday – Center, we've been hit, we're going in. God help us!"

The radio went silent. The two targets disappeared from the scope. On the aircraft list, USAir 223 and Southwest 2356 went from white to tan as the system lost contact with the two aircrafts' onboard computers. The whole room sat in stone silence for what seemed like eternity as the team digested what they had just witnessed.

Sean broke the silence looking over at his controller friends, "Charlie, Jim, what did you see?"

Jim answered first, "One of the things that caught our attention was the speeds. The speeds were deviating horrendously. Just during the last eight minutes the speed bounced between 50 to 420 knots."

"That wasn't all," Charlie spoke up. "There were at least five other aircraft that showed widely varying speeds. Bud, would these readings throw off 4DT?"

"I would hate to answer that without researching the code. I'm sure it would have an effect on it. It uses speed in its equation."

Charlie looked around at the tech heads in the room. "Can you guys bring up the 4DT historical data on the monitor?"

"Sure not a problem, give me two minutes," answered a young man who had to have been in his early twenties. Shortly, the center monitor showed lines of data scrolling across the screen. Step by step, they moved through the last eight minutes before the crash. Sure enough, 4DT calculated a three-mile in trail spacing on the two aircraft. Looking back through the data inputs from ADS-B, Southwest reported the speed ranging from a low of 52 knots and as high as 430.

The young lady from QA was busy on her calculator. "Southwest flew 57 miles in the last eight minutes. The actual ground speed calculates out at 427 knots."

"This is a critical issue," Charlie said. "How many times has this been reported from the control room?"

"There haven't been any that we're aware," Darrell answered. "I recommend we get the word to the controllers immediately to watch the speeds for abnormalities." The rest of the room concurred.

"What about the autopilots?" Charlie asked. "Why could they not be overridden?"

For the first time they heard from Stan Farrell, the NTSB representative. "That will have to be answered by the manufacturer. We don't have any information on the system yet. The black box is being diagnosed. We have listened to the cockpit voice recorder, and it seems as if the pilots were fighting the autopilot clear up to impact."

Sean couldn't believe it. "You're saying they could not get the autopilot disconnected from 4DT? Bud, were you aware of that?"

"I was not aware of the lack of a disconnect switch," Bud answered. "And it sure sounds like these guys did what they could to regain control of the aircraft to no avail."

"Bud, I would like for you to go through the data line by line, compare that with the software application. See if you can find the exact breakdown in the system. Jim will work with you. I will work with the NTSB on the autopilot situation. In the mean time Charlie and I will meet with the controllers. Darrell, is it my understanding that the controllers working these aircraft are on administrative leave?"

"Yes, Sean, they are. Both controllers asked to meet with Charlie once he arrived. I don't think they want to talk to management without union representation."

"Let me talk to them first," Charlie interjected. "I may be able to bring them around."

"Okay," Darrell responded. "They are waiting for your call."

Charlie was already at the Pizza Hut when Denise Derringer and Adam Wilson slid into the booth. He could tell by the look of the young lady and her coworker that it had been a tough day. Charlie got right to the point, "Tell me what happened."

"I tried to stop 'em." Denise started shaking her head as the tears ran down her cheeks. Wiping her eyes she continued. "I killed all those people. What am I going to do now? What else could I have done, Charlie?"

Charlie reached across the table and grabbed her hand. "Denise, stop it! No one is blaming you. Stop blaming yourself. I have seen the tapes. There was nothing else you could do. Now, just think back this morning to what you remember."

Denise wiped away the last of her tears and smiled, "Thank you, Charlie. It's just so dramatic. I've always known

209

that I work in an environment where a disaster could happen. I just never thought it would happen to me. Let alone be a midair that was caused by our system."

Charlie squeezed Denise's hand before letting go and leaning back in the booth. "Denise, Adam, when an error or any other breakdown happens in the air traffic control system, it affects us all. You two just happened to be at the right place at the wrong time. Go ahead, Denise, did you notice anything out of the ordinary leading up to the failure?"

"I was sitting all alone at Sector 29. I, or should I say, 4DT, was only controlling nine airplanes. Everything looked good, all systems showed green and white. No warnings or indications that anything was wrong. It wasn't until the clearance for the Southwest was transmitted that I almost jumped out of my seat."

"What did you see?" Charlie prodded. "That is, other than the obvious conflict with USAir that is."

Denise's voice crackled as she continued, "It was the speed, Charlie, the speed."

"Was that the first time you noticed the discrepancy?" he asked.

"No! I had seen it a couple of other times but it went back to normal, and I could tell by the histories that it wasn't the real speed. Just thought it was a fluke."

"Does that happen often here at CCATS?"

"What, me missing discrepancies or thinking things are a fluke?"

Charlie allowed himself to laugh. "No, Denise, the speed discrepancy. Has anyone noticed this happening before today?"

Denise and Adam looked at each other, shaking their heads, "No, we haven't heard of any."

"What can you tell me about the last thirty seconds?" Charlie continued.

"As you heard from the tape, I tried to verbally stop the Southwest once the computer had sent the clearance. Once the pilot responded with the message of the autopilot freezing up, I hollered to Adam to turn his airplane."

"I immediately did what she said," Adam spoke up. "As you know, I had the same response. That was when we tried to override 4DT and send manual commands to the autopilots. Obviously it was too late as the autopilots never acknowledged our clearances."

"You did the right thing, guys. You have no worries in speaking to management or the NTSB. I would recommend you take a union rep though. Some of these interviewers are heartless animals. They don't care about your feelings."

Just before midnight Charlie met the rest of the team in the hotel lounge. After bringing them up to date on the emotional state of Denise and Adam, he inquired about their findings.

Bud sat down his beer. "Jim and I got a good start on dissecting the data. We started back thirty minutes before the accident and worked forward. Our initial findings show that 4DT processed the data it received. The speed variation reflected in the data blocks were identical to what was transmitted by ADS-B."

"So ADS-B is the culprit?" Charlie asked.

Bud became adamant, "Oh! We are now certain that the speed data did have an effect on the logic. We are still puzzled why 4DT failed. Even with the confusion, 4DT should have recognized the rapid closure rate. This should have enacted the bailout procedure."

"What bailout procedure?" Sean questioned.

"It's a macro written into the program as a last-ditch effort to avert such a disaster. It is supposed to simultaneously send commands to both aircraft, which would automatically

211

make immediate adjustments to their flight path. It worked in testing."

"Good grief! The plot thickens. So where do we place the blame?"

"It gets even better," Bud slammed down his empty beer bottle. "Stan, tell 'em what you found out."

The NTSB rep had been sitting there quietly listening to the conversation and taking notes. "While you guys were reading code and interviewing the kids, I was searching online at the FAA archive document website. It appears as if during the early requirements stage of 4DT, the manufacturers and the users wanted a manual disconnect override switch located in the module that connects data link to the autopilot. In the memo I found, one of the developers of NextGen wrote an argument against the manual switch. He argued the chance of a pilot inadvertently disconnecting the system was greater than a failure within NextGen itself."

"Charlie, guess who wrote the memo?" Bud was giving Charlie a sick smile.

"It wasn't?"

"Oh yes, it was, the guy that turns your crank!" Now Bud was laughing.

Stan was confused, looking at the paper he had in his hand. "You guys know this Barney Williams?"

Getting back to his room, Charlie noticed he had a message from Carrie on his cell phone. Looking at his phone he knew he should call home. It had been a long day and he was tired. He lay back in his bed trying to process what had transpired. The day had started as a normal workday in Nevada and ended in a hotel room in Kansas.

Now he and Carrie were at odds, and if he didn't make it back by Friday evening, it would get worse. It seemed as though she was hit or miss these days as she worked her way through menopause. She acted as if life had passed her by and she had been left behind. The last few years, she had complained about the lack of time Charlie was spending with the family. He would find her in her garden crying about nothing. Charlie was now forty-seven and would qualify for retirement in a little over two years. Carrie had been looking forward to retirement so they could move back to Georgia. He wanted to stay until NextGen was completed, but she still wanted him to retire as soon as he qualified. They had this argument weekly, neither one giving in. She had even threatened to move back to Georgia as soon as Mitzy graduated. That was another thing. Mitzy was planning on going to Emery Riddle Daytona Beach to get her degree in aerospace engineering. That was going to cost a pretty penny. If he could just work another six years it would pay for her schooling. Charlie jumped as his phone rang.

"Charlie, this is Denise, sorry to wake you."

Charlie could tell by the sniffles that Denise had been crying. "That's all right," he yawned, "I wasn't asleep yet but moving that way. What's up?"

"I can't sleep. I keep hearing the pilots screaming may-day. It's so sad, all those people, and I could have stopped it. If I had just noticed it earlier, this would not have happened."

"Denise, don't talk like that. No one here believes you did anything wrong. I would have done the same thing you did. It is natural for you to have second thoughts on your actions, but you need to realize you are a victim here, not a villain."

Charlie spent the next hour listening to Denise spill her guts, getting a lot of her guilt off her chest. Finally, he got her calmed down enough she thought she could get to sleep. Thanking him for taking the time to talk with her, she told him he was her new hero and hung up.

Chapter 32

Thursday morning, the sun was just coming up over the horizon as Charlie walked into the dining room next to the hotel lobby. Sean was already there reading a newspaper and nursing a cup of coffee. Charlie grabbed a banana and joined his boss.

"Media's not painting a very good picture of us," Sean commented not even lowering his paper. "The article says here that the accident, while yet officially undetermined, looked suspiciously like it was caused by controller error."

"Not surprised," Charlie shook his head. "They're vultures looking for something to feed on. Hopefully Adam and Denise will understand the truth."

Sean looked up from his paper. The intensity in his eyes portrayed his concern. "That is one of your jobs. Only one of their own can get them through this unfortunate situation. We have a lot of work to do today, one job of which is to brief the controllers and meet with any one of them who desire clarification and confirmation."

"What else you got on our plate today?" Charlie asked, acting as if he wasn't even concerned about Sean's request of him doing an acting job as a psychotherapist.

"We're going out to the crash site. The recovery operation is still underway, but the sheriff's department has arranged to fly us over the site."

"What is the advantage of us witnessing this travesty?" Charlie asked. "I really don't see the need."

Sean smiled, "You never cease to amaze me. Charlie, you are leadership whether you like it or not. There are people out at the crash site that idolize you. It will encourage the recovery team to meet you. Remember you are the face of NextGen."

That brought a frown to Charlie's face. "Thanks for the reminder. That's all I need right now. What time is our flight?"

The Bell 206 Long Ranger was a beautiful bird sitting on the ramp at Gardner Municipal airport. The pilot, a veteran with many of hours behind the controls, was waiting along with his slightly younger copilot. "We will take you to both of the crash sites. The USAir came down just west of the village of Centropolis, and the Southwest crashed six miles west of town. It ended up in a field across the road from a little school. Fortunately, no one on the ground was hurt. Some of the kids were pretty traumatized though. It will be a while before they fly again." Once they were airborne, they leveled off at a thousand feet above the ground and headed west.

Charlie's eyes were glued to the ground as he watched the patchwork landscape pass by. Snow-blown terraced fields surrounded the dairy farms. Frozen farm ponds spotted fields where cattle were looking for something to graze. All of this made the landscape so inviting to those who chose to live a quiet life style here in the heartland. These people did not ask for the dramatic situation that now scattered their countryside. It would not take long before the last emergency vehicle would leave. Shortly thereafter, the last flatbed trailer with the remainder of the twisted metal would pull away from the village. All the visual effects of the crash would be gone, yet the emotional scars would remain. Many years from now, the parents would tell stories to their children of the day the airplanes fell out of the sky. Charlie wished he could leave the fast-paced life he lived and move to a down-to-earth place like this.

"Up there on your left," the pilot hollered, pointing to his ten o'clock position. Charlie was not prepared for what he saw. The images before him would forever be etched in his mind. Scattered out for what looked like about a half mile were pieces of a broken aircraft. It looked like it had started in the open field headed east and ended up in a wooded area just northeast of town. Emergency vehicles lined the road, and many were out in the field with lights flashing.

"Any problems with news media getting in the way?" Sean asked the pilot

"None at all with the TFR in place," the younger pilot replied.

"A TFR, what's that?"asked Sean.

"It's protected airspace, five mile radius, around each of the main crash sites below eight thousand feet," Charlie educated his boss.

They landed just outside the wooded area, as close as they dared to a large tent marked "NTSB." Icy wind hit Charlie in the face as he and Sean jumped out and headed towards the tent to check in. What had been just a frozen pasture lying dormant for the winter had now become a field of death and destruction. Coroners were scattered about the field recovering bodies and body parts, carefully cataloging the location of each one. NTSB agents were busy taking pictures of each piece of aircraft and mapping its location.

Rows of flat bed trailers lined the road, waiting for the time to come when they would move onto the field, and the cranes would start the meticulous job of loading each piece. The twisted pieces would be taken to a hanger set up in Kansas City, where they would be examined for clues. Whereas this case was pretty cut and dry as far as the reason the aircraft ended up this way, most accidents take considerable time to determine the cause. All at once, Charlie felt as if the cold wind was blowing right through him, and he experienced a sickening feeling in his stomach.

The kerosene heater in the tent helped take off the chill, but it did not remove the sickening feeling. It was just too much to take in, seeing the aftermath of such a disaster. Could there be such a thing as a computer error? He had always understood that computer programming was garbage in, garbage out technology. So how could a computer do all this? It had to be human error. Now, was the human error accidental or intentional?

"Charlie, get over here!" It was Sean hollering at him over the noise of the heater. "I want you to meet Seth Arnold. He is the NTSB boss and will be taking us on a tour. You warmed up and ready to go?" Charlie grimaced at the thought of witnessing anymore but nodded.

Their first stop was the flight deck, or what remained of the flight deck. The bodies of the captain and first officer had already been removed, and two NTSB agents with representatives from Airbus were busy removing the autopilot and Data Link equipment. Walking back to the east, they came across parts of the fuselage. Seats were strewn about alongside baggage and other personal items.

Then Charlie noticed the baby's car seat beside a small blanket. Immediately, a lump came to his throat as he thought about the child who had perished. One moment sitting there in the seat beside her parents, then the collision and all hell breaks loose as screaming passengers terrify the child. The plane tumbles towards the earth, disintegrating as it tumbles. At one point the seat separates from the others, and it drifts away slowly rolling end over end. The little blanket slips out of her hand, moving away from the child. Crying, she reaches out to recover her security. Charlie thought about security. Obviously the blanket, which had been her security, was about as secure as the air traffic control system which let her down. The

217

continuous freezing cold wind blasting in the child's face was more than the body could handle, causing loss of consciousness moments before she impacted the hard frozen farmland.

K9 crews were busy scouring the fields and wooded areas west of the crash site searching for more bodies. At last count twelve were still missing from the USAir Flight.

"Notice anything missing?" The NTSB boss brought Charlie's attention back to the task at hand.

"Where did the wings and tail end up?" Charlie asked in return.

"They're spread out from here to three miles west. It is quite obvious that the aircraft came apart shortly after impact to be spread over this distance."

Spending about an hour at the crash site, Charlie had the opportunity to meet a lot of the workers and left feeling that they did more for him then he did for them. Lifting off the field, the helicopter headed southwest for the six-mile trek to where the Boeing 737 went down. Along the way, Charlie saw the emergency crews walking through the fields below. About two miles from liftoff they came across the wings and empennage of the Airbus.

Four miles later, the Southwest site came into view. The helicopter circled around the Appanoose Elementary School before landing in the school parking lot. The 737 stayed together until impact, containing the crash site to the sixty-acre field across from the school. The last of the bodies had been removed, giving the FAA team more accessibility to the area.

After meeting each of the workers with words of encouragement, Charlie advised his boss it was time to go. In the air and headed back to CCATS, Charlie finally broke down. Sean put his hand on his friends shoulder as Charlie, with his head in his hands, sobbed.

"Charlie, you have done a great job. You have been holding all this in, even though it affects you too. You need to release those emotions as well. You want to cancel the briefing this afternoon?"

Charlie looked up with a slight smile, "No, we can do it. I may need your help, but these controllers were here and saw the accident happen. These folks still have to come to work every day and face the reality of a failed system."

"You ready to recommend shutting down 4DT?" Sean asked his lead controller.

"Playing on the emotions I am feeling now, I would say definitely. Let's wait until we get the facts before making the decision." The helicopter banked left as it entered the pattern back at the airport bringing CCATS into view.

Chapter 33

Charlie and Sean walked into the conference room. Eight quiet controllers surrounded the table, not typical for the type A personalities. Charlie had decided not to use any form of technical presentation but to listen to these controllers who had been in the area at the time of the accident.

After introductions, he got right to business. "Adam and Denise are on your team. While they were the ones working the airplanes, you are not exempt from the same stress they are experiencing. That is why I wanted to bring you guys together and hear what you are feeling. Please, don't hold back your emotions and concerns. So that we give each of you a chance to voice your thoughts, we will move around the table." He pointed to an elderly man sitting at the head of the table. "Carl, go ahead."

Carl was a thirty-year veteran controller who had seen his share of radarscopes. "Charlie, Sean, thanks for coming out here and spending time with us. This has to be the worst situation I have seen in all my years controlling airplanes. I was sitting next to Denise and felt horrible for her. Not only her, but for the rest of the team, and yes, including the supervisor, who did all they could to stop this from happening. My concern is for not only the flying public, but also our workforce. I think we need to take a step back and look at this program really closely. We should shut down 4DT, go back to manual control until the problem is found and fixed."
220

Charlie nodded, "Thank you, Carl, I do agree with your assessment. We are taking a real hard look at that option. As far as the controller workforce is concerned, this is not only affecting your team and facility. The ramification of this accident is a chink in the confidence of controllers nationwide." They continued on around the table listening to each of the controllers' concerns, which pretty much echoed their senior controller's sentiments.

Finishing up the briefing with the team, Charlie headed outside to call Carrie and bring her up-to-date on his return. Noticing he had a text message from Denise requesting he join her and Adam for dinner, he went ahead and called her instead. "Where are we meeting for dinner tonight?"

"Thanks for calling, Charlie, I am so still freaking out. I really didn't sleep much last night. This whole thing sucks. Did you see the papers today? They make me out to be at fault."

Charlie rolled his eyes and replied, "How many times do I have to tell you? You did nothing wrong. The media will do everything they can to find a news story. While this is a news story, and the FAA is very likely going to buy this one-you and Adam did all you could. Now, where is it you want to go for dinner?"

"Oh, yeah! Can we go up to Olathe? They have a Texas Roadhouse, and I'm hungry for a steak. Is that all right?"

"Sure, not a problem considering what you guys have gone through this week. Okay if I bring Jim along? He's been working at the center with Bud all day and could probably use the break."

"That would be great, Charlie. We will meet you at your hotel at six."

Hanging up, Charlie dialed Carrie's number only to get her voice mail. He left her a quick message reiterating his plans to make it home the following night. "That is strange," he

221

mumbled to himself looking at his phone. "She always answers her phone when I call. Bet she's still upset."

He stopped by the media room where he quickly went online and ordered a bouquet of flowers for his wife. By the time he got to the cafeteria, Sean, Bud, and Jim were well into their chicken fried steak and mash potatoes. "Think I will just skip the heart attack," he told them as he grabbed an apple and sat down. "What's new?"

"Jim and I are still working our way through the historical data, one line at a time. We should be finished sometime tonight," Bud continued. "I haven't found anything earth-shattering yet."

Charlie frowned, "Jim, I've got us a date with a steak house tonight. Will you be done in time to go?"

"Probably not, we have a lot of data to go through, and I would like to go home tomorrow providing we wrap this up. As you know, I've got a kid in the Christmas program tomorrow night."

"Yeah, I know. Mitzy's in it as well. Carrie threatened to dismember me if I showed up late. Sean, what about you? Want to go out for dinner tonight?"

"Love to, Charlie, but I already have plans tonight. The NTSB chief wants me to meet him over dinner to bring him up-to-date on our findings." Sean stood up. "Come on, Charlie, the mandatory briefing is about to start, and you are the guest speaker."

Charlie looked over at Jim, "Want your fifteen minutes of fame buddy? I will give you the limelight."

Jim laughed, "What, and miss out on a few thousand lines of code? Sorry, my friend. It's all yours."

The room looked more like a movie theater than a briefing room. The stadium seating gave the controllers a close-up view of the speaker. It was just after one thirty when Darrell Pence brought the room of 150 controllers to attention. Though normally not an easy task, this day was different. They had all heard of Charlie. Some of the stories were even true. He was one of them, and even in their time of doubt, they had great respect for him. The introduction was short and without substance as Charlie walked into the room and up on the stage.

"Thank you for the intro, Chief." Looking out over the controllers, he smiled. "You guys are why I'm here. I don't really give a darn about the management in this place or in Washington. You and I have been carrying the FAA for the last sixty-plus years and it will continue that way regardless of what you hear from those who do not wear headsets." That broke the ice and brought on an onslaught of applause.

"Now, let's get down to business. I understand how the rumor mill works in our environment so I want to set everything straight. Yesterday morning at nine fifteen local time, two airplanes collided in the sky just thirty-two miles west of here. Both aircraft crashed, killing 223 people, and, yes, it was a system failure.

At this time we will not put the blame on any one person, nor will we, regardless of what the media says, put the blame on controllers. All I can say about the cause is that there was a chain of events leading up to the midair. For starters, the ADS-B sent erroneous information to 4DT, second, 4DT miscalculated the closure rate based on these erroneous speeds; then the bailout procedure, a last ditch program, failed. Crew resource management taught us that layers of protection would prevent disasters from happening. The whole thing about the layers of Swiss cheese-if one layer did not stop an incident, another one would. This just happened to be a time when all the holes lined up. Give us time, we will address each of these issues, as well as many others, until you will once again have confidence in the 4DT system.

Earlier today, one of your own suggested we shut down 4DT until the investigations are complete. I don't know if that is going to happen. If it were my decision, I probably would, just as a precaution. We will keep you informed as the determinations are made. I would suggest you keep your controlling skills sharp, because you may be called upon to perform those tasks again. Now if you will give me just a few more moments, I want to share with you our experience.

From the day each one of you walked through the doors of your first facility, you understood what your job entailed. You knew that every time you plugged that headset into the jack that this could be the time your world came apart. You knew that every word you said and every move you made was being recorded. You knew that yesterday's disaster was only one control instruction away. How often did you look at your scope and see two aircraft moving away from each other and shudder, wondering how they missed?

Today, I visited the crash site. Today, I witnessed the destruction of two great airplanes which each of you has surely worked back and forth across this great nation. Today, I saw the empty seats scattered across the landscape, the luggage strewn about. I tell you this not for you to mourn or be depressed; now is the time our country needs us more than ever before. It is time for you to stand up and be counted. Be diligent in your scanning and prepared for any unusual situations.

For you younger controllers, never be intimidated. Years ago, as a new developmental, I was monitoring a radarscope when the radar controller cleared an aircraft to an altitude and put a different altitude in the data block. I, being a novice, thought about it for a second and then shrugged it off, thinking I had just heard wrong. I was intimidated. But ten minutes later, that aircraft lost separation with another, causing an operational error for the radar controller, and I could have prevented it. I determined from that day forward never to be intimidated and would question everything I even perceived to be amiss. Go back to work, my friends. You have a job to do."

224

The room applauded as Charlie turned the microphone over to the red-faced chief, who had to calm the controllers down for the counselor the FAA had hired. Charlie thought about sticking around for a laugh but decided against it. He had too much work to do. Back at his hotel he opened up his laptop and started his report.

Chapter 34

Denise showed up at six with the news that Adam had decided to stay home. His parents were coming into town and he wanted to be there when they arrived.

Great, Charlie thought. *I really shouldn't be alone with this beautiful young lady. She's twenty years younger than I am, but it still doesn't look good, and she's so vulnerable.* Finally he decided it would be all right. He would just be cautious. They headed up Highway 50 to Olathe for dinner.

It was a very pleasant evening with little discussion about the accident. Charlie listened to Denise tell him everything about herself from her childhood through her decision to be a controller. How her parents had been so proud of her and her grief in losing both of them in a tragic car accident just two years earlier. After dinner, Denise talked him in to taking her to a little park called Brookside in Gardner. The wind had calmed down a bit as they walked along the frozen stream. Coming to some old playground equipment, Denise ran over to the swing and begged Charlie to push her.

"Thank you so much for humoring me," Denise told him when she got off the swing and they walked on.

Stopping at a picnic shelter, Denise started to cry. Charlie wrapped his arms around her and held her until she stopped.

"You okay?" he asked as he wiped the tears from her cheek.

"This is where my parents used to bring me for birthday parties. There are too many memories here. Maybe we should go home." Walking back to the car, Denise held Charlie's hand firmly, and he had to admit to himself it felt good.

Back at the hotel, Denise followed Charlie into his room. No questions were asked, no answers were given. It was as if a mutual understanding had been reached between two people. Denise grabbed Charlie and kissed him hard and long. Charlie gently pushed Denise away. Sitting on the couch holding her hand, Charlie continued to listen to Denise spill out her heart. The battle raged within him. His desire to spend the night with this girl in his arms was being countered by thoughts of Carrie. He tried to justify his actions. After all, Carrie had been unfaithful to him once. Why shouldn't he enjoy that experience? What would Carrie do if she found out? He remembered the empty hurt he had experienced.

Looking into the eyes of this beautiful young lady, he knew what he had to do. "Denise, as much as I would love to spend the night with you, I can't. There are so many reasons. First of all, it is not right. As you are aware, I am a Christian and my convictions do not give leeway to sex outside of marriage, which leads to the second reason. As you are also aware, I am married. I have a wonderful wife. I love her beyond imagination and have no desire to hurt her. Finally, you are a very beautiful young lady and deserve more than a one-night stand. Somewhere out there, there is a young man whom you will meet, in God's timing. He will want to make you his best friend, like my wife is mine. Denise, I will be your friend and help you through this time in your life, but that is where our relationship stops."

By now the tears were sliding down her face as she smiled at Charlie. "Thank you for being truthful, Charlie. I just

227

hope someday I can find a man like you. Dad and Mom were Christians and raised me that way, but when I was twenty-one I turned back on their beliefs. I started drinking and hanging out with the wrong crowd. I haven't even been to church in years."

Charlie stood, helping Denise up and hanging onto her hands. "You have been through a couple of really tough days. You need to surround yourself with good people who will help you through the next few weeks. I suggest you get back in church. Is it all right if I pray for you before you go?"

Smiling, Denise responded, "I would love that."

Standing there in the hotel room, Charlie asked God to give Denise the ability she needed to make it through the tragedy that she was grieving over and for the changes she needed to make in her life. He thanked Him for his desire to remain faithful to his wife and his respect for Denise.

Giving Charlie a quick kiss on the cheek, Denise seemed happy now. "I came here thinking we were going to make love-- I am so happy that you showed what love really is."

Chapter 35

Friday morning

The meeting was scheduled for ten o'clock. The four from the FAA team, along with the facility chief, NTSB rep and his boss, Seth Arnold, were present. Charlie had spent all morning on conference calls with the controllers' union and had finally sat down with Sean for a heart-to-heart talk. The decision made, Charlie and Sean walked into the meeting. Sean listened as Seth Arnold described how the cockpit voice recorders revealed the last-minute efforts the pilots went through to shut down the autopilots.

Stan Farrell had a report back from the manufacturers stating that they have the technology available to install the manual cutoff switch anytime the FAA gives the word to do so. Bud and Jim both advised that no further discrepancies were found and that, as far as they were concerned, it was a good program as long as it received correct data. They recommended a patch be designed to overcome the speed discrepancies by cross checking ADS-B inputs with designers' recommended speeds. If at any time these do not correlate, alarms would warn both the controllers and the flight crews and disconnect the autopilot interface.

Sean stood up and addressed the room. "We have come to a decision. Tonight, during the midnight shift, we will be shutting down 4DT. We have not come to this decision lightly as it will have severe consequences. The union, along with Mr. Beckler, has made this determination and I support it 100 percent. We will still be using ADS-B and data link. The reasoning behind this decision is that ADS-B is all we have, and it did not fail as far as the position and altitude of the aircraft. Data link has shown no discrepancies. As the face of NextGen, Charlie will be giving a press conference after lunch. That is all I have, thanks for your help, and have a Merry Christmas."

Charlie was on the phone with the King Air pilots arranging for the trip home. A departure time of two thirty would get them home by six. Weather was not the best and the headwinds would add thirty minutes to their flight. As he was on the phone, a call came in from Carrie. He quickly hung up and called his wife back.

Carrie was crying, "I got the flowers and the note. I'm so sorry for being mean to you. The media is not saying nice things about you guys, and you don't need me to add to it. Will you forgive me?"

"It's all right, darling. You are mild compared to the media. You want what's best for our family. The media wants scalps. Be ready for the news tonight."

"Are you going to make it home for the Christmas play?"

"Yep, I'm giving a news conference here in an hour, and then we will be on our way. It looks like we will be at the airport by six. We need to spend some time together when this is all over. I feel like I'm losing you, and I don't want that to happen."

"Me neither, Charlie, let's get it together," Carrie sighed.

The press conference was held in the CCATS lobby with all three major networks present along with CNN and Fox News. All the TV cameras and microphones were a little intimidating. Charlie grabbed Jim and made him tag along.

"Ladies and Gentlemen, I'm sorry you need to be here today. It is so sad when you can no longer trust those who protect you. We will not discuss the history of NextGen since that is available online. Today we will only discuss issues pertinent to the accident.

On Thursday morning, the ADS-B sent erroneous information to the 4DT program. The 4DT program, using this information, failed to provide minimum separation standards, which should have triggered a last-ditch program. This program also failed due to a reality factor. The flight crews were extremely aware of their situation and tried to save the aircraft, sadly to no avail. More information will come out in the NTSB report. The NextGen team has decided, as a safety measure, to suspend the use of 4DT at all three centers, effective tonight. Are there any questions?"

"Does this mean the FAA is taking responsibility for the accident?" an elderly lady from AP news asked.

Charlie scratched his chin, "You don't expect me to be that easy, do you? The responsibility for this accident will be for the NTSB to announce. I can tell you that there are discrepancies in the 4DT program that our team has determined as insufficient for further use at this time."

The next question came from Fox News, "Can this happen again?"

"No, I feel that the measures we have put in place will prevent any further conflicts. As for whether it's safe or not, I plan on flying home as soon as this briefing is over. I will add that I have second thoughts as to the future of 4DT. I will keep them to myself for the time being."

Someone in the media grabbed that and had to ask, "Not too long back they made you the face of NextGen. Is that still the case? It sounds like it's losing your support."

Charlie sighed, one of many the last two days, "Yesterday morning, I walked around the scattered remains of two aircraft where 223 people lost their lives. Why did this happen? It happened because of a system I just happen to represent. That is why! We may have just moved beyond our limits. We may need to step back and think this thing through."

Turning to Jim, Charlie addressed the media, "This is my co-worker, Jim Gallagher. Jim, along with our programming manager, Bud Simons, worked hard over the last two days reviewing the program data. They are the unsung heroes on this team. Jim and I have daughters in a school Christmas play tonight. So, if you will excuse us, we have a plane to catch." With that they walked out of the news conference.

The King Air had been in the air about an hour when Sean called on the in-flight phone rang. "Charlie, the administrator isn't happy. Said we should have discussed the shutdown with him before making that decision. He doesn't want to shut down 4DT."

"What? Doesn't he know the dangers of leaving it up?"

"Probably doesn't care. He's saying we will get our butts handed to us by admitting the system is flawed."

Charlie couldn't believe it, "Listen, Boss. I don't care who blames whom. My responsibility is the safety of the flying public, but you are the boss. If you find you can't back me on this, then so be it. The blood of those who die will be on your hands, not mine."

"Come on, Charlie, you know me better than that. I have a meeting with the administrator when I land in an hour."

"Well, you know where I stand, and I can vouch for the controller union. They are there with me on this one. Let that hardheaded chief know he is getting absolutely no support on keeping this thing on line. I'll talk to you later," Charlie hung up with disgust and sat back in his seat.

"Not sounding good. What was that about?" Jim's curiosity got to him.

"The administrator wants to keep 4DT alive. I can't let it happen."

"How are you going to stop them? Are you overriding Washington?"

"We will see what happens after Sean's meeting."

As Charlie looked out the window into the building clouds rimmed with the golden glow of the setting sun, he was reminded of the Maui sunsets. Their first trip to the Garden Island had been to celebrate their tenth anniversary. Now they anticipated each annual adventure. Oh, how he wished he could go there right now with Carrie just to get away from the stress of the past week.

Then there was Denise. Should he tell Carrie about her? It was really a shaky time in Carrie's life to be throwing that at her. It may just send her over the edge. *Well, I didn't do anything,* he tried to convince himself. *I know I went over the line, and she needs to know, just not right now.* How he thanked God he was able to come to his senses when he did. He sure loved his wife, and those few moments of pleasure would have destroyed his family.

He tried to sleep, but every time he shut his eyes the images of the crash site would not leave him alone.

It was late when Sean walked into the 9th floor conference room. Bob Burkhammer, the new FAA administrator, was seated at the head of the table next to the

Secretary of Transportation, Terry Laverne. Four other people were in the room. They were introduced to Sean as "from the legal department."

"Sean, we have a problem," Bob said as Sean took his seat.

"Yes, you do," Sean replied, "and you can start fixing it by revealing what went wrong with your ADS-B. If I recall, you are the one that ran that program during development."

Bob's look of doubt told the story. "What do you mean ADS-B? The autopilot's the culprit. Leave ADS-B and 4DT alone."

Sean was fuming. "Dog gone it, Bob! You know that is a crock of crap! You have read the preliminaries and know darn well the autopilot was only the last straw. You just want to hang this on the manufacturers. It ain't going to happen."

Terry spoke up. "Sean, settle down. We have a lot at stake here and need to think this through. We have over fifteen years and billions of dollars invested in NextGen. One misstep will destroy what we have been working for."

Sean was now really perturbed. "Explain that to the families of the 223 passengers. I will go along with glitches in technology during its development but will not accept anything but perfection in its operation. If NextGen is the future, it will make it through this challenge."

Bob Burkhammer stood up as if that would make him look important. "Sean, we are going to override you and leave 4DT online. We have talked to Scotty Morris, and he feels the ADS-B problem was isolated and the other challenges can be fixed with a patch. Flight Standards will issue airworthiness directives to have the manual cutoff switch installed on all U.S. registered aircraft."

Sean sat there for a moment and then looked up at Bob. "So your final decision is to leave 4DT running even though the controllers feel it compromises safety?"

"Yes. They do not have the big picture and will have to learn to adjust. We will leave 4DT running and I have already advised the regions to make sure that happens."

"Great! If you want to be such an incompetent idiot, you leave me no choice other than to resign." Sean took off his badge and slammed it on the table. "I will have no part in the continuation of this type of compromise."

Sean walked out of the meeting with mixed emotions. With Charlie's help, he had come to realize the system was unsafe. He was convicted that no longer could he put his name on the program in its current state. Thirty-six years of government service and this is how it ends. He had to call Charlie.

"You aren't going to be happy, Charlie." Sean had called just as Charlie was walking into the house. They had made it in time for the Christmas program, which seemed to appease Carrie.

"What's up, Sean?"

"The secretary and administrator overrode us. They are keeping 4DT up."

"That is ludicrous! The odds are too high on a repeat, Sean. You can't let them do it."

"I know how you feel." Sean replied. "Problem is, I resigned."

Charlie was shocked. "What! Did I hear you right? Are you quitting?"

This made Sean laugh. "Not quitting, I resigned or better yet I retired. I've had enough of this, Charlie. I have been thinking about getting out anyhow. I just thought I could see NextGen through completion."

Charlie didn't know what to say. "Will they reconsider? Give me the administrator's number, I'm calling that miserable old...."

"That won't work, Charlie. They've made up their mind, and it's based on risk value. They feel the cost of shutting down outweighs the risk of staying online."

Carrie was harassing Charlie to get off the phone and barely whispered, "You have been working all week. Tell him you will be back to work next week and hang up."

Charlie gave her a stern look and got back to Sean. "What's our next move?"

"Charlie, do what you need to do. I am going to send out a press release tonight. You have any statements you want added?"

"You bet I do! I will have them ready to go in twenty minutes. Let's do this together."

Hanging up, he apologized to Carrie and begged for her to give him a half hour, and then he would be hers.

Sean read back over the press release to make sure he had covered all the bases. "At nine forty-five this evening I rendered my resignation from the Federal Aviation Administration. The position I have held over the last few years as the VP of NextGen operations has been one of great honor and respect. This ended this evening as a result of misunderstanding stemming from the midair collision over Kansas earlier this week. We, the NextGen 4DT team, after reviewing the discrepancies causing the accident, made the determination to suspend 4DT operations indefinitely. The FAA Administrator and the Secretary of Transportation have resisted the move and plan to keep 4DT operational. I personally cannot condone this course of action."

Sean let out a sigh matching his resignation and hit send. Charlie read the email that Sean had copied him. He quickly typed out his statement, which echoed Sean, concerning the team's decision. He added his feelings about the continuation of a failed system. He made sure to add drama from the accident itself.

Sean and Charlie's statements made third-page news the next day with hardly any notice. Fox News was the only channel to cover the resignation. They were looking for any dirt they could on the current administration and this seemed to be one of those things. They interviewed Sean, and he went into detail on the pitfalls of the program he had helped design. The FAA spin team who made him out to be a disgruntled employee countered him. After Charlie's first interview, he was told by his boss to either shut up, or face disciplinary actions.

Chapter 36

January in Ely, NV

Charlie was alone in the control room, running from scope to scope trying to keep the airspace organized. All the aircraft kept turning towards each other, descending to a single point in the center of the scope. Rapidly, he typed out commands to the aircraft. He had to stop them. It was no use. The aircraft continued on. He called for help. Over the radio, he begged for help, yet none would come. In slow motion, the airplanes came together, and over the speakers came bloody screams, as the aircraft plunged to earth. Charlie jumped, still shaking from the nightmare as he threw his feet over the side of the bed.

"You okay, darling?" Carrie asked, sliding over beside him. "Was it another nightmare?"

"Yes, this is getting ridiculous. Do you think maybe it's time I see a shrink? Maybe it would help."

Carrie rubbed his shoulders, "I think you need to keep away from work. You have been through a lot over the last few years, and it's time to call it quits."

"You may be right, darling, but they still need me. There are things yet to do."

"Charlie, you have a saying that puts this in perspective. Know the one I'm talking about?"

Charlie turned smiling up at his beautiful wife. "Yes, I do. When you pull your hand out of a bucket of water, how big the hole left in the water is, that's how much you will be

238

missed. Sure it will cause a few ripples, and the level of the water will go down. In the end it will smooth over, as if you never existed."

Carrie wrapped her arms around her man. "Not only that, my boyfriend. I need you worse than they do. Go see the doctor."

Wednesday morning at nine thirty, Charlie walked into the doctor's office. The sign on the door hit him with the force of a hurricane. "Roger M. Morgan, Doctor of Psychology," it read. All he could think about was the times they had made fun of the controllers who had walked through these doors. *I wonder if I am really this whacked,* he mused as the receptionist handed him a clipboard with a stack of forms to complete. He sat down on one of the uncomfortable seats next to an end table filled with outdated magazines.

Scanning down through the forms only antagonized his tired brain. Charlie did his best to fill in the blanks. He came to the one which asked for his reason for the visit. "Because my wife thinks I'm a nutcase," he said out loud, causing the others in the office to look at him with raised eyebrows. The door opened, and the receptionist called his name. He followed her down a poorly lighted hallway to a surprisingly pleasant room. The decorations were appropriate for softening the spirit, and the couch brought him from an antagonistic attitude to submission of the inevitable.

Dr. Morgan, a tall stately gentleman fitting the stereotype of a psychologist, walked through the door. "Charles Beckler," he read looking at the clipboard.

Charlie raised one of his eyelids, then let it drop back down to the closed position. "If that was a question, the answer is affirmative, doctor. Nice couch you got here. Think maybe I'll take a nap."

"It's fine with me, Mr. Beckler. For the fees I charge you can sleep all day, though a hotel would be cheaper."

That brought Charlie to a semi-alert position, and he smiled at the doctor. "They say you can help me. Is that so?"

"That depends," the doctor was being evasive, "if you need help."

"I really think I'm okay. I'm just having trouble sleeping at night."

"Tell me why you think you need a shrink instead of reducing your caffeine intake."

"It's the dreams, Doc."

"What are you dreaming about?"

Charlie looked around the room as if someone else would come out of the shadows and answer the question.

"What are you looking for, Charlie? I'm over here," questioned the doctor.

Charlie thought for a moment then replied, "It's hard to say. The dreams are so real they cause me to wake up in a cold sweat. My heart is pounding so hard I feel like I'm having a heart attack."

"What is the content of the dreams?"

"It's about work, Doc. They are coming together."

"Who are coming together, Charlie?"

"It's all the airplanes. Every one of them turns towards each other, and no matter what I do, I can't save them. Everything I do fails to solve the conflict."

"Charlie, I have heard this story before. Over the years I have worked with a number of your co-workers. Each of you shares that same dream. Your problem is real, and your mind is playing games with you. Let us take a trip down the pathway of your career."

Dr. Morgan got up from his chair and walked over to an ice bucket, where he pulled out a bottle of cold water and handed it to Charlie. "Charlie, you have an occupation that is unusual in a number of ways. The step towards a complete recovery is to look back at what has caused these symptoms. Once we have established the cause, we can one by one peel back the layers, returning you to a normal human being. Let's explore your schedule." Knowing the answer already, he prodded his patient. "What hours do you work?"

Charlie shook his head, "I can't even keep up with it myself, Doc. Let's see, on Sunday night I go to work at four and work until midnight. On Monday I go back to work at three and work until eleven. Tuesday I get up and go to work at either eight or ten. That changes every week."

Charlie paused for a moment in thought and took a drink of the chilled water. Dr. Morgan sat there with his pencil writing on a legal pad. "Continue."

"Okay, on Wednesday I go in at six thirty, for that is my briefing day."

"Briefing day?"

"Yeah, that's the day we only work traffic for seven hours and then spend the last hour listening to some manager spill his guts."

"Interesting," the doctor replied as he continued writing.

Charlie continued, "After briefing, we get eight hours off work before we come back and work the night shift."

Dr. Morgan looked up from his notes, his eyes peering above his glasses. "You work a day shift then return that night for another eight hours?"

"We only work the night shift every other week. The other weeks we come back in at six in the morning and work until two. It's a tradeoff, Doc. You either work the night shift and get it over with or work the next day shift and deal with the traffic."

Doctor Morgan put aside his notepad and looked over at his patient. Taking a deep breath, he continued with the questioning. "Why hasn't the FAA established a more conducive schedule for you guys?"

"I really don't know. From what I have heard over the years, they are concerned about equality in scheduling. They want everyone to get their fair share of traffic and day shifts."

"At the expense of sanity," mumbled the doctor.

Dr. Morgan picked up his legal pad and started writing. "Charlie, I am recommending you take some time off work to allow your body to heal. Until you get some sort of normality in your schedule, your nightmares will persist. Do you mind staying away from the center for a few weeks?"

Charlie smiled, "If nothing else, it will make my wife happy. Sure, whatever you want. You're the doctor."

"Okay, that is what I will prescribe, Charlie. It will do you good. That is all for today. Your homework is to spend your evenings with your family. Make sure you engage in activities that take you away from your work. We have a lot to do here, young man. I will see you on Friday morning."

Charlie walked out of the office where the cold winter wind blew right through him. Looking up at the dark clouds moving in across the mountains caused an unknown fear to chill his spine.

Armed with the letter from Dr. Morgan, Charlie arrived at the Center on Thursday morning. The closed-door meeting he had with his supervisor Nick Harton and his union representative was comical at best and pathetical at worst. Numerous threats of retribution were made by the Kool-Aid-drinking supervisor and the union rep countered with threats of grievances Charlie had never heard of. In the end, Charlie's request to fulfill the doctor's orders was granted, and he shook hands with his rep and left for a six-week vacation.

On the way home, all he could think about was the appointment he had the next morning with Dr. Morgan. Would he be able to reveal the true fears that kept him awake at night? Would the doc be able to see right through his callused skin? He was afraid of what the doctor may discover, but the challenge would be worth it. After all, the guy had managed to get him a six-week reprieve.

The next morning, Charlie was half asleep when Dr. Morgan opened the door. Yawning, he sat up, swinging his feet over the edge of the couch. "What's up, Doc?"

"Obviously you found a place you can sleep. How did it go at work?"

Charlie explained his encounter at work and the results. "Six weeks away from the bad place," he chuckled.

The doctor sat down in his overstuffed arm chair and, turning his pen end over end finally spoke up. "Let's go back to where we left off on Wednesday. Your schedule has caused an imbalance in your physical makeup, but there has to be something more."

Charlie snapped his head around, facing the doctor. "What do you mean, something more?"

"Charlie, when did the dreams start?"

"It was right after the accident."

"You had an accident?"

"Oh, I guess I didn't tell you that. It was the midair collision over Kansas in December."

"Were you talking to the pilots?" The doctor asked with a puzzled expression.

"No, CCATS were working the airplanes. I just went back to Kansas to help encourage the controllers."

"Did you do that?"

"Do what?"

The doctor could tell that now Charlie was now having trouble focusing on the conversation. "Look at me, Charlie." The firmness in the doctor's voice shook Charlie, and his eyes stopped their darting about and settled on the psychologist.

"I'm sorry, Doc, what did you say?"

"I asked if you were able to help the controllers."

"I really don't know if I helped them or they helped me. It was awful. There were bodies scattered all over the field." With that Charlie started trembling.

"So is that what you visualize about the crash site?"

243

"No, I was there, doc, I walked through the field where the airplanes crashed."

"Well, that explains a lot, Charlie. Let us explore a little more of the trauma you experienced before we move on. Please tell me the whole story, leaving nothing out."

For the next two hours Charlie replayed the investigation and the crash scene.

"I am most intrigued with the visualization you described when you came across the car seat and the baby blanket," Doctor Morgan commented when Charlie had finished. "Have you had any recurrence of the vision?"

"Many times, Doc. It just doesn't go away. I see that child falling through the sky." He hesitated shaking his head.

"What else do you see, Charlie?"

Tears were coming to his eyes. "It's Mitzy."

"The child is your daughter?"

"Yes, I see her face and hear her crying for me to save her. All the time I'm yelling to her that I'm sorry."

"How do these nightmares end?" he asked looking up from his notes. Charlie sat there stony silence, the dreams playing fast-forward through his mind. "Charlie, how does the nightmare end?" Dr. Morgan's firm voice brought Charlie back into focus.

"Everything starts spinning, and I wake up," Charlie whispered.

Dr. Morgan caught variance in Charlie's voice. Years of experience told him that the controller was not sharing everything. "Charlie, do you realize you were not alone at the crash site?"

"What kind of a question is that?"

"Just answer the question, Charlie. Do you realize you were not alone the day you witnessed the crash?"

"Of course I was not alone, Doc. There were over a hundred people working the site."

"Do you think they are having the same dreams you experience?"

"Why should they? They never created the mess."

"So you think the accident was your fault?"

"I think so. If I had been more forceful, it would not have happened. Why I signed off on the program to start with is beyond me. I just don't know why it had to happen."

Dr. Morgan could see that Charlie building a self-incriminating case against himself. The wrong move here would turn that case into a solid conviction. "It was horrible, absolutely, but it is not an everyday occurrence, it is an aberration."

It was all Charlie needed. "If this accident isn't the most gruesome and awful thing that can happen, what is? Doc, what's worse than people falling to their deaths from twenty-five thousand feet?" Charlie was almost yelling.

Dr. Morgan slowly tapped his pen on the pad in a soothing tempo, bringing softness to his voice. "Nothing...nothing's worse. Thank God this type of tragedy only happens once every few years. Charlie, I think you've had enough for today."

Carrie was nervous as she walked into Dr. Morgan's office. He had called earlier in the week requesting the meeting. She sat there fidgeting with her cell phone as the doctor looked up from his notes. "Carrie, I am concerned about your husband. Hours of questioning and listening to his fears has left holes in his story. While this is normal, I need to fill these holes in order to start the healing process. That is why I asked to see you alone." Looking back down at his notes he continued, "You and Charlie have been married for over twenty-three years so you know him better than anyone. What are some of the changes you have noticed?"

Tears were creeping their way into Carrie's eyes as she looked up at the doctor. "He's not been the same since he went

245

to Kansas. He spends all his time on the patio. It's cold out there, but he doesn't even seem to notice. When I go out to get him for meals, he jumps as I touch him." The tears were no longer creeping but were streaming down her face. Dr. Morgan handed her a box of tissues.

"What does he tell you about his time on the patio?" He asked Carrie as she wiped the tears from her cheeks.

"He doesn't say anything. Except one time I had gone out to get him, and he didn't respond to my calling. Then all of a sudden he screamed and pointed to two airplanes. He said they were going to hit. Obviously they didn't and he just sat there with a blank stare for the next ten minutes before I could get him to come in."

Dr. Morgan was busily scribbling notes on his pad so Carrie added, "There's another thing, Doctor Morgan."

"What would that be?"

Carrie looked around nervously as if she was ashamed of what she was revealing. "He seems to have lost all interest in sex. He tries, but it's just not happening. Do you know what I'm saying?"

"Carrie, you do not need to be embarrassed. This is normal considering what Charlie has gone through. We will be able to get him, or I really should say you two, through this tough time."

It had been three weeks since he first started seeing Dr. Morgan. Charlie was starting to get a grip on his role in the accident and looked forward to his conversations with the doctor. The thing that bothered him the most was the empty feeling in his stomach. It was as if all he had lived and worked for had suddenly disappeared. He slowly came to the realization that this was defying logic. He could no more be responsible for killing those passengers than all the other thousands of people involved in the NextGen program.

"So why am I experiencing this empty void?" he asked God, as he stared into a cloudless sky, "Why the numbing sensation?"

He thought of Denise, wondering how she was handling the situation. He had heard she was having challenges working the radar and had been reassigned to a staff job. Again looking deep into the darkening sky, he observed as the first stars twinkled in the cold evening air. "Why am I thinking of her? She has no business occupying my mind." For the next hour he sat there in agony knowing he had to tell the doctor.

Laying back on the couch, Charlie told the doctor what had happened that night in Kansas with Denise. After he had finished, Dr. Morgan smiled. "Charlie, you have just revealed the key to the puzzle. It was clear to me that something was missing in your story, but I had no idea that it could be an affair."

"It wasn't an affair, Doc, I didn't let it go that far," Charlie protested looking off into space.

"Charlie, look at me. It was an affair. While the physical completion of the affair never transpired, the emotional affair ran deep, and that sometimes can be just as destructive. Carrie never mentioned this encounter. Have you told her?" Dr. Morgan knew the answer even before Charlie spoke.

"I haven't found the right time to do so, and I would appreciate it if you didn't tell her."

Dr. Morgan shook his head, "I won't tell her, but you will, Charlie. The fear that is constantly nagging at your conscious is the encounter, not the accident."

"Doc, I want her to know, but I'm afraid of what she will do. Our relationship hasn't been that strong lately."

"Why is that, Charlie?"

"I don't really know, it's just that I don't share with her as much as I once did."

"Could that be because you're hiding something from her, so you're scared talking with her would somehow bring it out? Charlie, the longer you wait the harder it will become. Is Carrie here now?"

Charlie's eyes got wide and then he dropped his head, knowing what was coming next. "She's in the waiting room."

Dr. Morgan picked up the phone and in a couple of minutes Carrie walked into the room.

With questions in her eyes she sat down next to her husband and grabbed his arm. She looked at him with concern as she could feel his body shaking. "Thank you for joining us, Carrie. As you are quite aware, we have been dealing with this situation as if it were post traumatic stress disorder. It's hard to tell if a controller is disorientated as they normally are considering their schedule. Are they suffering from this stress reactions or PTSD? In this case, it appears to be three-fold. Charlie not only suffers from the stress of the changing work schedule and the trauma of the accident on his mind, he has another force working at destroying his stability. I am going to let Charlie explain it in his own words. Go ahead, Charlie."

With tears of regret and sadness, Charlie repeated the story he had earlier shared with Dr. Morgan.

Carrie sat there emotionless as her fears became reality. When Charlie told her they had not slept together, she broke down and cried. She had read relationship books enough to know that something had happened. She had expected worse. All she could hear was Charlie asking for her forgiveness.

Turning to her husband with tears of mixed emotions she wrapped her arms around him. "Of course I forgive you," she cried.

Chapter 37

Maui

It was not the cabin of the Gulfstream, but it wasn't coach, either. Charlie and Carrie were on their way to Maui. The six-hour flight from Las Vegas to Kahului, Maui was made less painful by the upgrade to first class. Sipping on an Island Breeze, they talked about their future with little mention of the past. Charlie listened as Carrie explained how much she desired for Charlie to retire and they move to Georgia. They could travel, and even spend a lot of time at the beach home. "We need more time together walking in the sand," she explained.

Charlie raised his eyebrows, "Only walking?"

All she could do was smile. "That was almost fifteen years ago. You were younger back then."

"I'm still young at heart, my girlfriend."

Carrie settled into reading her book, and Charlie was soon asleep. It was obvious he had recovered from any form of PTSD he may have experienced. But Carrie knew she was struggling. They had been married for twenty-three years. Not all of these years had been blissful. She knew Charlie loved her, that was not the question. Sure, he had resisted when confronted with the opportunity to be unfaithful. What was tormenting her was her past. She had not been that strong. She had let her husband down. She knew he had forgiven her, but she was not sure she had done the same. Now she was being tormented by his faithfulness. It was almost as if it would have been better if he had gone ahead with the affair. At least then they both would have been broken.

Carrie nagged at herself while looking at Charlie. *Those are crazy thoughts. It would not have been better. Why did he even tell me about Denise? Did he do it to make me look bad? Why did he even allow her in the room? He knows better.* She went back to her reading hoping this relationship book would give her some answers.

The humidity was evident as they got off the airplane. Walking through the terminal brought back the memories of their first trip here to the Valley Isle. It had been their tenth anniversary and Carrie's parents had given them the trip to celebrate. This trip could be an answer to their prayers and instrumental in healing their marriage. Now, thirteen years later, Charlie wondered if the island still had that touch. Even though Carrie said she had put the Denise situation behind them, her actions indicated otherwise. Maybe these two weeks would be enough to rid her of any lingering doubts in their relationship.

They drove east on Highway 360, better known as the Road to Hana, in the Jeep Wrangler. Top open allowed the tropical breeze to blow away the worries of this life. Their plans were to spend the first night in Hana and climb the Pipiwai trail to Waimoku Falls the next morning. Their first stop was in the town of Paia for a few groceries. A couple of miles down the road, they passed Hookipa Beach, where they stopped to watch the kite surfers as their colorful sails pulled them across the waves. Every so often one would attempt to break the bounds of earth and become airborne. It was to no avail, and they always returned to the sea.

It was a beautiful drive to Hana. Stopping off at the pullouts, they enjoyed the waterfalls. They drove through stretches of highway where the growth created a canopy bringing a cool reprieve from the sun. The rainbow eucalyptus trees with their fluorescent colors lined the road, and wild flowers gave contrast to the rich green foliage. The sun was settling into the western sky as they pulled into Hana. Tired from a long day's travel they found their villa on Uakea Road overlooking the Pacific Ocean. It was Saturday evening, and the birds were adding music to the sound of the waves beating against the lava.

Carrie threw together a salad as Charlie grilled the mahi mahi. Sitting there on the lanai, Charlie could imagine ninety-five years earlier when two army lieutenants first flew from California to Oahu. It took twenty-six hours in their Fokker Trimotor C2, compared to just over five today.

After a good night's rest, Charlie and Carrie hiked up the two-mile Pipiwai trail to enjoy the four-hundred-foot falls. They took their time, stopping to watch the many birds which seemed interested in the humans who were invading their habitat. In the late afternoon, they arrived at the Kaanapali Beach Club, tired and ready for two weeks of rest and relaxation. At five-thirty the next morning Charlie's phone rang. Not recognizing the number, Charlie rolled over and went back to sleep. Ten minutes later, the same number rang again. This time they left a message. Again he ignored it, until it rang a third time. "I'm on vacation, leave me alone! he yelled as he grabbed his phone. "I think it would be a good idea to throw this thing in the ocean."

Carrie rolled over wrapping herself around her man. "You know you can't do that. You have a daughter who may need you."

"Mitzy, need me? Right, all she needs is my money," Charlie retorted as he listened to his voice mail. "Great! It's the new union facility rep."

"Here, let me call him. I can take care of your light work," Carrie laughed as she snatched his phone.

251

"I don't think his concern is for our vacation. He's got bigger fish to fry."

"Okay! Go ahead and ruin our vacation by spending your time on the phone," Carrie pouted. Then, thinking of something she had read in her relationship book, she apologized, "It's all right. I know it's important for you to do your job." Then smiling again added, "I may have to declare an emergency here to get some quality time. I think you know what I mean by quality time."

Chapter 38

"You want to do what?" Charlie could not believe what he was hearing.

"Yes, Charlie, the leadership feels it's necessary to preserve the integrity of the system," George Wilson, the union representative for WCATS, replied, "You know better than any of us, it's not safe."

"I understand that, but you know it's not legal. We will all get fired. You know as well as anyone they are looking for any reason they can to get us old farts off the payroll. Have the rank and file voted yet?"

"Not yet," George answered. "The voting will take place next week. We are doing online voting to speed up the process. I really think it's going to be a landslide. Charlie, the controllers all across the country are scared. The Kansas accident could happen again, and they know it. We need you to help us with the media. They, as well as the flying public, still trust you even if our boss doesn't. Will you be back by the end of next week?"

"Dang it, George," Charlie almost yelled. "I'm here on a much needed vacation alone with Carrie, and I plan on keeping it that way. We will be home in two weeks. You also know that I am under a gag order from our wonderful employer. I can't talk to the press."

"That is where you are wrong, Charlie. You can't talk to the press as a controller, but you can represent the union. They can't touch you for that."

"Okay, but they can fire us for striking." Charlie couldn't believe they were even discussing this action. Even talking about it could lead to a hefty suspension.

"If you're not coming home for two weeks, we will set it up for the media to interview you over there. Can you take an hour out of your busy schedule for that?"

Charlie heard a tint of sarcasm in his coworker's voice. "Sure, make it here at the resort, and I will discuss the unions stand on 4DT, but not the strike. You guys are going to have to do that dirty deed. Just make sure I have the documentation that I am representing the union."

As Charlie expected, the word got out fast. The calls started coming in from all over the country. To the controllers, he advised that the system was unsafe to use. As far as his answer to a job action, he reminded them that it was illegal and they could, and probably would, lose their job. Would he vote for a strike? That would be a personal choice he would have to make when it came time for him to submit his ballot.

His old buddy Jim finally got through. "So, you have heard? I have mixed feelings, Charlie. We have put so much effort into this thing to terminate it."

"Tell that to the families of the Kansas crash," Charlie quickly continued. "A rotten egg still stinks, regardless of the hen that laid it. I think 4DT can be saved, but operations need to cease until it is perfected."

"Have you heard from Washington yet?" Jim asked.

"No, but I do have four messages on my voicemail that I haven't gotten to yet. Two messages from the 202 area code, which I assume is from headquarters. No big hurry on getting to them after what happened to Sean. I sure miss the old days."

"Yeah, I miss the Gulfstream. Sandy still talks about the Aspen trip."

"Yeah, we kind of miss it, too. We still have a lot of living left to do Jim, so don't get stuck in the past. Speaking of that, you may want to watch the news in the morning. They're sending the media here to Maui to interview yours truly."

"Seriously! What about the gag order?"

"We got it covered, just watch the news and hang on for the ride."

"Last time I heard that from you the FAA clipped your wings," Jim laughed. "You take care and don't forget about Carrie, or she'll find herself an aloha type of guy."

"Not funny, not funny," Charlie grumbled as they said good-bye.

Sure enough, two of the messages were from headquarters. The first was the administrator's secretary asking Charlie to call. The second was from Bob Burkhammer himself.

"Thanks for returning my call, Charlie. We have a crisis on our hands, and I was told you're on vacation."

"Yeah, we're on Maui trying to recover from stress your management team has created."

Charlie had no love for the arrogance Bob had shown ever since Congress had confirmed the long-time FAA employee. Bob had never controlled airplanes. Coming from a technical background, he had worked his way up through the ranks on the back of the NextGen programs. Having this strong technical expertise created an adverse bias towards the controlling work force.

"Don't go that direction, Charlie. You know I had nothing in that. We inherited this mess."

Charlie had heard this drum beat before. "How long are you going to keep this charade up, Bob? You're always blaming the old administration, never taking any responsibility yourself. You aren't fooling anyone. What do you want?"

Bob sighed, "You controllers never change. At least I know what you're thinking. Charlie, I have been hearing rumors and am hoping you can help me fill in the blanks."

255

"What rumors have you been hearing?" Charlie wasn't about to play his hand.

"Don't act stupid. You know as well as I do that the union is considering job action," Bob huffed. "We're getting a lot of questions from the media, and we don't have the answers. Give me something to work with. Good grief! We can't let this get out of hand or every one of you will get fired."

"Thought that's what you wanted," Charlie continued to poke the frustrated administrator. "I would love to, but now is not the time. There are too many doubts with 4DT. The flying public would lose confidence."

"So, now you're admitting to a flawed system."

Charlie wasn't just poking now, he was kicking the bear in the butt. "Are you ready to suspend 4DT indefinitely? You know the union would consider that a positive move."

"No! We are not taking down 4DT. How many times do I have to tell you? I built the system, and I know it works. You idiots need to figure out it's not the program, it's the controllers."

"Now you're telling me you built 4DT, next thing you'll tell me is you invented the Internet. Let's cut the crap, Bob. What do you want me to tell you? It's obvious you're looking for something to hang your hat on."

Bob felt drained, "Are the controllers going to strike?"

"On the record, I would say they are disappointed and concerned about the lack of safety portrayed by 4DT in its current state." Charlie said in a matter-of-fact statement.

"What about off the record?" Bob asked.

"Is there really such a thing, Bob? Or is this off-the-record statement going to end up being part of a testimony in court? Nevertheless, off the record, you need to get your ducks in order. Unless the winds of dissention change, you will have the opportunity to test your 4DT with managerial staff. You and I have come a long way together with this program, and I want its success almost as much as you do. The difference is that I have spent the last twenty-three years controlling airplanes and you've spent that time building and managing programs. Will the controllers vote on a strike? Understanding the mentality of a controller, I would have to guess that they will. Another thing, something ingrained in us is the need for providing a safe passage between point A and B for the flying community. Take that away and you take away the very core of our existence. It would be my bet that a strong majority would rather risk their jobs before compromising this principle."

Bob jumped in, "Well, that's exactly what will happen if they do. The President said it would be August 3rd all over again if they do go out." Bob was referring to the controller strike of 1981.

Charlie had to just shake his head and absorb the comment he was sure Bob did not mean to share. "So you're telling me a contingency is already in place for a controller strike? Why did you call, Bob?"

"I already told you. We want to avert this calamity," he responded.

"I understand that, but why did you call me?" Charlie was about to give up on this worthless conversation. He had heard his phone beep no less than a dozen times while talking to the administrator. He knew there was work to do, and he was supposed to be on vacation.

Bob continued, "Charlie, even though we have our differences I know you're an honest man with high moral integrity. I just thought maybe you could convince your coworkers not to go through with this. I know I may be telling you something I shouldn't, but the President is serious about the legality of a job action. He will not even be giving them a chance to come back to work."

"Thanks for the vote of confidence. I wish I could say the same for you, but the FAA and I are on different worlds right now. You decide to suspend 4DT, and we will see what we can do to avert what you called a calamity." And to throw in a little formal goodbye, Charlie concluded, "Good-bye, Mr. Burkhammer, you have a good day."

It was ten o'clock when Charlie finally came out of his temporary office to find Carrie was nowhere to be seen. He knew he should have thrown the phone away. He found her lying out on a beach chair catching some sunshine. He could hardly believe she was forty-six and could still turn him on in that bikini.

Carrie looked up as Charlie slid into the chair beside her. "You okay?" she asked.

Charlie sat there for awhile looking out over the waves with their whitecaps glistening in the morning sun. In the distance the island of Molokai poked up out of the sea, shrouded in clouds. Their dark rainy bases gave way to bright whimsical tops drifting higher into the pure blue sky. He was interrupted from the mesmerism of the scene by Carrie touching his arm.

"You okay, darling? You seem preoccupied."

"Guess you could say that. Things are a mess back home." As an afterthought he added, "And they think I can fix it." He covered his face with his hands and visibly shook. "Why are they bothering me? I really can't help. I really need my doctor." Charlie was almost sobbing.

Carrie wrapped herself around her man and whispered something in his ear that brought a smile to his face. "That would be beyond my wildest dreams." After a pause she added, "Maybe it would be my wildest dream."

They spent the rest of the day uninterrupted on the beach, soaking up sunshine and playing in the waves. As the sun began to set, the firmament turned all colors of yellow and orange, making the colors dance among the clouds creating splotches of dark pink and purple.

Carrie had her head lying on Charlie's shoulder. "Hey! No one has called. What did you do with the phone?"

Charlie, with a big grin, leaned over and kissed his beautiful wife. "Shut it off and put it in the safe. It's going to stay there until we go home. I really don't give a darn about the job, the union, the FAA, or the administrator. So if they really need me, let them find us. For the next two weeks, I am yours. Let's go make this night a memorable one."

"It already has that potential. What better way to spend it than here on the beach together. I am anticipating many awesome memories."

Picking up their things, they walked beside the pool and up the steps by the waterfalls to the lobby. Ascending inside the glass elevators up to their room, they witnessed the last glitter of light as the sky darkened into the night.

Chapter 39

On Monday morning, a knock on the door woke the love birds. It was the bellboy delivering a package from the mainland. It contained documentation which showed Charlie as a representative of the union in releasing official information to the news media. Along with these documents was a schedule of media events planned for him that day and on Friday after the vote.

"I thought you told them only one hour," Carrie fumed. "I really think you should cancel the whole thing."

"I don't know what's worse. Doing the interviews or discussing this with the union. Don't you worry, I will be strong."

"One more emotional outburst like you had yesterday and I will be calling Dr. Morgan," Carrie warned.

Charlie laughed. "You seemed to like the emotional outburst last night."

"That kind of outburst is always appreciated with this girl, cowboy. What are our plans today?"

The press release and interview was schedule for one in the afternoon local time, and would be covered live on all the cable news channels. As per the media's request, at precisely twelve forty-five, Charlie walked into the transformed conference room. He was greeted by a sharply dressed lady who introduced herself as the local news agent who would be hosting the breaking news report. Charlie apologized for not

260

wearing a suit. Leading him to the podium at the front of the room, she coached him on the cameras. His inquiry about who would be asking questions brought blank stares.

"Oh," Charlie responded, "there may not be any questions, is what you're indicating?"

The reporters in the room laughed as one of them spoke up. "We have no idea what we're covering right now, that's our position."

"You will find out shortly, but let me give you a hint. You may want to reserve your trip back to the mainland on a ship." Knowing instantly that was not necessary Charlie joked, "You guys can scratch that. I will be flying back to the mainland myself in ten days."

Right on key, reading from a teleprompter, the host announced the breaking news live from Maui with Charlie Beckler, representing the air traffic controllers' union. Charlie walked up to the podium and looked at the cameras lined up in front of him.

"Thank you for coming out here this afternoon. For you who came from the mainland, I feel your pain." This brought laughs from reporters. "I have been asked by the union to explain our dispute with the Federal Aviation Administration in relation to the computer program known as 4DT. This four-dimensional trajectory program was first used last August with great success early on. Then, as you are all aware, last December two aircraft were involved in a midair collision over Kansas. This was due to a deficiency in the computer programming which has been identified as an isolated incident.

The NextGen system had removed the controller/pilot interface which would have prevented this tragedy. After this accident, the controllers experienced extreme stress stemming from the lack of direct control and minimal support from the FAA management. Controllers are being held responsible for separating aircraft when their hands are tied by the system. The program built to replace them is now destroying them. It is of the opinion of the union that safety is being extremely compromised with 4DT, along with the data link/auto pilot interface. The union has persistently requested a suspension of these programs. The FAA administrator, along with his management team, has rejected this idea as unnecessary. It is their opinion that this is overreacting on the part of an overpaid workforce. The controllers now have been driven to the precipice of compromising the principles they have lived by for the last eight decades. The controller workforce must now decide how they will move forward. In two hours, online voting will commence, asking for a consensus on the future of this organization. I will now take your questions."

"Mr. Beckler, am I to understand that the controllers are going to strike?"

"I cannot answer that question. I believe my statement said they would be voting on how to move forward. As far as a strike, that would be illegal and grounds for dismissal."

"But is that not what the vote is asking for?"

Again Charlie just smiled at the reporter. "I will be here speaking with you again on Friday morning and we can discuss the contents of the vote at that time."

"Is it safe to fly?"

"As I said in the beginning, I will be flying home in ten days. As to the degree of safety, as long as our controllers are controlling the skies, it will be the safest mode of transportation."

"Looking back at your career, I find that you have been controversial in a lot of issues and seem to have always come out on top. Is this going to be the most challenging one?"

"I have always stood by our motto to ensure a safe, orderly, and expeditious flow of air traffic. Dealing with challenges is just part of the job." Charlie responded. "I am still a firm believer in the overall program and its future, but just like anything else, it has bugs that need to be worked out. Take 4DT down for however long it takes, and then bring it back as a reliable system, and all of us would look at it in a different light. Is this the most challenging? Let's leave that for the historian. Next question."

"Is it true that you are working directly with the administrator on trying to divert a strike?"

"I don't know where you get your information. Yes, I have talked with the administrator. He is aware of our concerns with 4DT and is unwavering in his determination to keep it operational."

Another reporter raised his hand, "What will happen if the controllers do strike?"

Charlie now was skating on thin ice. "According to the contingency plan I was able to get a hold of, it would be twenty-four hours before the FAA could get personnel into place. Even this would be extremely scaled back, using all available managers and military controllers. Most of these individuals have never been certified on our equipment. So as to your question, it would be twenty-four hours with only essential aircraft flying, then minimal operations with questionable safety." Charlie paused and smiled. "I have a beautiful wife waiting for me to take her sightseeing, so only one more question."

"What are your personal feelings on a strike, and what are you recommending to the other controllers?" This question came from someone that looked more like an FAA mole than a reporter.

"I personally believe in obeying the law even when I disagree with it. The law states that a strike would be illegal and grounds for dismissal. The question then lies with the level of conviction. Is my conviction to the law stronger than my conviction to the safety of the flying public? That is yet to be determined. How do I advise my fellow controllers? They have to look at their own consciences and make that decision. The ramifications of their actions will likely change their lives both financially and emotionally. Thank you for your time."

Chapter 40

It was dinnertime in California and late evening on the East Coast when the online voting opened. The number of controllers logging onto the independent website overloaded the servers. On Maui, it was the middle of the afternoon and no matter how desperately the reporters searched, they could not find Charlie. Charlie had tipped the valet, who had taken the Jeep next door where Charlie and Carrie met him with their beach towels and hiking shoes. They drove north for about fifteen minutes where Charlie pulled off onto a dirt trail leading towards the sea.

"Do you know where we're going?"

"Not really, girlfriend," Charlie answered looking down at his GPS, "but twenty bucks got me these coordinates from a local. Don't know if they are real or not, we will soon find out." The handheld GPS showed a dirt lane ended in about a mile, not far from the ocean. Parking the Jeep, they grabbed their stuff and headed down a very narrow path. Winding back and forth down the cliff toward the sea was nerve-racking in itself.

Finally reaching the rocky shore, Carrie was disappointed. "Where's the sand?" Charlie grabbed Carrie's hand and pulled her towards a hole washed into the sheer wall. "I am not going in there." Carrie said with a no-nonsense tone. "There could be live things in there. Worse yet, there could be dead things in there."

Charlie laughed, "Stay right here, I'll be back in a moment." He disappeared into the cave creating quite a concern for Carrie.

"Don't go far," she whimpered. Two minutes later he returned without their stuff.

"Come on, grab my hand and follow me."

Twenty feet into the cave, the dampness gave way to a light off to the left. Charlie assured his freaked-out wife. He crawled through the hole into a much larger cavern. This one had sand on the floor and led out onto the beach. No more than a hundred feet long it led up to a grove of trees creating a beautiful scene. Completely isolated, the couple spent the afternoon in total harmony.

Much later, while driving back to the condo, Charlie held Carrie's hand and said, "It looks like the magic is still here."

She smiled back at her husband, knowing that, yes, their marriage was again on a firm foundation.

Back at the Kaanapali Beach Club, they were greeted by a handful of reporters trying to get information out of the previous "face of NextGen" now turned union representative. Charlie held up his hand and explained that he had no information at all as he did not have his phone with him and had not even been online since the earlier interview.

"Mr. Beckler!" It was a lady from guest services. "We have had a considerable number of calls requesting to speak to you. We set up a special voice mail for you. Here are the codes necessary to get into your voice mail." She handed him a paper.

Charlie thanked her, and he and Carrie stepped into the elevator. Sliding his arm around his wife, Charlie mischievously squeezed her bottom as he kissed her. "Thank you for fulfilling my wildest dreams."

After getting Carrie to agree to an hour of work, Charlie turned on his laptop and logged in. First check was the news which had totally misconstrued his statements. Well, it was not his first run in with the media. He expected nothing less. Reading a couple of other statements from FAA headquarters was even more disgusting. Checking his email, he was not surprised at the three hundred messages in his inbox. Most were from fellow controllers he knew.

Flagging most of them for future reading, he clicked on the one from Jim Gallagher. "Charlie, what have you done with your phone? No one is able to reach you. Give me a call as soon as you get this message. All hell is breaking loose at work. With management's encouragement, supervisors are harassing the controllers like we've never seen. The vote is going strong, and last count showed 65 percent have voted with a 92percent for the strike. This is scary, brother. We need your help."

Charlie read a dozen more emails all with the same general message as Jim's. All across the country, management was using intimidation techniques to discourage controllers, especially the younger ones, from voting for the strike. Next, he logged onto the voting website and entered his password. The tally had risen to 85 percent with still over 90 percent in favor of striking. Looking at the question asked on this vote, he read, "Are you for or against a general work stoppage against the FAA for requiring our workforce to control aircraft under a flawed system?" There were only two choices. Charlie hesitated for a couple of minutes as he gave thought back to August 3rd, 1981.

The controller union had been pushing for a shorter work week, better working conditions, and higher wages leading up the late summer strike. It was carefully planned for one of the busiest airline schedules, for the greatest impact. They got what they wanted in the way of impacting the industry. It cost the major carriers over thirty million dollars a day and stranded tens of thousands of passengers. What they didn't get was the public opinion supporting their illegal strike.

Would it be any different this time? Charlie had to ask himself. Would the public outcry be for the support of the fifteen thousand controllers, or would it be for their heads to roll? After all, things are different this time. We are not asking for money or less work. As far as the working conditions, all we want is a safe system. Is that too much to ask? Surely the public would understand. What if they don't? What happens then? We would all potentially get fired and that would really suck.

Look at what happened after the last strike. Many of the fired controllers lost everything. The stress from the loss of employment along with pressures of potentially going to jail caused many couples to separate, leaving broken homes. Is it worth it? His conviction on the safety issue was a solid one, but were they outweighed by his concern for the controllers and their families? Finally he made his decision, clicked the box, and hit enter. His hour was up. He said a little prayer for his coworkers knowing that a very turbulent ride was in the near future for all of them.

Chapter 41

By the time Charlie awoke on Tuesday morning, the media was in full swing. It was afternoon on the East Coast and the results of the vote had been leaked. Of the 14,260 certified air traffic controllers voting, 12,406 had voted for striking and 1854 against. The news channels tried to downplay the vote and reassure the public that it was still safe to fly. The FAA headquarters put out a statement that per chance the controllers did perform this illegal, ill-advised action, NextGen would be able to take up the slack. Secretary of Transportation, Terry Laverne restated that any controller walking out would meet the same fate their predecessors did in 1981. Interviewing passengers at the local airports brought a multitude of different comments. It was obvious that very few passengers were even aware there was a problem with NextGen.

A red light flashing on the house phone told Charlie that he had a message at the front desk. "Mr. Beckler, there's a gentleman down here in the lobby looking for you."

"I'm not speaking to reporters. Tell him I'm on vacation and to come see me on Friday at the press conference."

"He says he's not a reporter, but he wouldn't give me his name. Do you want me to send him up to the room?"

"No way! I'll be down in a couple of minutes. Oh, and have security standing by, just in case." Charlie hung up the phone.

"Meet me at the restaurant for breakfast in twenty minutes," he told Carrie as he pulled on a T-shirt that said "Big Kahuna" on the front. "We need to get away from here as soon as we can today. It looks like the vultures have found us."

Downstairs, Charlie was shocked to see an old friend. "Sean! What the heck you doing here? Are you working for the media now?" Charlie gave his old boss a big bear hug.

"I am unemployed, my friend," Sean responded. "Are you scheduled to meet with the press today?"

"Not today! Not that I will be able to avoid them. What are you doing here? I know this is not coincidental."

"You're right, Charlie, it's not. We need to talk in private. For some reason, there are too many ears and eyes around this place."

"Let me call Carrie. We can go up to our place."

"Let's not do that, Charlie, I wouldn't want to intrude."

Sean handed Charlie a piece of paper and said, "Have a great day, Mr. Beckler, enjoy your vacation."

Charlie just stood there bewildered as Sean turned and walked away. Walking over to the open-air restaurant, he picked out a table overlooking the ocean. After ordering a cup of coffee, he opened up the paper Sean had given him.

"Charlie, your room is bugged. The FBI has been trailing you ever since you got here on Saturday. If you can shake them, meet me at these coordinates, 21° 1'17" North 156° 36'32" West, this afternoon at two. Please be careful." He was folding the paper when Carrie slid into the chair beside him.

"What was that?" she asked as he put the paper in his pocket.

"It was just some information on the controller situation," Charlie told her as he leaned over and kissed her cheek. He hated lying but not knowing who may be listening, he didn't want to tell her the truth.

"Who wanted to see you? You must have run them away. I had really expected to be waiting half the morning."

"Just a reporter thinking he could get a scoop," Charlie lied, again. "What do you want to do today?"

Carrie was looking over the brochures that she had picked up at the concierge's desk. "I really think I would like to take a helicopter tour. Can we do that?" That gave Charlie an idea.

Charlie didn't know if it was paranoia or reality, but he did notice a car following them as they left Kaanapali. It was still behind them as they arrived at Air Maui. Online, Charlie had reserved a private complete island tour from one of the best helicopter tour companies on the island. Taking a flight in the American Eurocopter with its 180-degree unobstructed view would be perfect.

As they were waiting, two men came in dressed in khaki pants and Hawaiian shirts. Charlie recognized them from the car that had been following them and laughed at their less-than-clever disguise. They tried not to make eye contact with Charlie and Carrie as they approached the counter and requested information on tours. As they were walking out the door, Charlie overheard the older one growl at the sales clerk, "What do you mean the flight's full? There are only two of them."

After the pilot introduced himself as Captain Jack, he explained all the safety issues, and they strapped in. While the Turbomeca Arriel power plant spooled up, Charlie pointed at the two "tourists" and their pilot headed out to a helicopter. "Could you find out what tour they're taking?"

"Sure, one second." The pilot clicked his transmitter and questioned the sales clerk.

"They purchased a private charter, which means they can go anywhere. She said they really wanted on this flight with you guys. Do you know them?"

"Less than they know me." Charlie smiled at the pilot then asked, "You said you flew in Desert Storm. You want another mission?"

"Keep talking!" Captain Jack replied as he continued to flip switches as the noise level increased.

"Those guys are trying to follow us," Charlie explained as he told Jack the rest of the story. "We need to get away from them and be at a beach on the northwest end of the island in an hour. If you can do all that and give us a spectacular tour, there will be a tip you can take home to Mama."

"I have only one question for you. Do you get airsick?" Captain Jack lifted the ASTAR off the pad and sideslipped out toward the taxi way. Speaking briefly with the tower, he pulled up on the collective and moved the cyclic slightly forward. Like an elevator, the airport dropped beneath them as they headed southeast towards the sloping hills and over the Kula forest reserve. Turning east, they flew low over the lush landscape, hugging the hills, and dropped down into the valleys. Sensational waterfalls met them in every one of the tropical canyons they traversed. They stopped a couple of times to embrace the incredible, God-created beauty of the water falling hundreds of feet just fifty feet in front of their noses. They circled Hana then headed west. After discussing the situation with Carrie, they decided Captain Jack would drop off Charlie at the beach and take Carrie back to get the Jeep.

"We have company!" Captain Jack pointed out the right side of the helicopter. Sure enough, only two hundred yards away, was another Air Maui Eurocopter trailing them.

"They sure are persistent. You can at least commend them for that. Still think you can shake them, Captain?" Charlie asked.

"Not only can I shake them, but I can make their heads spin in the process." Looking over at Carrie, he smiled and warned, "Tighten your seatbelt, little lady. We're going for a ride."

Carrie looked a little peeved at Charlie. "If this guy doesn't kill me first, you will pay when we get home."

Charlie laughed as Captain Jack dropped the aircraft towards the earth and headed up the Iao Valley. Clouds covering the ridges on each side soon encompassed them. More than a little concerned, Charlie looked over at the pilot who seemed to be enjoying his mission. "Aren't you a little nervous about the cumulous granite in these clouds?" he asked the cowboy-turned-pilot.

"Nope, haven't you heard that if you can't see it, it's not there?" All of a sudden he brought the helicopter to a forward stand still and pulled all the way back on the collective shooting them upward at almost fifteen hundred feet per minute. This took the breath right out of the two tourists as Captain Jack yelled, "Yee haw!" Popping out of the clouds they slid down the northern slope of the mountains. He turned towards Charlie and gloated, "They won't find us for a while. They're still back in the valley looking for us. Old Tom will be pissed. He's been calling for a position report. He can't find us and thinks we might have crashed."

"You going to let him know we're all right?" Charlie questioned.

"What, and ruin our cover? I'll call him once I drop you off. Until then he deserves some discomfort. That will teach him to trail me like that."

Flying out over Honokohau Bay Captain Jack turned back towards the shore. Finding it deserted, brought them to a soft landing on the rocky beach. "Take care of my girlfriend." Charlie grabbed Captain Jack's hand while slipping him a hundred dollar bill. He quickly exited the helicopter and fought the wind created by the spinning rotor as N405AM quickly took off and headed west.

Charlie walked up to the grove of trees next to the parking lot for the bay. Sitting down on a rock, he felt alone. Here he was on an island with no transportation, no phone, and not a soul within sight. Fifteen minutes later, a car pulled up, and Sean got out looking around and then at his watch.

"Over here!" Charlie called from beneath the overgrown mango tree. "Here, have a seat in my new office," Charlie joked as Sean, with briefcase in hand, sat down on a rock next to his old friend.

Looking out over the water, Sean took out his hanky and wiped the sweat already forming on his forehead. "Sure is a far change from the musky granite offices of Washington. I think the people that live in poverty and snorkel these waters are far happier than the wealthy people we know that live in the capital."

"You really have to come to reality once in awhile, Boss. I know you didn't bring me out here for a lesson in philosophy, so what's up?"

Chapter 42

Pulling a stack of papers from his briefcase, Sean handed one to Charlie. "Remember when I told you they wouldn't shut down 4DT based on risk value? Read it."

On the top it read "Top Secret" followed by the subject line "Operational Risk/Value NextGen." It was from the Congressional Aviation Subcommittee chairman to the president of the United States. Reading the contents brought on a numbing chill despite the tropical heat and humidity.

Mr. President,

Upon completing an extensive research and study of the NextGen program, the following shortfalls have surfaced:

1) *The four-dimensional trajectory program under extreme conditions has shown signs of weakness. In 4 percent of the tested scenarios, it failed to provide adequate control reducing separation below the allowable standards.*

2) *The data link program has failed to release control during testing under extreme situations. Further testing of the data link program should be performed before implementation.*

3) *Security in the development program has been compromised. Upon reviewing all documentation it is the subcommittee's opinion the level of security necessary to develop a program out of the reach of terrorism has been lacking.*

The Congressional Aviation Subcommittee under majority rule is asking that the following corrective steps are taken prior to the implementation of the NextGen 4DT program:

1) *4DT software is improved to the benchmark of 99.999999% percent reliability factor. This has always been the level required with a proven safety record.*

2) *An override cutout switch is required in all aircraft equipped with 4DT/data link/autopilot direct connect. This switch will allow any pilot in a last ditch situation to override 4DT.*

3) *A complete scrub down of all software programs to be conducted only by United States citizens with a security clearance issued within the last thirty days. The committee understands the immensity of this task and has allowed for additional time and funding to complete this requirement.*

Thank you, Mr. President for your consideration in regards to this report. Senator Kirk Frances, Chairman Congressional Aviation Subcommittee.

Charlie looked up at Sean. "We could have told them this without an inquiry. Why hasn't this been brought to the public's attention?"

"Oh, that's not all!" Sean handed him another paper. This memo was from the president to the chairman.

Thank you for your diligence in the investigation of the NextGen air traffic control program. This administration has reviewed all the concerns you have brought forward and has concluded that they are unwarranted and void of any substance.

1) The 4DT software has proven to be trustworthy in all requirements. It has overcome all skepticism encountered during development. The program has risen to the level of reliability necessary which was established by the Federal Aviation Administration design team.

2) Requiring an override switch to be installed in all aircraft would be costly and is not necessary.

3) Security with this program has always been a top priority with this and previous administrations since the conception of NextGen. Therefore, security has never been compromised, making it unnecessary to spend the taxpayers' money needlessly on such a task.

In conclusion, we will move forward with the implementation of 4DT as planned next week in all three of the major air traffic control facilities.

"That was the week before we went live last August," Charlie explained.

Sean just nodded his head and handed Charlie another paper. This one was a response from the Chairman, advising that they would start withholding funding if something wasn't done to delay the program.

"Obviously nothing was done. What happened?" Charlie asked.

"This is where it gets interesting. It appears there was a closed-door meeting between the president's chief of staff and the chairman. Inside sources say that the president has some dirt on Senator Frances that would lead to an indictment, and he shut him up with threats of leaking it to the press."

"All this went down prior to Kansas. You would think his conscience would bother him." Charlie couldn't believe that the government had become so corrupt.

"It did Charlie, between you and me. You don't think these documents just fell in my lap, do you? After the accident, the senator contacted me asking for help in looking into these issues. Said it was keeping him awake at night. Here are copies of the emails from the last two years between the administration and the chairman. There's some pretty incriminating stuff."

"Why are you giving them to me? I am just a burned out controller," Charlie replied, feeling very sick to his stomach.

"Charlie, you are an icon in the world of aviation. You're a good old pilot and a controller who has moral fiber. You are what most parents want their kids to become. Remember, you are the face of NextGen."

"If I hear that one more time, I think I'll puke," retorted Charlie with a smile at his old boss, who was looking very tired and exhausted. "Let's go get a drink, we need it. It won't take long before the goons find me and will start asking questions again."

They walked to Sean's car and drove down to the resort. Sean advised Charlie not to try and contact him. "I will stop by in a couple of days. In the meantime, use whatever information you want in the decisions you make. I trust your good judgment, Charlie."

Charlie was sitting at a table by the pool when Carrie arrived, closely trailed by two very disgruntled faux tourists. He jumped up, kissed his wife, and nodded an aloha greeting to the two FBI agents. "I should invite them to join us for dinner," he suggested sarcastically, looking at Carrie for approval. Not surprisingly, he found nothing to encourage him.

Charlie and Carrie spent the next two days avoiding the media and, after ditching their "tourist" friends, spent another afternoon at the hidden beach. Much of their time was spent discussing the future and the effects of the upcoming strike. They wondered how they would handle the pressure. Charlie no longer listened to his voice mails and retreated more and more into seclusion.

Sitting on their lanai as the sun was setting on Thursday night, Charlie slipped his hand into Carrie's and, looking into her eyes, asked her one more time. "Is this the right thing to do? Will you stand behind me?"

Carrie smiled at her husband and squeezed his hand. "I am not willing to stand behind you, but I am willing to spend the rest of my life standing beside you. Yes, it is the right move."

Chapter 43

The news on Friday morning was as expected. The air traffic controllers had gone on strike. Only seven hundred controllers had reported to work for the day shift, which normally would have consisted of over forty-five hundred. The stations were broadcasting live from in front of the facilities, showing controllers carrying their picket signs. Not one was asking for more money, shorter work weeks, or better working conditions. There were signs that read "KANSAS APOCALYPSE – JUST THE BEGINNING" and "Forecast for today - Aluminum rain showers." Other signs depicted different viewpoints, but all were on the issue of safety.

Unfortunately, the media didn't spend much time on the safety aspect but went to the airports where they reported thousands of canceled flights. The reporters instead interviewed the most vocal of the stranded passengers, who did not show any support for the controllers responsible for this dilemma. They interviewed the FAA administrator, who reminded the viewers that the striking controllers were now criminals and would be prosecuted as such. He also advised that the computer system was operating normally. As soon as he could get the supervisors, managers, and military controllers into work, flight schedules would return to normal.

Charlie had just sat down with his coffee when a local reporter came on in front of the control tower over at the Kahului Airport. The intra island flights and those coming in

280

from the mainland were on schedule. That could not be said about flights scheduled for the lower forty-eight. They were delayed by up to four hours. The next reporter got Charlie's attention. She was introduced standing in the lobby of their resort.

"Right here in Maui we have the man who not too long ago was being heralded as the face of NextGen." An old picture of Charlie at the Las Vegas convention showed up in the top right corner of the TV. "Air traffic controller Charlie Beckler has been vacationing here on the island with his wife for the last week. Was it because he was anticipating the strike? No one has heard from him since last Monday, when he spoke to the media on behalf of the union. We have heard that later this morning he is scheduled to speak to the press. We will be anxious to hear what his take is on the work stoppage."

Charlie looked at his watch. It was almost noon on the East Coast. He had one hour to put together his statement. He had thought it through and felt comfortable with the decision he and Carrie had made. Things would be different, but they would adjust. He shut off the television and headed for the shower.

The room came to attention with a look of surprise as Charlie walked in with Carrie. Charlie had never introduced his wife to the public. She stayed right by his side hand in hand as they walked up to the podium.

"Good morning, folks. For those of you who were here Monday morning, I apologize for your agonizing week stuck here on the island." At the back of the room, he noticed the two men that had been following them all week. "I believe some of you took advantage of the helicopter tours. We found out it's a great way to see the island.

This morning I advised the FAA Administrator that I was submitting my resignation, effective immediately." Charlie

281

noticed the eyebrows rise as he continued. "To clear the air, I am no longer speaking on behalf of the FAA or the union. From this point forward, I am only speaking for myself and the safety of the flying public. On Monday morning, I told you that each controller would have to deal with his or her own conscience concerning the voting. Taking my own advice, my wife and I spent the last three days soul-searching. As you know, it is illegal for a federal employee to participate in any action contributing to work stoppage. I signed an agreement twenty-three years ago giving up my right to strike. While I will not judge or condemn my fellow controllers, I cannot, with a clear conscience, go along with the strike. Having arrived at this decision, my intentions were to return to work after this vacation was over.

So what has changed? I will not work for this administration as it is corrupt and dishonest. A couple of days ago I received classified information that I'm not at liberty to share. There are enough incriminating details within these documents to indict the individuals involved. Simply put, it is scary how low our government leaders are willing to stoop. At this time, I will not reveal the source or the evidence, but it is enough for this controller to give up his career for fear of retribution.
As for what happens next? That will be up to the Senate Ethics Committee. We have discussed this with the chairman and it should be made public shortly. That's all I have for you."

Questions started flying at him, which he ignored except for one about safety. "We'll still be flying back to Ely next week. If any of you are scared, you can fly with us. Has safety been compromised? Sure! You have just removed over 85 percent of your professional controllers. Safety is compromised and will be even more when the scabs start working tomorrow. I do support our military controllers, but, give them a break, this is not the traffic they are used to working. They'll do a stand up job. Will it be enough? That's yet to be determined."

"What are your future plans, now that you're resigning?"

Charlie scratched his chin. "Spend more time with my beautiful wife. We have a lot of making up to do. Hope to start here on the island as long as you guys leave us alone. I think that would be a good idea considering I am now unemployed."

"Will you be staying in the aviation industry?" Charlie just waved his hand as if to say that's not even a consideration; grabbing Carrie's hand, he walked out of the room as a private citizen no longer a civil servant.

Riding up the elevator his arm around his wife, he asked her, "What do you want to do with your unemployed boyfriend?"

She smiled at him, "I know where there's a cave we can crawl through." Even though the accumulative stress would soon go away, a lot of work still lay ahead.

Later, laying by the pool, Charlie heard, "It's a beautiful day to catch some sun." Charlie recognized the voice as he looked out from under the book he had been reading to see Sean slide into the lounge chair beside him. "Enjoying your retirement?"

"Unlike you, I didn't retire, I quit." Charlie sat up, "What are you up to today? Taking down a president or another congressman?"

"Funny. Thought maybe I could bring you up to speed on what's going on in the real world. You won't answer your phone or return messages anymore."

"I am on vacation, Sean. One week ago I was making almost two hundred thousand a year, now I'm a bum. Give me one more week, and I will reengage." Looking out at Carrie swimming in the pool, he continued, "Right now all I want to do is spend time with Carrie. The good Lord knows I have neglected her the last few years."

Sean studied his friend, who at one time was the standard-bearer for morality and work ethic. "It will all be over in a week, Charlie. At five o'clock eastern time tonight, the President will be revealing the future of air traffic control. From my inside sources, it's not pretty."

"First of all, why is the president involved? And not pretty from whose perspective?" Charlie cut in.

"Let's just say the term *radar controller* will become obsolete. Just thought you would want to get upstairs and watch the news."

"That's okay, I will do it from the bar. I may want a drink the way you're talking. When are you getting off this island?"

"Not until you're out of here. Those are my orders." Motioning to a waitress, he hollered, "Over here!" The waitress brought them each a cold strawberry daiquiri. "I thought you could use a drink, got Carrie one too."

Charlie was now sitting straight up, sunglasses up on his head. "What do you mean orders? Who are you working for?"

"KGB, Mossad, Scotland Yard, whoever pays the most." Sean laughed. "Really, Senator Tessil asked that I keep an eye on you. His sources revealed that the goons would be here and thought it would be a good idea if you knew."

"So why are they so interested in us and our vacation?"

"First, it's not us, it's you. Why the interest? You have the ability to save NextGen or destroy it."

Charlie rolled his eyes. "That is a little over exaggerated, wouldn't you say?"

"No, you may not be the only one that can control airplanes, but you are the only controller the flying public recognizes and respects. It's time to watch some news."

The newscast started out with footage of stranded passengers, airplanes sitting on tarmacs, and picketing controllers. The newscaster emphasized the national emergency as all air traffic had come to a standstill.

Interviews with angry passengers tore Charlie to the core. "At least they're not scattered over the fields of Kansas," he muttered.

They interviewed a controller at Dulles who reiterated that all they wanted from the strike was safety. When asked how he felt about the threat of getting fired, he replied, "If I get fired, which I do expect will happen, at least I will be able to sleep at night. As far as the administrator and the rest of the incompetent FAA management, all I can say is the blood of the flying public will be on their hands." The reporter went back to the East Room of the White House where the podium was set up waiting for the President.

Walking briskly, the president, followed by the secretary of transportation, entered the room.

Good evening, ladies and gentlemen. This morning at 8:00 a.m. we were informed by the air traffic control union that a strike would be taking place. We responded with an order for all controllers to check in at their facility no later than 2100 UTC today. To disregard this order would be grounds for termination and replacement. Five minutes ago, this deadline expired. I am sorry to announce that only thirty-five out of the thirteen thousand chose to comply. The striking controllers will no longer be treated as federal employees but will now be treated as criminals. As to any leniency we might show, that will be up to the Attorney General. I have asked that the governors have their National Guards protect the facilities from these insubordinates, and I have been assured the governors

285

have complied with my request. While we are saddened at the uncertain future of the families of the now-fired controllers, the problem was of their own making. As to the future of the air traffic control system, we are happy to announce we have replacements ready.

For the last three years, we have been training and equipping replacements for such an emergency. As you know, the NextGen program has revolutionized the system to the point we no longer need the highly paid radar controllers to maintain a controlled environment in the National Airspace System. The Air Traffic Specialist of the future will know more about computers and computer software than the art of separating airplanes. If you're concerned about the lack of this skill, let me assure you that you need not be.

Let's look at the example of the phone most of you have in your pocket. Fifty years ag,o cell phones were practically unheard of, used only by the very elite. Today almost every adult owns a cell phone, which not only maintains a constant communication link, but it will tell them where they are and how to get where they want to go. It connects them to the internet and tells them when to wake up in the morning. This is accomplished all on a piece of hardware that fits in your pocket. Now if this is where we are with technology, why do we need the human factor to calculate distance between aircraft? We need computer savvy specialists to make sure the computers do their job. We foresaw this change in the industry taking place, and we have met the demands of the change. Thank you for your time. Do you have any questions?

"Thank you, Mr. President. The controllers are striking for reasons of safety. Are you aware of these safety issues and why would they not be addressed?"

"Good question. We have looked at all the safety issues presented by the union and found none of them have merit."

"What about the Kansas accident? Did that problem get fixed?"

"I am sure it did, otherwise we would have shut down the program." The President motioned to another reporter.

"Thank you, Mr. President. My question concerns one of your employees, or I should say previous employees. Charlie Beckler, who was the face of the NextGen program, resigned this morning. Were you aware of his resignation, and what do you know about the statement he made this morning about a corrupt and dishonest administration?"

Charlie almost spit his drink out of his mouth at the mention of his name at a presidential news conference. Looking around, he was happy his fellow vacationers were not looking at him. The president frowned and shook his head. "I have lot of respect for Mr. Beckler. He served his country well. I really don't want to speculate as to his blatant accusation of wrongdoing by this administration. I can tell you that I will not tolerate corruption, and that includes false accusations. Mr. Beckler was a great asset for NextGen and will be greatly missed."

"You are an arrogant idiot!" Charlie growled at the television, "You are so full of crap you stink."

Sean kicked Charlie under the table as people started looking at him. "Let it go, Charlie. Judgment Day is coming."

Chapter 44

Slipping down into the Jacuzzi with Carrie by his side, Charlie looked up into the clear night sky. Mesmerized by the twinkling stars, memories took him back to another night when the skies were empty.

It had been a day that would live forever in every American's memory. It was September 11th, 2001. Charlie had started his shift that morning when a coworker arrived with the news that an aircraft had hit the World Trade Center. He had stayed at Sector 16 while his coworkers gathered around the computer terminal at the supervisor's desk monitoring the Internet.

He recalled the time a B-25 Bomber hit the Empire State Building back during World War II on a foggy morning. With today's navigational equipment and radar services provided, how could this happen? It never crossed his mind that terrorists would use an aircraft as a weapon. When the second aircraft hit, all doubt was removed, and it became evident that these were intentional suicide missions.

Within seconds of impact, general information bulletins started coming off the printer. The first one read, "All aircraft are to be landed ASAP. Any pilot questions are to be given the phrase 'Due to National Emergency' this includes VFR aircraft." The next one, three minutes later, read, "Ground stop all aircraft to all airports until further notice due to National Emergency." Being on the West Coast and early in the morning

288

controllers, didn't take long getting the airplanes on the ground. And finally a message went out, "Special Notice: due to extraordinary circumstances, and for reasons of safety...attention all aircraft operators. By order of the Federal Aviation Command Center all airports/airdromes are not authorized for landing or takeoff. All aircraft are encouraged to land ASAP." An hour later, they received a message stating, "All law enforcement aircraft and rescue aircraft are released."

Charlie had been as awestruck as the rest of the world at what had transpired the remainder of that day. He and his coworkers spent the rest of their shift watching for primary targets of any unauthorized aircraft. They were filled with uncertainty as to whether they would be going home that night. By early afternoon, the swing shift started arriving, and Charlie had been allowed to leave. Later that night in his Jacuzzi, he had become very aware of the empty skies.

The knock on the door startled the still-sleeping vacationers. "I told them we didn't need housecleaning today." Charlie complained as he grabbed his robe and stumbled to the door. Opening the door, he was greeted by a courier delivering a certified letter. Signing for the letter, Charlie thanked the man and closed the door.

"It's from the FAA," Charlie answered his wife's inquisitive look.

"Oh, the cash award you were looking for?" she joked, knowing that the letter was one of more serious content.

Mr. Charles Beckler,

This letter is to inform you that, due to insubordination, your employment at the Western Center for Air Traffic Services has been terminated. In order to receive your final paycheck, it is imperative that you send your

289

federal identification badge and parking pass to your place of employment no later than February 28th.

Robert L. Burkhammer, Federal Aviation Administrator.

"Wow! He must have stayed up late last night getting these things signed," Charlie sighed looking at his official occupational death certificate.

Rubbing his shoulders, Carrie reminded him, "He can't fire you, remember? You quit."

"Still feel sorry for the guys receiving these this morning. Even though we knew it was coming, it's still a slam to a person's confidence. Only time will heal the pain that is being felt this day."

The morning news was centered on Bob Burkhammer and a couple of his goons explaining the change from air traffic controllers to air traffic service specialist. "Each specialist will be responsible for four stations simultaneously. This is possible by allowing a computer to assist with the system monitoring. When everything is going smoothly, no intervention is needed. It's only when something is amiss that intervention is needed. At that time, the specialist can focus on the challenge at hand. All scenarios possible have been compiled in dropdown boxes. All the specialists have to do is analyze the challenge and pick the proper solution using the new ATC service program.

We have not previously introduced this program knowing that the radar controllers would not be receptive to a predetermined fix package. Implementations of this program, along with the specialists already trained in its operations, are on their way to their predetermined facilities from the Aeronautical Academy. Upon their arrival, they are ready to resume normal flight operations. It's sort of like plug and play, as we say in computer language,."

The ATC Service Program worked as planned, and by Saturday morning all flights were back to normal. The news had settled down, and the media vultures had disappeared. The Beckler's flight was uneventful, and the tired couple arrived home late Saturday night.

Sunday afternoon, their living room became the gathering place for many of Charlie and Carrie's friends.

"I really don't know what to say." Charlie tried to comfort his old coworkers. "We all received the same letter. It was one we expected. We will live with the decision we made with no regrets. Have we changed things? Probably not! We have stood for integrity and have had our knees cut out from under us. Where do we go from here? I really don't know."

Chapter 45

The atmosphere within the Centers changed drastically. The few radar controllers who did not go on strike were reassigned to the training department. They were told that it was to assist in training the plug-and-play specialists. It became obvious that the real reason was to get them out of the control room. Their Type A personalities was no longer conducive to the new FAA. Their type was replaced with tech-head geeks who had no desire for joking around and making fun of their coworkers. They sat in their positions like stone-faced zombies, never speaking a word, never taking their eyes off the monitors. Even better, they were always back from breaks on time and never disobeyed supervision.

Within a year, an updated version of the 4DT was installed, which removed any resemblance to a radarscope. This change was a dagger in the heart of those who had for so many years sat in front of a scope, communicating with their airborne counterparts. All this in the name of progress was considered safer and more efficient.

Air traffic was on an upswing as more unmanned flights began hauling freight, and the mass production of very light jets was in full swing. With fewer delays and less time circling airports, the flying public soon forgot about the dinosaurs of air traffic control. A year after the strike, there were still a lot of homes for sale around Ely. The specialists replacing the strikers were not being paid nearly as much as the old controllers, making it impossible for them to buy the dozens of foreclosed homes stretching up and down the Beckler's street.

Charlie had been busy flying back and forth to Washington, testifying as Congress tried to sort out the shenanigans taking place in the Aviation Subcommittee and the White House. In the end, the success of the new program and its savings covered a multitude of sins. With the success of this revolutionary program, all that became of the cover-up was a congressional censure of the President and Senator Kirk Frances.

Charlie filed a lawsuit against the FAA on the grounds of management misconduct creating a hostile work environment leading up to his resignation. His suit was settled prior to trial for an undisclosed amount but did include Charlie's retirement. Charlie soon became the target of almost all the major aviation consulting firms. He no longer desired to live under the bondage of a job and rejected many lucrative offers. The one he had to take was from Sean. Having started O'Leary Aviation Consultants after his resignation from the FAA, Sean's fledging company rapidly became a powerhouse within the aviation community. Just having Charlie Beckler registered as one of the consultants created a buzz with his clients.

Tyrone Cava had just started his shift at WCATS. He had been one of the first air traffic specialists to arrive at the facility, and he was proud of his job. He had first been approached by the FAA three years earlier when he graduated from Emery Riddle with a degree in aviation science. He had almost turned down the job when the recruiter would not tell him exactly what he would be doing or where he would be working. "Let's just say it's exciting and along your line of education. We will tell you everything you need to know once you're sworn to secrecy." Where the recruiter almost lost him with lack of details, he hooked him with the thirty-thousand-dollar signing bonus and the promise of paying off his student loans. So Tyrone had signed the five-year contract and three weeks later found himself with seven thousand other recruits at the academy in Oklahoma City.

They were housed in newly constructed barracks on the grounds secluded from the outside world. For the next three years, they learned about their future jobs, and then used their education to develop the ATC service and simulator programs to enhance their skills. Two weeks before the strike, the agency finally revealed their new jobs. Each specialist was given a facility based on earlier surveys. Tyrone had asked for somewhere in Georgia close to his family. How he ended up in Ely, Nevada, instead of Georgia would always be a mystery. Not wanting to be a complainer, he kept his dissatisfactions to himself. *This is not the time to be daydreaming,* he reminded himself as his attention was drawn to an incongruous situation.

The data was not adding up between a Citation Jet and an American B757 descending into Salt Lake City. He moved the slew ball over the flight plan, and a window opened up showing the closure rate between the two aircraft was inconsistent with preset parameters. He clicked on the dropdown box that sent a speed readjust message to both aircraft and a data of the transaction to the program director sitting at the front desk. *These situations are happening way too often,* he thought as he sat back in his chair and resumed the monotonous task.

Sitting at the command console at the center of the control room, Nick Harton was sipping coffee with his feet up on the counter. This job had become so boring since the controllers had been fired. He grumbled that these darn kids don't even know how to argue. If they had an emotional bone in their body, it never showed. A message appeared on his computer monitor. Dropping his feet down, he reached up and hit the enter button, allowing the contents of the message to appear: "N539CL/AAL391 Speed anomaly/Speed reset/Successful." He added his acknowledgment to the package and sent it to the data center in Atlantic City where it would be collaborated with all the others across the country. *Wonder what I'll do when the fix doesn't work,* he asked himself. *Guess I'll just read about it in the news the next day.* He laughed at the answer to his own question then more seriously realized he should be looking at what had been going on. He picked up the phone and called an old friend of his who worked at the tech center.

"I really don't know, Nick," Brent Mitts responded to Nick's concern. "You guys are not the only ones. We are now getting over thirty a day and have yet to figure it out. Once we get the common denominator, we can work on a fix."

"Could you send me the data on the last couple of weeks?" Nick asked. "I would like to do a little research on my own."

Brent hesitated, "I'll send them to you on your FAA webmail, but they are sensitive, so keep them to yourself."

"I would appreciate it. Give me something to do while sitting here babysitting the zombies."

Nick said good-bye to his old friend. If he could find the common denominator, it might be worth a promotion and he could be out of this jailhouse job. *Wonder what it would be like working an office job working day shifts Monday through Friday. That would give me a normal life. Maybe they would give me the position as safety manager. It'd sure be nice to have weekends off. Twenty years in this job and still working Saturday evenings."*

Nick logged onto his FAA email. The requested files were already there. As he scrolled down the spreadsheet, he was overwhelmed at the vast number of reported anomalies. He found the one he had just transmitted an hour ago and noticed four more from around the nation had already happened since then. Amazingly, there were over seven thousand intercepts in a year. This put a lot of pressure on these kids to make the right decision. He saved the file to his thumb drive and went back to his daydreaming.

"Mr. Harton?"

Nick jumped as Tyrone startled him out of his trance. "What's up, Tyrone?"

"Well, I just had that challenge with the Citation jet and have some concerns. At the academy, we ran thousands of ghost operations and never once experienced these problems."

"Wait a minute," Nick interjected, "what's a ghost operation?"

"

It's where we were piping in live data from the facilities and running parallel operations without interfering with live traffic."

"Wow! I didn't know that was possible. You kids design that program too?"

"Yeah, that was an easy one. All the data is available on the Internet if you know how to get to it."

"So, is it accessible to anyone? Say a cyber terrorist decides to send it a worm virus or something?"

Tyrone shook his head, "No, it is a one-way-only data stream. A hacker may be able to get all the data but would not be able to transmit anything into the ERAMS system. I have been researching the programs and went back to its origin."

Nick had his feet back up on the counter with his hands behind his head. "That sounds intensive. Find anything interesting?"

"I'm not really a good judge when it comes to interesting, but I did find a variance in the programs," Tyrone continued. "In 2008 a fix-it program was installed in ERAMS that never made it to the academy. It seems that interfacility communication challenges required the patch. I have found

296

records of the patch but unable to find the patch itself. It seems to be no longer available."

"Thanks for your work on this, Tyrone. You bring up some great concerns, but, being realistic, live traffic has always played out differently than simulated. If you can find a guy by the name of Charlie Beckler, he could help you with a lot of your questions. He was one of our radar controllers who went out on strike. What a shame, screwing up his life like that."

Tyrone just smiled at Nick and headed for the break room. He knew Charlie from church. He just hadn't put two and two together. First of all, Nick was all messed up on Charlie striking. He had resigned. He would talk to Charlie on Sunday.

"I really am not interested in discussing it here," Charlie told the young man who had approached him after church. "If you want to stop by the house tomorrow, I will give you a history lesson on ERAM." Tyrone jotted down Charlie's address and assured him of his intentions of following through the next morning.

Sitting on the back patio with a cup of coffee, Charlie gave Tyrone a *Readers Digest* version of NextGen origin and his involvement in the program.

"What about the ERAM's fix?" Tyrone asked when Charlie had finished.

"You're going to have to be a little more specific," Charlie responded, "There have been a lot of fixes to ERAM."

"The one I came across had to do with communications between ERAM and the old Host computers."

Charlie shook his head. "That happened before I became involved. But something that might interest you is how the fix came about." Charlie went on to tell Tyrone about the million dollar contract and the mysterious virus that was allegedly installed in the system. "We have spent millions more trying to find the darn thing. It was finally concluded that it was flushed in an upgrade or deleted by a security program."

"I'm thinking the Trojan horse is raising its head," Tyrone offered, looking up from his empty coffee cup. "We have been experiencing a number of anomalies and the number is increasing daily."

"So why do you think it's a virus and not just a program discrepancy?"

"Charlie, we ran these programs for three years at the academy without a problem. This is different. It's as if the thing has the hiccups," Tyrone explained. "Nick Harton thinks it's because it's live traffic, but I know better. I helped write the simulator program, and the logic leaves no variance to these kinds of anomalies. How did I come to the conclusion it may be related to the ERAM fix? It was the only program never installed in the academy computers."

"Why was it never installed?" Charlie asked.

"Simple, we didn't need to connect to the old Host computers. By the time we built the simulator, all the facilities were operating using ERAM."

Shaking his head, Charlie looked at Tyrone with all seriousness. "This program has been doomed from the beginning, we just didn't know it. It has a lot of potential, and the day will come when it will work with the reliability we have come to expect. They need to start over and do it right. Good luck, Tyrone. I wish you the best."

Chapter 46

Friday morning, July 4th, was a busy day. It seemed that everyone had somewhere to fly to that day, contributing to a traditionally busy holiday weekend. Jet Blue flight 777 nonstop from Boston Logan Airport to Las Vegas had just finished boarding. The Airbus 320 was fully loaded with 150 passengers and a crew of five. At the helm was Captain Pat Eastin and First Officer Robin Thibert. It would be a long five-hour-and-thirty-four-minute flight to Sin City.

"What a great way to spent Independence Day," Pat commented as they finished up the preflight checklist. "At least we should be there before the fireworks start. Have we received the clearance yet?"

Robin pushed a couple of buttons. "Just came through the data link. It's already been accepted by the autopilot."

"What routing did they put us on?" Captain Eastin inquired. "Not that it really matters. We have to fly it anyhow."

Scrolling down the display, First Officer Robin Thibert found what she was looking for. "We're departing Runway 4R, via the Highland 6 departure, Manchester transition direct Syracuse, then via Q2703 to Bryce Canyon then via the Full House High Profile 3 arrival. And let's see, initial climb to 8,000 on departure."

"Flight plan acknowledged," Captain Eastin grunted. "Let's close this thing up and get out of here on time."

Ten minutes later they departed to the northeast making a climbing, slow left-hand turn around the city of Revere direct Manchester. Two hours into the flight, they were over central Wisconsin on time and enjoying a smooth ride at flight level three-four-zero.

At the same time, sitting on the ramp at Salt Lake, Captain Kurt Hufford was complaining to maintenance about data link and the autopilot acting strangely. The flight for Las Vegas was already ten minutes late, and the passengers would soon be getting antsy. The Captain made the correct decision to delay the flight even longer, giving the technician time to run testing on the new equipment. Finally, at 6:33 p.m. local time, Skywest flight 2347 departed on Runway three four left on the Edeth 4 departure making a left turn direct to Milford where they would join the Full House High Profile 3 arrival into McCarran.

Ten minutes later, the flight reached its cruising altitude of thirty-one thousand feet and transmitted their request for direct Luxor. Five seconds later, data link lit up with a command clearing them direct Ksino. "We'll take what we can get," Captain Kurt Hufford told his First Officer, Nolan Selmer.

At 7:15 local time, Jet Blue 777 had started a maximum profile descent out of FL350 just twenty-two minutes from touchdown. At the same time, Skywest 2347, still flying straight and level showed twenty-three minutes out. Tyrone was monitoring all four Las Vegas quadrants during the evening arrival rush.

Just fifteen years earlier, to handle this same traffic, it took six seasoned controllers working six different scopes. A lot was on his mind this evening. Tyrone had finally made contact with Abdur. Abdur, who was now living in seclusion in a small town in Montana, at first did not want to talk. After

Tyrone had revealed his meeting with Charlie, he had agreed to meet with the young specialist.

Tyrone had scheduled a few days off and was planning to drive up to meet with the aging programmer the following week. As most geeks do, he had been making a list of questions. He was not concerned as much about the reason why, he already knew that. His questions were more technical concerning the language used and proof of the existence of the Trojan horse, even though it made sense now with the way 4DT was acting.

"What the heck!" he exclaimed as two aircraft started flashing alert.

Ted Whistler jumped up from the supervisor's desk. He hadn't heard an outburst like that since before the strike. *Maybe that type A personality can be acquired,* he said to himself as he looked over Tyrone's shoulders. "What you got there?"

Tyrone was busy punching the keyboard. "It's something new. Skywest is to arrive a minute ahead of Jet Blue."

"That's new?" Ted seemed puzzled. "Doesn't that happen all the time?"

"4DT doesn't show a blow-by, and he is behind the Jet Blue. Something's not right."

"Slow the Skywest down," Ted prodded.

"I have already thought of that. Sent an override and got a negative response."

"The pilot rejected a clearance to slow down?" Ted asked.

Tyrone was getting irritated. "It was either the autopilot or 4DT. I don't know, and I would appreciate it if you would either leave me alone or come up with some good ideas. We don't have all day here."

"Just listen to you. I thought we had fired all the controllers!" Ted mumbled as he shut his mouth and watched Tyrone at work.

"This is not good!" Tyrone's fingers were now flying across the keyboard. "It's not working, it's not working!" Beads of sweat were forming on his forehead as he tried to slow down the CS100 Bombardier Skywest jet.

"What's happening?" Ted demanded.

"I don't know. I am not getting any response from the aircraft. We're showing connection. I've sent text messages directly to the pilot requesting he override 4DT."

"Did he get them?" Ted was now a little more subtle about his questions.

"Yet to be determined, I have not received confirmation." The monitor showed the two aircraft five miles apart; within a minute they would know.

Tyrone buried his head in his hands. "This is not what I got hired to do. This is not supposed to happen."

At twenty-six thousand feet, eighty miles north east of Las Vegas, the two aircraft were descending on a converging path. Jet Blue Captain Pat Eastin was the first to notice the converging aircraft on their display. "That guy's closing fast. He should be pulling his speed back."

He was adjusting the range when the terminal collision avoidance system warning activated. The speaker blared "Warning traffic, stop descent now. Warning traffic, stop descent now."

Captain Eastin hit the disconnect switch on the autopilot and pulled back on the sidestick to bring the nose up. "It's not responding. Robin, check yours."

Robin pulled back on the controls with the same results. "Captain, it looks like the autopilot didn't disengage."

Captain Eastin went back to punching buttons while keeping an eye on the Skywest jet screaming at them. He pushed the throttles forward. "Full power will at least slow down the closure rate."

Robin monitoring the gauges, "It's not responding to the throttle either. We have lost control of the airplane."

"Check the manual, see what we can do. We have about two minutes."

On the Skywest jet the TCAS had alerted the crew to the impending collision. Captain Kurt Hufford and First Officer Nolan Selmer kept trying everything they could to regain control of their rogue system. Having already retarded the throttles, they watched as the airspeed stayed nailed on 315 knots. "The only option we have is cut off fuel flow to the engines," Nolan advised his captain.

"I don't like that idea, but go ahead and kill number two, that should give us the descent rate we need to get under this guy."

The First Officer reached above his head and pulled the fuel cutoff switch. "Number two responding, winding down. I'm trimming for single engine operations." The aircraft increased the descend rate to three thousand feet a minute.

"Keep working on finding a way to shut off this autopilot, Nolan." Captain Hufford in the Skywest grumbled as he tried to retake control of the jet. "Why did we agree to this satanic program anyhow?"

"Found it!" Jet Blue First Officer Robin Thibert exploded. "Disconnect the fuses from the autopilot, data link, and the ADS-B."

"Cut them now, I'll be ready to take control. This guy is getting close." The captain grabbed the sidestick as Robin turned around, looking for the right fuses. "Hurry it up, Robin!" Captain Eastin hollered as he was now able to see the Skywest jet at their two o'clock position closing. It seemed like an eternity for Pat. He so badly wanted to push Robin out the way and pull those fuses. "The autopilot is the second row down, third from left."

"I got it!" Robin answered, "Found the other two, Captain. We're going dark."

Warning lights started flashing all over the panel as Robin pulled the other two fuses, and they went from a highly equipped aircraft to flying stick and rudder. The Airbus shuttered as the twin power plants went to 100 percent and Captain Eastin applied full left aileron. The Skywest jet filled their windscreen as the left wing lifted.

After trimming up the Skywest jet, First Officer Nolan Selmer scrolled quickly through the emergency checklist hoping for the answer to pop out. "We did not cover this in ground school."

Captain Kurt Hufford looked over at the youngster half his age. "Nolan, ground school only prepares you to learn. Start pulling fuses, we have to stop this thing!"

"Which ones should I pull first?" Nolan asked as he turned in his seat and started running his finger down the labels.

"Autopilot, and do it now!" Captain Hufford now had visual with the Jet Blue Airbus, and they were going to hit the sucker.

"The autopilot fuse is out, " Nolan answered as he looked around at Kurt, who still could not get any response from the yoke.

"Try the data link and the ADS-B."

As Nolan pulled the plugs on those two systems he heard the captain yell, "Hold on!"

Pulling back hard on the stick and applying right aileron, Captain Hufford could see faces looking out through the windows of the Jet Blue Airbus as the right wing started up.

The CS100 Skywest impacted the Jet Blue Airbus with enough force to sheer off its left wing at the outboard aileron. Captain Kurt Hufford watched as the winglet and the outer part of their wing disintegrated. The impact took off the outer three feet of the right wing of the Airbus. The jet veered to the left briefly before the captain threw in right rudder to counter the impact.

Looking back over his left shoulder he could not find the Airbus. "Nolan, start number two!"

"Starting number two!" Nolan's hands were shaking so bad he didn't know if he could do it.

The excitement in Kurt Hufford's voice was one of pure adrenaline. "Let's get this thing down to ten thousand. When you finish starting two, reengage data link only. We need to communicate with ATC."

First Officer Robin Thibert looked at the nose of the Skywest regional jet as it came into view from behind the right wing.

"Turn it hard, Captain!" she yelled. In horror, she watched as the two wing tips sheered each other off. Their Airbus shook violently as the airfoil was drastically altered. Captain Pat Eastin continued the left turn away from the stricken Skywest aircraft and pulled the throttles to idle, not wanting the airplane to lose anymore of the wing.

"Send out a mayday, Robin. We may be going in. Reboot data link only, nothing else."

Robin pushed the data link fuse back in and, within seconds, the ready light glowed green. Pat was able to level off at ten thousand feet and turn southwest. Looking down for familiar landscape, Captain Eastin was glad he had flown this route a few times in his last twenty years of flying. Who would have thought he would have to use pilotage as a way of navigation again in his career.

"We have communications with WCATS. They want to know if we have contact with the Skywest."

The Captain had to find humor in such a question. "You can tell them we had contact and would rather not repeat the process." Scanning the sky, he found the crippled aircraft off their left side about seven to ten miles. "Tell them we have the Skywest in sight and want to land at Nellis. I am not taking this thing downtown." Pat was referring to the McCarran airport next to the strip in Las Vegas.

"Roger, Captain," Robin replied as she was busy typing on the keypad, but to herself she wondered why they had had to give up voice communications.

The words started scrolling across the monitor "Mayday, mayday, mayday."

Data showed the two aircraft occupied the same airspace at exactly the same time. Ted just stared at the monitor. It revealed both aircraft moving apart, descending rapidly. Two minutes later, a text message from the Jet Blue scrolled across the screen. "Hit wing tips, aircraft under control. Landing Nellis AFB, eta 7 minutes."

Tyrone, numb from the message, was startled when Ted screamed at him. "Find out about the Skywest! I'll call Nellis."

Tyrone started typing and shortly got a response back from the CS100. "Left wing damaged, we have minimal control, slight left crab. Unable to stop descent, unable Las Vegas, will try to make Nellis."

Tyrone responded to both aircraft. "Use extreme caution. Both of you are landing Nellis. Equipment will be on standby. All other aircraft clear."

Fingers flying across the ERIDS screen, he located Nellis airport. "Jet Blue 777, if able use runway 21 right. Skywest 2347, if able use runway 21 left." Hitting the send button, he sat back and waited. It seemed like an eternity before the response came through.

"We have the Skywest jet in sight, and we're trying for 21 Right."

"Skywest is in a strong crab for 21 left, doesn't look good. Gear is down, having trouble maintaining directional control. Have emergency equipment standing by."

Tyrone quickly typed, "Switching you to Nellis control." Then, knowing this may be his last transmission added, "I'm praying for you." Then he hit the manual transfer switch, and the aircraft were gone from his screen.

Captain Kurt Hufford was using full left rudder to keep the aircraft upright as it approached runway two one left. The gear showed three greens and, as planned, the airspeed ten knots above normal. Nolan continued scanning the sky until he had visual on the Jet Blue Airbus descending for runway two one right.

"I got our bogey in sight, Captain. It looks like they're under control, should not be a factor."

"Not a factor. That's a fine choice of words. Keep an eye on our neighbors, and be ready to kill the engines when we land. The last thing I want is a fire. Is the cabin ready?"

"Cabin is secured and ready for a crash landing." Even the sound of that statement made the young first officer grimace.

For those on Las Vegas Blvd. passing by the base, they witnessed a strange sight as two airliners were making simultaneous approaches to Nellis. They had seen large aircraft arriving at the base before, but not two at a time and not domestic carriers. Only the most educated aviation enthusiast noticed the missing section of wing from the left side of the Skywest jet. They continued to watch as the aircrafts touched down, first the Airbus which, even though it seemed to skid sideways a little, was not all that abnormal. The Skywest was a different situation. Just before it touched down on its mains, the damaged left wing dipped and hit the pavement.

"Left rudder!" Kurt yelled at his already nerve frazzled copilot, applying right aileron to compensate for the lack of lift on the damaged wing. The airplane slammed onto the runway still fifteen degrees off centerline. The last minute move of the experienced pilot saved the lives of his passengers as the aircraft's nose moved just enough to the left to keep it on the runway. Both engines now spooling down, Kurt eased his viselike grip on the control stick and let the aircraft coast down the ten-thousand-foot runway. Sweat dripping from his brow, he high-fived his first officer and thanked God for getting them safely on terra firma.

Chapter 47

Midsummer

It looked more like an insane asylum than an air traffic facility, Charlie thought as he walked into the control room.

It had been two years since his resignation. He never expected he would return to this place. After the strike, Carrie had left for Georgia to spend some time with her parents, and Charlie had stayed behind to tie up some loose ends in Ely. He was busy packing his suitcase for an evening flight to Georgia when Sean called. A lot of arm twisting later, he agreed to take on this job. "You know controllers," Sean had emphasized.

"Yes, I know controllers, and these people are not controllers. We had the ability to suck it up and move on. Good grief, Sean. I can't even stand these people. They took the jobs of my friends. I say let them slobber in their misery."

"Come on, Charlie. It's a fifty-thousand-dollar contract. I will give you half."

Charlie grumbled something unintelligible and responded, "What's the duration of the contract?"

"Three weeks, maybe four," Sean answered. He was obviously delighted. "Does that mean you will do it? You know it's the right thing to do. You're already in town."

"Okay, but if they give me even one little piece of crap, I'm out of there. You know this is blood money."

"Thanks, Charlie, let's do lunch sometime."

"Not if I can help it. Every time I talk to you I have more work to do."

"Look what the cat dragged in," Nick gloated as Charlie arrived at the command console.

Charlie had never appreciated Nick's humor or his management styles. How happy he was not to be working for this son of Satan anymore. "Yeah, the cat did drag me in. It will probably be the same cat that drags your lazy butt out of here. What did you screw up now?"

"I don't know what you're talking about. Who let you in here? You know this is a restricted area."

Charlie leaned against the counter and flashed his badge at the pathetic manager. "It seems your boss thinks you need some professional consulting. Maybe we should start with recommending your removal."

Nick's face was redder than a beet. "Wait a minute. I am an integral part of this program. I'm working on a confidential fix to your 4DT screw-up."

Charlie laughed, "Don't get your dander up. You will always be a manager. No quality needed. I've work to do, so I will leave you to your devises, and if you have any questions as to my authorization, call the front office. I am sure they will help you sort out your Napoleonic complex."

Charlie headed back to his old area, where he sat down behind one of the specialists and tried not to interrupt her concentration. He noticed the specialist soon started shaking. He could tell she didn't have a lot going on, so he spoke up and introduced himself.

"Hi," she replied, "I'm Laurie Cronin, have been here for two years. It's still new, but we are getting used to it."

"You're getting used to what?" Charlie asked the young lady.

"I don't really know." She started shaking, almost sobbing. "It's so strange. It's like we are trapped here with a job to do. One we don't understand."

Charlie gently put a hand on her shoulder. "It's okay. If you don't mind, I would like to speak with you off the sector." The request brought a smile to Laurie's face, and she nodded her head.

Ten minutes later they were sitting at a table on the patio. "I know who you are." Laurie smiled as she sat back in her chair playing with the hem on her blouse. "My uncle was at the convention in Las Vegas where you spoke. He thinks you are what aviation needs. He would really like to meet you someday."

Charlie laughed, "Vegas! That was a long time ago. Times have changed. Let's talk about you. How did you get this job?"

Laurie relaxed a little as she explained. "It started with my first airplane ride with my uncle. He's the one who wants to meet you. This turned into a love for aviation. I never expected to be involved in air traffic but wanted to work on the electronics on airplanes. I thought that maybe someday I would get a job with an airline."

Charlie listened to the young lady, knowing she was missing out on her dream. "So how did this job come about?"

Laurie smiled at Charlie, "When I graduated, I started looking for work. Just like the others. That is when I was contacted by a recruiter. The rest is history."

Charlie wrote down a couple of notes on his iPad and continued. "So, Laurie, what is happening in there?" He was referring to the control room.

"Mr. Beckler, I don't really know for sure. I was told I would not be controlling airplanes, only monitoring the system. Now it seems as if every day, things get worse. We are constantly required to make instantaneous decisions. I don't like it, Charlie. I want to quit."

Charlie looked at the fear in her eyes and softly asked, "Why haven't you?"

Laurie frowned. "The contract. They paid off my student loans for a five-year contract. Now I'm stuck for three more years. I don't know if I can do it."

Charlie tried to encourage the girl who was young enough to be his daughter but sent her back to a job she was never equipped to handle. He spent the rest of the day interviewing a number of other specialists.

Over the next two weeks, Charlie interviewed over fifty of the specialists and spent hours monitoring the young professionals at work. Having been away from his wife long enough, Charlie jumped a flight back to Georgia on Friday night. The three-hour-and-twenty-five-minute flight from Salt Lake to Atlanta gave him time to write his report.

After interviewing fifty-four specialists and spending twenty hours monitoring these specialists in operation, I have come to the following observations:

The Federal Aviation Administration, in preparation for a new style of operations, hired seven thousand highly educated individuals to replace air traffic controllers. They did this in order to change the personality style of the work force that had, for eight generations, endured the stress of maintaining a safe air traffic environment. It is now the opinion of the FAA that knowledge outweighs control and is accomplished with smaller salaries. While this change has reduced labor cost, it has also reduced the level of experience, compromising safety.

Charlie shut his laptop and sat back in his seat, looking out the window at the fluffy clouds passing rapidly below. Deep in thought, he drifted off to sleep. His dreams were unsettling, with the interviews of the specialists occupying his mind.   Waking up with the inspiration to continue, he started typing.

My observations reveal that there is a transformation happening within the specialist workforce; they are slowly changing from specialist to controller. While this may sound like a ludicrous idea, I will explain. The nature of this job requires a person to make instantaneous decisions while maintaining a constant awareness to the surrounding environment. This is accomplished with the ever present realization that a mistake would not only end your own career, but it could potentially take the lives of hundreds of people.

The FAA has made the argument that due to enhanced equipment, the stress is no longer a factor. My rebuttal to such a naïve statement is one I have witnessed over the last two weeks. Each one of the specialists interviewed was scared. This fear is derived from the number of instances where human interference was required to maintain a safe operation. It is not by choice, but due to the necessity of the job, that this transformation is created. These young specialists have no desire to be controllers, but their situation demands it. In conclusion, I would suggest it's not the person who makes the job; it's the job that makes the person.

Chapter 48

By October, the system was undergoing rapid transformations as the technicians tried desperately to stabilize the shaky program. The anomalies had become the normal. A specialist could expect to be challenged at least once during each session, sometimes two or three times. With every update, the problems seemed to multiply. On October 17th, during the early afternoon hours, 4DT's primary and secondary programs shut down. For thirty minutes, the specialists had to become controllers and make timely decisions. It was a madhouse in the control room as these previously emotionless specialists became psychosomatic controllers working out perilous situations. The problem was never located, but the system seemed to have mysteriously stabilized.

Over the next three weeks, the system seemed to continue to get stronger. There was no answer as to why. One of the software engineers from Atlantic City was busy deciphering the shutdown when he came across an unusual phenomenon.

Picking up the phone, he called his boss. "Mr. Morris, this is Andrew Lang down in software research. Could you come down here? We have a situation that's beyond my pay grade."

Scotty Morris had been with the NextGen program from the beginning and was looking forward to retirement. He told himself on the way down the three flights of steps to the

314

software research department that forty years with the government was enough. "Maybe the youngster should have come upstairs," he mumbled as he held his proximity card up next to the sensor.

"Watch this code," Andy explained. "It's changing every few seconds. I have been watching it for the last fifteen minutes, and it hasn't stopped."

"Is there a hacker in there manipulating it?" Scotty asked the most obvious of questions.

"That's not possible," Andy replied, "This system isn't connected to the outside world. It terminates here for testing."

"So, where's the command to change coming from?"

Andy scratched his head. "I don't know, but it has the smell of a virus. Do we have any records of a virus in the system?"

A light came on in Scotty's head. "I don't believe it. I wonder if this could be the Trojan horse?"

"There's a Trojan horse?"

Scotty sat down and watched as the code again started a rapid scrolling motion and stopped at some strange symbols. "What in the heck is that?" he asked.

"Not that I can read it, but it looks like Arabic," Andy replied, picking up his phone calling his friend Lonna, who knew Arabic.

Two minutes later, Lonna arrived. Reading the screen, she turned white. "Where did this come from?"

"We don't know," Andy answered. "What does it say?"

"It's a threat from Al-Qaeda," she explained. "Violent death bestowed on all Americans. I pray to Allah that all your airplanes fall from the sky." Lonnie looked puzzled at the two men in the room. "I thought Al-Qaeda was annihilated a long time ago. Is this a joke?"

Andy highlighted the text and right-clicked. Going to properties, he was able to locate the origin. "It looks like this language was installed in '07. It's been lying dormant for over seventeen years. It is a Trojan horse."

"Get everyone you can on this now. This could be the reason for the shutdown. If it's not deciphered soon we may need to take down 4DT," Scotty told his young programmers. "You have my authorization for all the overtime you need. You can use engineers from other departments too. Man! This is not good. I have to call Washington. Keep me informed on the progress."

Scotty headed back upstairs. "Why did you do it, Abdur?" he asked out loud as he finally made it up to the third floor. He knew this was the virus that for so many years had evaded them. At least now they had found it. The question still remained. How much damage had the Trojan horse already done? Thumbing through his contact information, he found Sean O'Leary's number.

"So the old boy wasn't lying," Sean replied to Scotty's description of their find. "Why are you calling me?"

"We need to get in touch with Abdur. Do you know where he is?"

"Sure do. But don't be surprised if he doesn't return your call. You treated him pretty badly the last time you two were together."

"Could you call him for me? He will listen to you," pouted Scotty.

Sean laughed. "If you remember, the FAA decided I was no longer relevant. So if you need me, I will be happy to do consulting at a price."

Scotty's anger was starting to show. "It wasn't this office that caused your demise, you old fool. At least give me his number. I'll call."

Sean again laughed at Scotty's huffiness and gave him the number. "You may want to start with an apology. Abdur would like to forget his past, not have to relive it through you."

316

"What about Charlie, could he help?"

"Charlie is retired and has less respect for you than Abdur has. He is somewhere in Georgia right now. I think he's heading back to Ely next week for a follow-up on a job. Good luck Scotty! Oh yes, and congratulations on finding the ATC doomsday virus. Think I will stay on the ground for awhile."

Bob Burkhammer was busy with meetings all morning. Things had settled down within the agency since the controllers had been fired. It sure had been a great idea to plan ahead in anticipation of the strike. It had been almost three years, and it felt great not to have the challenges of employee unrest to deal with. It was now time to work on the growth of the industry and his legacy within the agency.

"Mr. Burkhammer, you have a call on line one. It's Scott Morris from the tech center. He says it's an emergency."

"Emergency! Everything is an emergency when it comes to the tech center. Bet their coffee machine is broken." Picking up the phone he hit line one. "What's up, Scotty?"

Scotty explained the find. "You may want your people formulating a contingency plan if this thing goes south. We are getting everyone we can on it, but we have no idea how deep the virus goes."

Bob sat there in shock. He knew the virus story, but it was his understanding that nothing was ever located. "Thanks for the update, Scotty. We will take care of a plan. You keep on the fix." Hanging up the phone, he spent the next ten minutes turning his pen end over end deep in thought knowing he had to do it and it was going to hurt. With that knowledge, he called the Secretary of Transportation.

Terry Laverne was not happy. "Say again why we can't shut down the program?"

Bob again explained, "We no longer have air traffic controllers. They are only specialists. The shutdown two weeks ago for a half-hour was chaotic at best. To take it down for even a day or two would be disastrous."

The secretary talked a little softer now as the information started sinking in. "So what are we going to do?"

"I think it's time to bring in the president."

"I'm kind of thinking maybe Homeland Security," Terry added. "It is an attack on the homeland. At least DHS should be apprised of the potential national emergency."

"You ready to face the President on this one?" Bob knew the president didn't need this on his plate.

"Don't mind at all, Bob. We will see what he's made of. Have you called O'Leary?"

Bob was quiet for way too long. "I didn't really plan on it. Is it necessary?"

Terry sighed, "You know as well as I do that you have to. Swallow your pride and make the call. It will probably save you your job."

"Thanks for the vote of confidence, Boss. I'll make the call."

"Am I to assume this is not a call to check on my health?" Sean prodded Bob after the small talk had subsided.

"NextGen has been hit with a virus and we need your help."

Sean did not reveal to the administrator he had already been apprised of the find. "So what you're saying is that you now want me to help you shut down 4DT? If you had have listened three years ago, we would not be having this conversation today."

Bob winced, "Thank you for that reminder. We need a plan, Sean. This thing is likely to disintegrate in a matter of days. I am going to give you the opportunity to use your conscience as far as how much you charge the tax payers."

Sean already had a plan. He and his associates had been working on it for over two years. "I will get back to you on the cost of the contract. I can assure you it will not be one on monetary value. To what extent does this meltdown encompass?"

Bob hesitated, "That is classified, but I gather if I'm asking you to come up with a plan you need to know. The president and the Homeland Security secretary are being brought up to speed as we speak."

"Great! Keep it out of the media as long as you can. Set up a meeting with the president and all involved parties. I'll be at headquarters in two hours."

Chapter 49

"Good evening, Mr. President." Sean acknowledged President James Banister as he entered the situation room. He was ushered to an empty chair across from the first year president.

"Thanks for coming, Mr. O'Leary." The president replied. "Bob has filled me in on your history with NextGen. So you were the one working with Charlie Beckler?"

Sean looked around the room at some familiar faces and a couple he had never seen. "Yes, I do have a history with NextGen. Are you a friend of Charlie's?"

"I don't know if you would call us friends. I was at the NBAA convention in Las Vegas when Mr. Beckler gave that sensational speech a few years ago. We met in the VIP room afterwards. Whereas he probably doesn't recall our meeting, I sure do. It changed my perspective on a lot of things, including running for this job. Mr. O'Leary, what sort of plan do you have for us?"

"First of all, gentlemen, we are on the verge of a national emergency. Since my demise with the agency, my team and I have been spending our available time putting together a contingency plan per chance our worst fears were realized. I understand this sounds a little presumptuous on our part so," Sean noticed the nodding in the room, "so let me help you through that. Most of the people in our association have been deeply involved in the NextGen development. With a

320

feeling of responsibility ever since we became aware of the possibility of a virus, we started looking at the what-if-scenarios.

"Let me start with the best-case scenario and work my way down." Sean turned on his iPad and connected to the situation room's projector. "Let's start with a simple 4DT shutdown. The air traffic service specialists are not air traffic controllers and will be unable to handle the volume of traffic now populating the airspace. Within six hours of losing 4DT, over 80 percent of all aircraft will be experiencing over two-hour delays. Within twenty-four hours, over 30 percent of your specialists will resign. One week after 4DT shutdown, you will be lucky to get over 20 percent of your flights even in the air."

President Banister motioned to Sean. "I have a couple of questions. First, are you sure this is not the worst-case scenario? And second, what is your answer if this happens? "

"No, Mr. President, sorry to say it is not. Unfortunately, there are a number of far worse scenarios that could take place. As for a solution to this emergency, we are ready. Mr. President, I have on standby thirty-five hundred retired and fired controllers on a ready list who would be willing to assist in maintaining a seamless air traffic system if the need arises. I understand that, under the law, these fired controllers are unable to return to federal service. We have had our attorneys prepare a contract which you can sign under the National Emergency Act that will temporarily give my company the National Airspace System. Please understand, Mr. President, I have no desire or intentions of a long-term takeover. The contract is open-ended to be terminated by the completion of a 4DT replacement or by executive order of this White House."

"What do you think, gentlemen?" President Banister looked over at the secretary of transportation and the FAA administrator.

Bob was shaking his head. "There is a lot of speculation in what Sean's saying. I think we should hold off on this kind of drastic measure. We don't know for sure if it's even going to happen."

"What if it does, Bob?" The president asked. "Are you ready to take that responsibility? Don't you think we should at least be prepared?"

Secretary Terry Laverne spoke up. "We brought Mr. O'Leary here for a reason. If it's all right with you, Mr. President, I would like to see what he has to say."

President Banister shrugged his shoulders, "Go ahead, Sean. What is the worst case scenario?"

"The worst could be aviation Armageddon. It may sound like a scare tactic, but it could very well become a reality. Our concern is the networking between all the components of NextGen. We did this at the request of the user and the architects of NextGen with much reservation. They contended that the ability to access all data whether it is flight information, security, or weather would far outweigh the risk of a single source. Now all components of the system probably have this virus."

"So you're saying security is affected with the virus also?" The secretary of homeland security, Penny Hankins, spoke up.

"Considering your department has not released access to these programs to our company, we cannot confirm the extent it has infiltrated your system." Sean continued, "We are to assume they are infected."

Penny grimaced, "This could get even more serious. NextGen Security is tied into our department's network. This virus has the potential to spread to all levels of the nation's security system. What do you recommend we do?"

Sean gave the secretary a nervous smile. "I am not the expert on virus containment. We do have our software engineers working on a scrub program for NextGen, but even with that, it is our company's recommendation to build a brand new program to ensure its reliability. My first concern is with aviation. Once we get that stabilized, we can assist with your network.

Sean continued to explain how national security and aviation had been joined at the hips.

"Here is the challenge we have with security tied to the NextGen program and the virus."

"After the terrorist attacks of September 11th, Homeland Security required all facilities be protected. As a result, some of the departments really took this to heart and integrated defenses into each of the facilities to extreme. Even local technicians could be overridden if NextGen security thought it was being threatened. So, to answer your question, Mr. President, the worst case scenario would be not only a complete loss of NextGen but also an errant program that internal security would not let us shut down."

The room sat in silence. Finally the President spoke up. "Mr. O'Leary, I would like to speak to Charlie Beckler before I make a decision. Can you get him on the phone?"

Charlie had just sat down to dinner with Carrie and her parents when his phone rang. He shut off the ringer without even looking at the caller. He felt the vibration as the caller left a message. He pulled the phone from his pocket and groaned, "Oh, great! I just ignored the White House." That got the attention of the others sitting at the table. "At least the caller I.D. says 'White House'.

He put the phone on speaker as he listened to the message. "Charlie, this is Sean. I'm at the White House and we have a situation. We need you to call as soon as you can. The president would like to speak to you."

Without hesitation, Charlie returned the call to the White House.

The President got straight to the point. "Charlie, this is James Banister. Are you available to answer some questions for us?"

Charlie chuckled, "I think I can clear my schedule for a few minutes, Mr. President."

"I understand you're now a consultant with Sean O'Leary? The agency sure messed up losing you." Charlie was now puzzled.

"I'm honored, Mr. President, but how do you know me?"

"Charlie, you probably don't remember me, but I was in the VIP room in Las Vegas many years ago when you gave a great speech on aviation."

"Sorry, Mr. President, but things were spinning that night, and I don't recall."

"That's all right, Charlie. I have been a fan of yours ever since and wondered what happened to you. As you are aware from working with Sean, we have a problem here. What is your take on the plan to bring back in the radar controllers?"

Charlie sat in silence pondering the answer.

"Are you there, Charlie?"

"Yes, Mr. President, just thinking this through."

"That's what I like about you, son. You never make rash decisions. Do you think it will work?"

"Sir, we are very aware of how severe a virus could affect NextGen. The sooner you can get air traffic controllers into the facilities, the greater chance you will have in averting this disaster. Will it work? My concern would not be with the thirty-five hundred hungry controllers. As long as the system gives them something to work with, they will give you service and safety. Considering the deterioration over the last few days, I would not give NextGen more than another thirty days before it's totally gone."

Now it was silent in the situation room as the leaders of United States sat there stunned by such a realization. Finally, the President thanked Charlie for his input, and the call was terminated.

The President leaned back in his chair, looking at the ceiling. Finally, he looked at Sean. "Mr. O'Leary, we are going to move forward with your plan. I would like for you to put the machine in place and have the controllers standing by. In the mean time, Bob, you set in motion the necessary logistics at the facilities to receive these controllers. Let's get it done as soon as possible."

"Mr. President, we will be ready to move in as soon as we get the word from Bob. To lessen the impact, we will be placing as many as we can into their last facility. The others will take a little more time. Do you want us to move forward with 4DT replacement?"

"It is in your hands, Sean. Do what you need to do to fix this thing."

Chapter 50

Sunday evening November 16th

WCATS was running scared as the specialists sat stone-faced in front of their monitors, diligently watching the aircraft movement. With each anomaly, the specialists would wipe the sweat from their brows as the situation passed. A sigh of relief came late in the evening when the rush was over and traffic settled down to just a handful of aircraft per hour. Tyrone signed out at eleven and headed home, exhausted from the day's work. On the little paper in his pocket were eighty-seven dash marks, one for each of the fixes he was required to make over the last eight hours.

I can't take any more, he told himself on the short drive down to Ely. *At least we have controllers coming in next week to help. I sure hope they don't blame us for taking their jobs. We didn't know what was going on. How could we have known?* Even if they did, he would tolerate it in order to get some relief from the past two months. He had heard that Charlie would not be among those returning to WCATS. It was too bad because Charlie sure had a way of raising morale.

Tuesday morning November 18th
0730 Local time 1430 UTC

Nick Harton was on the phone with the facility chief. "We have a problem here. 4DT is not taking commands.

Systems engineers tried to reboot 4DT, and it wouldn't let them."

"Is 4DT doing its job?"

"Yes, as far as separations standards, but we are under light traffic right now. In two hours, we will be approaching the level red, and I question its ability to maintain any level of safety."

"So, do you recommend we leave it running, or should the engineers shut down the whole system for a cold start?"

"I think we are better letting it go for awhile. I don't want these kids working traffic without it. As much as I hate to admit it, we sure could use a few air traffic controllers in here right now."

"Hold on, we're only days away. It will be bittersweet."

One hour later the operational error detection program alarm sounded, drawing Nick's attention to a display. The OEDP showed two aircraft within two miles and only three hundred feet apart. Nick quickly typed in an explanation that would later be reviewed. No sooner was he finished when it sounded again. This time the aircraft were even closer.

Frantically, he called his boss. "We have to shut it down! We've had two errors within five minutes. Hold on just a minute. Make that three! We just had another! We need it shut down now!" The excitement in his statement showed fear he was not accustom to portraying.

The phone rang beside Nick. It was the program director from CCATS. "We are experiencing the same thing. Doesn't respond to any commands."

Nick was not surprised at the call as 4DT had become a thorn in the side of aviation. "We are going to do a complete shut down and see if that helps."

"We tried, it didn't work."

"The problem still existed after the restart?" Nick asked.

"We don't know. It wouldn't let us shut it down. When the engineers tried to shut down the programs for a restart, it locked them out of the computer."

"What? It's locking the system engineers out of the program also?" Nick asked. "What about a power shutdown?"

"Think about it, the power switching is all networked within the network. They tried to get into the power supply room and it has locked the doors, not allowing anyone in."

Nick was at wit's end. "Thanks. We will get on it here and see what happens. Maybe we better call headquarters."

"We already have. They are clued in on our situation. Do what you can and stand by for a conference call. If you're able to make a breakthrough on this thing, call us. We are hanging on by our teeth here, and the outcome looks grim."

An hour later, the phone rang again; this time it was headquarters. "Please standby for the administrator," the voice said.

Two minutes later, Bob introduced himself. "Ladies and gentlemen, what has happened this morning unfortunately is the worst-case scenario. We are not going to spend much time with niceties as there is much work to do. First let's quickly introduce ourselves so everyone knows who's here. Go ahead folks, quickly."

Nick jotted down the names as they were read off. Terry Lavern, secretary of transportation, Penny Hankins, secretary of homeland security, Scotty Morris, Atlantic City software manager, Sean O'Leary, O'Leary Consulting. Besides these mentioned were facility and program managers from all three centers and most of the major approach controls.

"As I said, we have experienced what we had hoped would never happen. A virus planted during the days of ERAMS installation has now taken over NextGen. Not only has it taken over, it has shut out every attempt at human interference. So far, all attempts at physically shutting down power have been met with a security system second to none.

Unfortunately, that security system is now our enemy. Most of you know Sean O'Leary from his days involved in the development of NextGen. He has been retained by the president to assist in recovering the airspace. Listen to what he has to say; he is our only hope. Go ahead, Sean."

"Greetings, managers. We have very little time to take back NextGen. The metamorphous is transpiring much more rapidly than previously expected. We have alerted all previous air traffic controllers in your area and, thanks to Homeland Security, have sent agents to get them. They should start arriving within thirty minutes. We are going to start with staffing each position with a controller and have the specialists monitor them, giving them technical advice.

Please do not argue with these controllers. They are cantankerous and will not take crap from anyone. We have engineers on their way to the centers, which will be looking for alternative ways to shut down 4DT. Once 4DT is shut down, our controllers will be able to manually control the airspace. That's all I have at this time."

Next, Bob explained a little more about the O'Leary contract and how to treat the influx of highly volatile controllers and ended the conference call.

Chapter 51

The middle-aged guard with an AK47 cradled in his arms approached the Lincoln Navigator as it pulled up to the secure gate leading into WCATS. "Sir, you can't get in!"

"These are the air traffic controllers we were ordered to deliver," explained the driver, irritated by the guard's lack of awareness as to who was in the car and the nature of the emergency transpiring within the walls of the center.

"I know who you are," the guard responded chewing on his gum. "I've worked here since this place opened. I've cleared these clowns through this gate more times than I care to count. Have to admit I miss all the controllers; they were more fun than the geeks coming in these days. We can't get the gate to go up. One of the guards went to get a facility engineer to help and found out the whole facility is locked down. Not letting anyone in or out. Heard the security computer malfunctioned. Someone said it is attached to the air traffic control program."

The driver looked back at the controllers with a nervous glance and then back at the guard who was digging a piece of paper out of his shirt pocket. "What is the plan?" he asks the guard.

The guard looked at the paper than back at the driver. "We received this from an unverified source a few minutes ago. All phone lines are shut down between all ATC facilities and the outside world."

"Let me guess! Computer controlled?" responded the driver.

"You guessed it! Anyhow, they got the word out via ham radio for all the controllers in our area to be taken to Ely airport. Just don't let this get out to the press. They have been calling every ten minutes trying to get information about what is going on down here. If it weren't so far from civilization, they would be swarming this place."

"This is ridiculous," Charlie complained as he fished out his phone. He dialed Sean's number only to hear, "All systems are busy at this time. Please try again later." He called O'Leary's home office only to hear the same thing. He called Carrie on her cell phone, no response. "It looks like all outside communications have been affected also," he told Jim. "We could be in for a long day."

The driver turned the car around and headed south to Yelland Field, a small municipal airport just north of Ely. Recently, two airlines had started regional jet service to Las Vegas and Salt Lake. It had taken three years to get the runway lengthened and a control tower installed, even with the pressure of the FAA coming into town. The new GPS approaches with precision vertical navigation had made this airport a showcase for technology.

"What are we doing now?" Charlie quizzed as they pulled into the airport and headed for the ramp.

"Can't really tell you," the driver replied as they pulled up to a hanger with the door partly open. A sign on the door stated, "Fly History, WWII Aircraft Restorations."

An elderly man was sliding open the hanger door revealing an old DC-3 with army markings. "Greetings!" he yelled over the noise of a jet being run up on the ramp. "The rest are in the lounge area just through that door."

Charlie and Jim had already grabbed their bags and were headed through the door, needing some serious answers. This thing was getting stranger by the minute, and they were ready to take control as soon as they could assess the situation.

In front of the crowded room, a smartly dressed gentleman in a dark blue pinstriped suit was deep in conversation with a small group of pilots. The old leather jackets they wore were adorned with patches from another era. They looked like they had just arrived from the European Theater of WWII.

He grabbed a bottle of water from the table in the back and took a seat in the last row next to Jim. Looking around, he recognized most of the controllers in the room. They had all gone on strike in opposition to 4DT. After being fired, they had revealed to the media of the flaws within the system. He noticed a couple of the guys the guards had escorted to the gate when they lost their temper back in 2021 during the first NextGen failure. Charlie caught Rich's eye from across the room and motioned for him to join them.

"What have you heard, Rich?" Charlie asked as the grizzly old Philadelphia Steelers fan took a seat next to his former comrades.

"Not a darn thing," Rich replied. "The goons picked me up ten minutes ago, and they haven't said a thing. I keep hearing something about flying below the radar. Guess the suits haven't got it figured out, we don't use radar anymore."

"I heard the radar is still turning," Jim interjected, "used by the military for overseas training."

"Does anyone really know what happened?" one of the old Salt Lake Center controllers asked. "Heard rumors it could be solar flares. Did anyone ever even research what one of those could do to this thing? Maybe that's what happened."

"I don't think so," was all Charlie could get out of his mouth. One of the suits up front interrupted the conversation, bringing order to the room.

"Ladies and gentlemen, my name is Officer Matthew Franklin with the Department of Homeland Security. The deputy chief of WCATS contacted us this morning at ten thirty-five with some very disturbing news. I expect most of you will understand the severity even more than I do. At seven thirty a.m., prior to the morning rush, there was an apparent systems failure. At first there were the normal miscalculations with the system, which were easily handled by TCAS. Once the software engineers investigated the problem, the whole system started getting shaky. At this point, they decided to go to backup. That is when things started to fall apart." He paused when the murmuring in the room became disruptive.

"We told those idiots it was a disaster waiting to happen," explained a disgruntled old goat who had transferred down from Oakland.

"Excuse me," Matthew growled, "what's your name?"

"Don't matter, can't fire me again. Don't work for you guys anymore. The name is Mike Johnson. I spent almost thirty years separating airplanes and all I got for it was a pink slip and my own psychotherapist."

"Well, Mr. Johnson, nobody is firing you, and we have all read the newspapers and congressional reports on how you older controllers felt about NextGen, but as you know, technology has to move forward, and that it did. Even though it left you in the dust, it now seems to need you. We have a problem here that sitting around arguing and pointing fingers will not help. We have requested your services today, not because you were on the cutting edge of technology, but because of the uncanny ability you had at controlling airplanes. You guys were the best, but unfortunately you were not able to give up that control to a computer. Now, let's get back to the problem."

"At nine thirty this morning, NextGen took over the system when software engineers attempted to shut down 4DT. How this happened, we don't know. What we do know is that it is connected to the security system, at not only this facility, but also the entire FAA nationwide. We are getting a continuous stream of data coming out of the system, but it is not responding to input from any human source. When engineers tried shutting down power to the mainframes, the system considered it a threat and locked down the facilities. Now no one can get in or out. Once the calls went out to ITT for assistance, NextGen took these calls as hostile actions and shut down the phone systems. Our only contact with the inside is via a portable ham radio one of the SE folks was storing in the basement for emergencies."

The controllers sat in silence. As Charlie looked around the room, he could see the fear in the faces of the thirty controllers who had been brought to this hanger. They were perplexed as to why they were there instead of the geeks that monitored aircraft in today's world.

"What about the specialists off duty? Why not use them?" someone in the front asked.

"Good question," responded Matthew, "one I can answer. The specialists know the new system. They can describe it inside and out, how it works and what it should look like. But when it comes to controlling airplanes outside the box and processing information on the run, you can forget about it, they are at a loss. That is why you people are here."

327

Chapter 52

Charlie had been patiently waiting for things to settle down before he raised his hand. Matthew Franklin acknowledged Charlie with a gentle rebuke. "We aren't ready to field questions, sir, what do you want?"

Charlie stood up. "I'm Charlie Beckler, a consultant with O'Leary Aviation Consultants. We have been planning for this scenario. Has anyone been able to get in contact with Washington?"

Matthew's mouth dropped, "I'm sorry, Mr. Beckler, I did not recognize you. I wasn't told you'd be here. Get your tail up here. You should be giving this briefing."

Charlie walked to the front of the room and shook hands with the Homeland Security officer. Matthew continued, "We have been receiving orders from Washington via an old analog fax machine. Thank goodness for garage sale items. That is how we got the go ahead on the ATC Armageddon plan. Am I to assume you are aware of that plan?"

Charlie smiled at the stuff-shirted government stereotype and answered calmly, "Sir, not only do I know it, I wrote it. Loosen up a bit and have a seat. There are things to do."

Looking around the room at the now-silent air traffic controllers, Charlie smiled. "Friends, your day has come. The piece of crap that took away our jobs has now taken over our airspace. Not only did it take away our airspace, it has now taken our customers hostage. One thing it cannot take away is our dignity. Today, we are going to return this airspace back to the rightful owners. The recovery plan is simple. We disconnect from the future and embrace the past. How? We destroy what brought us here and dust off the old."

By now the question marks in the eyes of the thirty controllers were very evident. "As I said, we at O'Leary Aviation Consultants have been expecting this meltdown for some time and put contingencies in place. That is why we are here. Now, if you noticed outside on your way in, there was an old DC-3 being pulled from the hanger. Those of you from Seattle will be leaving on the Gooney bird in a few minutes. I suppose you think a G5 would be better, but let's think about it. What does a G5 have that a Gooney Bird doesn't?"

There were a lot of shrugs when finally someone hollered, "A computer!"

"That's right! We have to revert back to the past prior to the days of bits and bytes. We knew if we could get some WWII aircraft, we would not be subject to the virus infecting the high tech aircraft of today. Sorry, no first class on this flight."

"That's good for Seattle, but what about the other four facilities?" Jim asked.

"Don't get antsy!" Charlie patiently replied, looking at Matthew with raised eyebrows, "The Commemorative Air Force on their way?"

Matthew nodded and grinned, "Yes, sir, there are two B-25s and three B-27s coming in from an air show in Phoenix. They should be here in about fifteen minutes."

Charlie thanked the officer and turned back to his friends. "You guys have worked them, now you get to ride 'em. Let me tell you about the recovery plan."

Ten minutes later, as Charlie was finishing, the meeting was interrupted by the thunderous sound of an aircraft passing over the field. "It sounds like our ride is doing a flyby," Charlie commented as the rumble settled down. "Gotta love flying cowboys. If NextGen don't kill us, these guys will."

"How old are these aircraft?" someone asked. Charlie, acting like he was counting fingers and toes, said, "Let's see, this is 2025 and they were built in 1945- that would be about 80 years. Man! Can we say metal fatigue?"

"We taking your car or mine?" someone hollered before the meeting was brought back to order. One of the Seattle controllers was questioning Matthew about the consequences of the recovery plan.

"My job is to protect the homeland," Matthew was explaining, "I don't know all the ins and outs about the job you guys did. What I do know is that the FBI gave us your names as the best that ever controlled the skies before NextGen and, looking at you, I wonder where they got that information. So, considering you somehow got the title, you will have to think on your feet and help with the execution of this plan. We will be working it from here. Just remember not to turn on any computers until you hear from us. There will be a member from the DHS waiting for you to assist with communications. Okay, it's time to go. The pilots will direct you to your aircraft. Good luck, people!"

Turning onto a left downwind for runway one eight, Billy was no more than two hundred feet above the deck. Turning to his copilot, he hollered, "You wet yourself yet, Earl?"

Earl Hartley smiled back at his old friend. "I haven't flown this low since I gave up crop dusting."

Billy turned final as Earl got the gear down. Just two hours earlier, they had been sitting in a briefing room discussing the upcoming air show when the call had come in from Texas. An aide had handed him a paper that read, "ATC Armageddon – ELY" The crews had been briefed and knew their mission. Fly as low as possible and get to Ely, Nevada as soon as possible. Ten minutes after receiving the message, they departed runway 3 right, staying under three hundred feet headed north.

Flying low over the Arizona badlands, they continued a slow climb reaching the western end of the Grand Canyon. Billy broke as many of the Federal Aviation Rules as he could; he even descended below the canyon rim. They crossed the Utah state line just west of St. George. They flew up canyons and down valleys. Finally after two hours of hair-raising aviation, they rounded the Schell Creek mountain range, and the Ely airport came into view.

By the time the controllers made it to the ramp, all five historic aircraft had landed and were not quiet about their entrance onto a crowded ramp. The first to board were those heading for Seattle. Six old saggy-eyed controllers who were the best in the business years ago now became the hope of the Northwest. The old DC-3 Gooney Bird proudly took to the air and turned towards Seattle. Slowly it disappeared heading up the valley northwest of the airport.

Charlie, Jim, Rich, and two others crawled into the belly of Billy and Earl's bomber. Before they shut the door, Matthew handed Charlie a folder. "These just came though from Washington." he hollered over the roar of radial engines coming to life.

Strapping in, Charlie sat back and opened the folder to be faced with large print 'Operation ATC Armageddon.' Charlie had to ask himself why in the world he insisted on using that name as he started reading.

"Charlie, the majority of domestic aircraft have landed. The crews became aware of the precarious situation early on and used the hardwired disconnect to disable the autopilot. That is the good news. The bad news is we still have ninety-two international flights coming in from overseas. These flights have not been equipped with the disconnect switch mandatory on domestic carriers. We have yet to discover what the impact will be to these aircraft. We will fax further information to Palmdale. Be careful," It was signed "Sean." Charlie read back over the cover sheet. Ninety-two jumbo jets, that's still a lot of metal up there.

That's when it hit him, and a lump came to his throat. This was the day Carrie and Mitzy are flying back from Europe. Charlie quickly scrolled down through his text messages until he came across the one Carrie had sent him two days ago. "We will be on Air France flight 75 from Paris arriving LAX 6 p.m." They were still five hours out. They would be entering U.S. airspace within a couple of hours. Suddenly, the mission took on new meaning. Charlie scribbled a note and handed it to Jim. Jim's eyes showed he understood. He leaned over and gave his buddy a quick hug of confidence that all would work out.

The Mitchell bomber headed south, climbing over the mountains and dropping down into a valley intercepting Highway 318. They followed it south until they came to State Route 93 and followed it to Las Vegas. The plan had been to go around McCarron in order not to get picked up on the Nellis radar. Twenty miles north of Las Vegas, Earl asked about the turn to the west.

"Not going to be a turn. It's time to go downtown," Billy answered, drawing out the downtown.

"Billy, what the heck are you talking about? We are to stay clear of all populated areas. It's no time to go rogue."

Billy smiled over at his old buddy. "This is the only time on God's green earth I can get by with this, and I don't plan on missing it. Get your camera out."

At three hundred feet Billy took a left off of Interstate 15 and lined up over Las Vegas Boulevard. At 260 knots the eighty-year-old bomber flew down the Las Vegas Strip. Earl was looking up at the tops of the casinos flashing by as the poor controllers no longer had any concern about NextGen. These boys were sucking the cushions out of their seats.

339

"Hang on!" Billy hollered back to the five scared-stiff controllers. As they screamed over the intersection of Tropicana and Las Vegas Boulevard, he pulled back on the yoke and performed a beautiful barrel roll to the right, leveling off just above Interstate 15.

Once Charlie could breathe again, he looked over at Jim, whose white knuckles looked like they would never release the arm rest and croaked, "And they say controllers are crazy!"

"We have company," Billy told Earl and pointed to their two o'clock position.

"What is it?" Earl scanned the sky in the direction Billy had pointed. What looked like a small aircraft was closing in on their position.

"It looks like a drone," Earl said as he pulled his binoculars out of his weathered flight bag and adjusted the focus. "It's a Predator, and I think it's stalking us."

"What makes you think that, Earl?"

"Well, it's paralleling our course at our speed and altitude. That is no coincidence."

"You're right. They don't fly those things at three hundred feet. You know somewhere down there they are watching us."

"Captain, it's armed, it just lowered its missiles."

Billy was looking at it now and scowled, "This is not good. I wonder how they found us?"

"Well, first of all, that trip down the strip wasn't supposed to be part of the air show," Earl huffed. "What you going to do now?"

Billy pushed the throttles forward but the Predator had no problem keeping up. "I thought those things had a top cruise of 140 knots. If we can't out run it, let's shoot it down."

Earl looked over at his captain over the top of his aviator glasses. "Now you are crazy. We never even showed the boys the guns."

Billy turned around and motioned for Charlie to come up front.

"Yeah, I see the Predator and I had fifty caliber training in the Navy. I saw the guns; do you guys actually have ammo?"

"Twenty boxes in the back. How about the others, do any of them know how to shoot?"

"Rich was a weapons officer for a while, I'm sure he can handle it. That thing can kill us from two miles away. How're you going to get us close enough to hit it?"

Billy chuckled, "You get ready. I will bring the bird in for the kill."

Charlie quickly explained their dilemma to Rich who headed for the tail.

Strapping on the old cloth helmet, he plugged the headset into the antiquated jack. Clicking the transmit button, he found himself talking to Captain Soother.

"Tail gunner is armed and ready," Rich said in the best macho voice he could come up with. In reality, he was about to throw up. In the turret above the wings, Charlie had also strapped in and acknowledged his guns were ready.

"Okay, gentlemen, we will need to test the guns before we engage. Only a short burst, and then be ready to fight. I'm sure the Predator will respond." Two "Roger, Captain" replies came back through the intercom.

"Okay now!" Billy commanded. Immediately, he heard the guns go off in the rear as the plane gave a light shudder. He made a hard right turn heading right at the Predator.

Meanwhile on the Predator, the computer system was humming. It had terminated contact with its human source thirty minutes earlier when a command to land had been contrary to its original program. Receiving an updated command from WCATS' 4DT program, it processed the data and found it to be more realistic to its mission. It turned to a heading of 180 and picked up its speed to top cruise. Within fifteen minutes the threat came within range of the Predator's sensors. It could easily terminate the threat at that moment and locked onto the aging aircraft. Not having yet received the command from the rogue program to fire, it made the decision to monitor the situation until it concluded a threat was imminent.

Taking up a position a mile off the right wing of the aircraft, it continued to scan ADS-B for the aircraft's identification. It checked its armament and lowered its two AIM-92 Stinger missiles. Five minutes after taking up station, the sensors picked up sounds of gunfire. In micro seconds the data base recognized the gunfire as that of a fifty caliber machine gun. It then picked up a deviation in the flight path of the aircraft as the distance between the two quickly closed. Its status changed from monitor to defense.

Charlie almost lost his lunch on the two G turns as the world around the turret spun in circles. The slick, bug-looking Predator entered his gun sites.

Hearing Rich yell, "Yee haw, take this!" Charlie knew Rich was ready to splash the unmanned aircraft as well. The exhilaration of the moment was overwhelming. The antique guns still had what it took. As the Predator tried to make an evasive maneuver, the fiberglass shattered by the fifty-caliber shells disintegrated, and the fuel erupted into a ball of fire.

"That was easy," Rich bragged as he started back down the fuselage.

"Not so fast," he heard Billy inform over the intercom. "We may have more company."
Sliding back into position, Rich quickly pulled on his helmet and plugged in his headset. "What is it, Captain?"

"Don't know for sure, but we finally got through to Homeland Security on the Guard frequency, and they said we have additional unmanned aircraft roaming the skies near here. I'm just assuming if they somehow get wind of what we did to their little brother, they may get upset."

"You trying to tell me they are thinking now?" Rich asked.

Charlie answered for the pilot. "Not only are they thinking, but they are taking their orders from 4DT. Once we terminated the Predator, 4DT became aware of us as a threat and will do what it is programmed to do and terminate us. I suggest we stay at stations all the way to Palmdale. How did they get the radio working, Captain?"

"Thanks for the education, Charlie. My understanding is the emergency frequencies were left out of the data base. With data link taking over communications, they were not needed anymore. Fortunately, old aircraft like these still had 'em."

"Guys, we just got a message from the military. It seems they had a total of seven Predators in the air when this went down. We shot down a lone one operating here in the south complex, but the other six obviously got the word and are heading our way. Last reported sighting was sixty miles south of Independence, California heading southeast at about three hundred AGL." Billy's voice sounded somewhere between that of a scared hillbilly and a teenage pilot flying the English Channel eighty years earlier.

"Can we make Palmdale before they get us?" Charlie asked.

"Don't think so, but the good news is that these are not armed with missiles," Billy replied. "The bad news is that they are armed with guns."

"Guns," echoed the two new gunners in back.

"That's right, gentlemen. The Predator was undergoing tests for a new role as surface attack aircraft. That's why there were six of 'em, and now they are looking for revenge. Keep your eyes peeled and let's get a gunner in the nose."

Charlie jumped down out of the turret and grabbed Jim. "Just aim and shoot," he told his friend, showing him how to operate the turret.

Grabbing a box of ammo he slid down into the gunner's position in the nose of the rumbling aircraft. "How much more can this thing take?" he asked Billy once he got the headset on and the ammo loaded.

"Don't rightly know, nose gunner, but you might want to keep your eyes on the horizon. If you spend too much time looking at the ground, it's going to freak you out."

"One o'clock coming in high!" Jim hollered from the turret. Six buggy-looking Predators with guns blazing were diving at the old bomber. Billy turned hard left just before being peppered with bullets.

"How bad we hit?" Earl looked back at his passengers who looked like they had just wet their pants.

"Just a few hits here in the tail," Rich responded, "I'm okay, but the Predators are turning back this way."

The right engine started smoking. "I'm feathering number two, Earl. Trim the rudder."

"Roger, Captain. Can we keep this thing airborne on one?"

"You bet, but I don't know what we're going to do with the Predators. Have everyone prepare to ditch if they hit us again. It would be better to land in the desert than get shot down."

"Captain, we have more problems, additional aircraft coming in from eight o'clock high," Jim advised.

"What type are they, and how many?" Billy was now starting to set up the aircraft for ditching.

"It looks like... I don't believe it! You got friends out here, Captain?" Billy asked.

"Mitchell bomber, Mitchell bomber, request you make a right turn heading two-eight-zero and leave the fighting up to us."

Billy recognized the Texan drawl as that of his buddy, Jeff Atwater. "You guys are just in time, Mustang. You bring any help?"

"Yep! All six of us, and we are looking for some game. Seen anything worth shooting around these parts?"

Rich watched in fascination as the old P-51 Mustangs, the two Hellcats, and the P-38 Lighting made heyday of the Predators. Within seconds, all six Predators were scattered throughout the Mojave Desert. Turning back direct Palmdale, the old bomber with its three gunners still solidly attached to their seats was joined by six fighters of the same era. "If you don't mind, Billy, we'll fly shotgun for you. We heard you needed some help getting your boys to Palmdale."

Billy growled, "We would have got 'em, but thanks for your help, boys. And we'd love the company."

Chapter 53

Twenty minutes later, the old Mitchell bomber made a smooth landing on runway two two at Palmdale regional airport. As soon as the propellers stopped spinning, the controllers hurried out of the aircraft and into a waiting van. The white government van drove the five controllers across the old airfield to the mothballed Los Angeles Air Traffic Control Center.

It had been thirteen years since Charlie helped close this place, and it didn't look any worse for the wear. The trees surrounding the center had shed their leaves for the winter, and the grass was a dull green. The place had the resemblance of a high-security prison, with at least a hundred troops lining the perimeter. "This is just like the government," Charlie commented as a guard checked their identification at the gate.

"A computer virus takes out the National Airspace and they send out the National Guard," Jim laughed. "Remember, this is our castle, and these are our guards. Welcome home, Charlie."

The van came to a stop in the circle on the west side of the center, close to the front doors. Charlie remembered the days when they had been allowed to park here. After 9/11, all vehicles were moved away from the building for security. The five controllers, now in their late forties, looked up at the place where their careers had begun. So many hours of training that had caused so much anxiety in their lives. So many years spent building the strange friendships that only existed within these walls—walls where they had spent more of their waking hours with each other than with their families.

One of the guards opened the glass door leading into the lobby. The stained glass window still decorated the lobby, along with some old magazines and a board with the names of the managers who had long ago retired. Up the stairs in the control room, they found a group of people at the operation manager's desk.

"Welcome to your old home, gentlemen." A tall chiseled-faced man introduced himself as Neil Moffitt from Homeland Security. "You will be setting up shop in area C. Airway Facilities has assured us that they will be ready in twenty minutes for the system start-up."

Charlie looked around for someone he knew, but he recognized no one. "Do we have direct contact with Washington?"

"Yes, we found a hardwired phone in the basement to open a line with headquarters."

"Good," Charlie replied, "we'll use the line in the area to synchronize the takeover time."

Over the North Atlantic

Aboard Air France Flight 75, Captain Renee DuPont and her first officer, Andre Lafevre, were sitting back relaxed, watching the miles tick by. The ADS-B monitor's range was extended out to its maximum as was customary on the overwater operations. They could see a number of their competition moving west along the same track. Andre had always enjoyed this part of the flight. He would scroll through the aircraft they were tracking to see where each one was heading. He loved seeing such places as Miami, Dallas, or New Orleans, different destinations he hoped to someday visit. He even found one heading for Hawaii. That would be a great place to take his young wife and their two toddlers.

These flights back and forth between Paris and Los Angeles were getting old. Maybe soon he would get a new route. He was watching a British Airways flight from London on its way to JFK when he noticed the destination change. "Look at this, Renee, they just changed their destination, JFK to some fix. That's strange."

Renee looked up from the magazine she had been thumbing through. "What's strange about a destination change? It happens all the time."

"Maybe, but not to a lat/long fix. I wonder where it's going." He pulled an old WAC chart out of his bag and started looking for the fix.

He now had Renee's attention and she was watching the display when another aircraft changed its destination. "Check this out, we have another one." As quickly as she spoke, three other aircraft changed their destinations. "This is definitely not normal."

Renee started typing out an enquiry message to the Oceanic area, located at ECATS, when the chime rang. She looked over at the data link display, which showed an incoming clearance. She hit the read button, and a new route came up showing a lat/long as their new destination. "Look here, they want us to change destinations. We can't do that." She hit the reject button, and the screen scrolled through some computer code. An unable message showed on the screen. The flight management display scrolled the same style of code before settling on the new destination. "Something is not right," Renee said with a puzzled expression. "Find out where this thing is asking us to go."

Andre had his ruler out and was drawing on his map. Two minutes later he looked as if he had seen a ghost. "There is no airport at this fix. It's a big lake southeast of Las Vegas."

White House Situation Room

"Just how am I going to explain this to the American people?" President Banister yelled at Terry Laverne.

The Secretary of Transportation was taken aback by the outburst of his old friend. "What I'm telling you is we have no idea how to stop it. We have ninety-two jumbo jets out there with dibs on ninety-two different high-impact targets. It's like we have ninety-two missiles heading our way with no way to stop them."

The President was pacing the floor again. Pacing had become a habit with so much turmoil going on. Turning to his secretary of defense, he asked, "What if we shoot them out of the sky? We do have the weapons to accomplish that, right?"

Secretary Hugh Riss gave his boss a sick smile. "We have the weapons, but they're not usable."

"Not usable? Why not?" The President was fuming.

"Mr. President, the virus has infected Homeland Security which controls our anti-aircraft batteries. We have engineers working on the fix, but this could take time."

"So, let's get this right. We have ninety-two aircraft heading towards our shores, all aimed at taking out our infrastructure, our national defense is inoperative, and you guys have no idea how to stop this virus-induced Armageddon? Does anyone have even a hint of a plan to reduce the impact?"

Bob Burkhammer sheepishly looked out above his glasses. "O'Leary's plan is in place if you're interested."

The President shook his head. "This is absurd. We have to go to the crazy Irishman for a plan to save the country. Where is he?"

"He's over at Headquarters working with our contingency team."

"Get him over here now! This crap has gone too far." the president fumed.

Los Angeles Air Route Traffic Control Center

Dust was all over the place as the controllers surveyed their old, yet familiar, scopes. First of all, we need to clean these things," Charlie told the guys.

"No more cobwebs than in your head, Charlie," Rich laughed. "Sure good to be back. When are we taking over the airspace? I'm ready to control some airplanes."

"That is up to Washington. We go operational when they give us the go-ahead." Charlie's thoughts were on his family aboard Air France Flight 75. He wondered where they were and prayed just maybe that aircraft had the cutoff switch. Even if it didn't, they could still make it here safely. After all it was only ninety-two airplanes and they weren't all heading for LAX. The guys got busy with old brooms and rags wiping down the twenty-five year old scopes and the surrounding areas. A technician was busy hardwiring an old analog phone to a speaker.

Suddenly, voices started coming out of the speaker, and Charlie instantly recognized Sean's Irish accent asking for someone to answer.

"Sean, this is Charlie. As you can tell, we made it to ZLA, where are you?"

"We are at FAA headquarters working out a plan. Stand by for the takeover; it may take about an hour to get this all ready to go. I have to head over to the White House for a briefing. Once I know the takeover time, I'll be back on line."

"Good, we'll be ready. I'll have some stories for you when this is all over."

"I bet you do, anxious to hear them. Oh! And, Charlie, the CATS facilities are all locked down no one can get out, and we haven't come to a conclusion on how to shut them down. Got any ideas?"

"Remember the antique bomber scenario during contingency planning?" Charlie was referring to using the old bombers to destroy the centers.

"I forgot about that. We'll get right on it." Sean was gone, and the guys went back to prepping the area for an air traffic control resurrection.

White House Situation Room

"We can do it in two hours," Secretary Riss advised the president and the rest of the group when he got off the phone.

"Okay, it's five minutes before five now. Let's have this go down at eight thirty. That'll give the eleven o'clock news plenty to talk about." The president was obviously perturbed. "Are you sure this plan will work, Mr. O'Leary?"

Sean was tired of defending their attempt to save this soon to become known as "Aviation Armageddon." "We have no way of knowing until it happens, but what I do know is you're sacrificing three facilities and eleven hundred lives to save twenty-five thousand airline passengers, thousands of United States citizens on the ground, and massive damage to our infrastructure. While you, Mr. President, are the one ultimately responsible for the welfare of our country, we all share the burden to insure that happens. Those federal employees trapped in those three Centers will be making the ultimate sacrifice to save the nation."

Silence fell across the room as those in attendance realized what Sean had just said. He had brought to light the fact that entire groups of air traffic specialists had been given a death sentence.

Bombing mission

351

Earl looked over at his Captain. They had just taken off from Palmdale flying east and were slowly climbing above Lake Arrowhead when the call came. "Mitchell bomber, change your destination to Edwards AFB."

Billy keyed up responding with a simple "Wilco" and made a left turn towards the dry lake bed some sixty-five miles to the northwest.

"What do you think this is all about?" Earl asked.

"At some point in your life, you just follow instructions, Earl. This is one of those times. I have been shot at one too many times today, so I think I'll just follow orders for awhile."

Earl didn't reply. He, too, had experienced the fear of being the target. They were on short final for runway two four at Edwards when he called "Gear down" and broke the silence.

A follow-me truck met them as they taxied off the runway. It led them to a bunker at the southwest edge of the complex. Shutting down the engines, they saw two trucks approach the aircraft pulling trailers with bombs.

"I think we have another mission, Earl," Billy smiled at his wide-eyed copilot. "I wonder where these things are going."

A fit older gentleman met them as they opened up the door. "Welcome to Edwards, gentlemen. My name is Scott Scholl, and I will be you're bombardier today."

"Our what?" Billy asked.

"I guess you haven't heard. We have a bombing run to make. They called me ten minutes ago. I was over at the officer's club for a few drinks when this lieutenant comes rushing in looking for me. I thought I was in trouble until he explained."

The sound of machinery working underneath the aircraft was a little unnerving to the flight crew, but Billy asked Scott to continue. "Well, obviously I was never in World War II, but I have dropped bombs from these things in air shows."

"That's comforting," Billy responded, "we have a drunken bombardier. Now what are we going to bomb?"

352

A well-dressed officer stuck his head in the plane. "Gentlemen, step out here. We need to discuss your mission."

The lieutenant took them to a van which sat running next to the plane. Billy nervously looked back at the technicians cranking the four bombs up into the belly of his aircraft.

"They know what they're doing," explained the lieutenant. They are well trained at handling explosives."

That comment did nothing to ease his apprehension, but Billy followed the others into the large van.

"Afternoon, gentlemen," an older Air Force general looked up from the map he was hunkering over. "You have been ordered to carry out a dangerous mission, but it is necessary."

"Where are we delivering these bombs?" Billy asked.

"That would be Ely, Nevada."

"We were just there. You want us to take these to the airport in Ely?"

General Paul Deering pointed down at the map. "Your target is the Western Center for Air Traffic Services."

"You want us to bomb a government facility? Are there people in there?" asked Billy incredulously.

"Yes, Captain, we want you to level this facility. If the occupants of the building are unable to evacuate..." he paused, "I'm sorry. These are the casualties of war."

Billy and Earl looked at each other with doubt on their faces. "Sir, I do not doubt your position, and I know there has been some sort of hostile takeover, but we thought it was just a computer virus. Why do we have to bomb the place? But don't get me wrong, I am up to the challenge."

The general looked more than a little relieved he wasn't going to have a fight on his hands with these flyboys. "The security system has total control over the facility and will not let anyone or anything into the facility to shut it down. The system engineers have even cut the electrical lines going into the

353

Center. When that happened, the generators started up and are providing back up power."

"Why don't you guys take some tanks up there and blow up the generator building?"

"We tried that using an old M4 Sherman tank from the Nevada National Guard. It didn't work. One of the twenty-seven batteries hidden around that placed took it out when it was still a quarter of a mile away."

"Dang, General, and you want us to fly this thing into that hornets' nest?"

"Not only fly into the hornets' nest, but destroy it. Your squadron is at Indian Springs refueling and will join up with you about twenty minutes after your departure. Your route of flight will take you through Dreamland. As far as we know, there are no aircraft or weapons activated along your route of flight. Even so, keep your eyes open. We would hate to have you shot down before you reach your target."

"Will those batteries you're talking about be a factor?" Billy asked.

"Most likely they will. Make sure you come in as low as you can and max speed. Once the sensors pick you up, all hell will break loose, and you will most likely experience anti-aircraft fire along with surface-to-air missiles."

Looking over at Earl, Billy could tell this was going to be one hard sell. "Come on, give us a bone. We need some reason why we should risk this mission. What's the incentive?" The general looked tired and somewhat irritated by the request. "How about saving twenty-five thousand airline passengers' lives?" he asked, "and a whole lot of collateral damage when ninety-two airplanes crash? Just go do it and be diligent."

Inside WCATS

The monitors were busy scrolling through lines of computer code. As much as he tried, Tyrone could not make heads or tails of what it was doing. One thing he knew for sure was that this was not what the program architects had planned. Most of the specialists had joined the managers in the conference room where they were waiting for information from the outside. He was going back through his notes trying to find an answer to the virus. He hadn't heard Nick Harton come up behind him.

"Give it up, Tyrone, they're going to bomb this place."

Spinning in his chair, Tyrone's expression said it all. "How long do we have?" he asked.

"We have ninety minutes to figure out how to get out of here."

"You have been here for a long time. Is there a way out?" Tyrone questioned his boss.

"None that I'm aware of. The airways facilities people are going over blueprints searching for some hole in the structure where we can cut through. Time is running out."

"Well, I for one am not giving up!" Tyrone said defiantly. "I will work on this thing until they blow it up. Are there any safe rooms in the basement?"

"Not any unlocked ones."

"The basement should still be the safest place when we get the crap blown out of us," Tyrone replied as he turned back to his typing.

In the conference room, one of the managers from airway facilities was informing the rest of the group the latest information on their demise. "Unfortunately, the walls that were built to keep terrorists out are the same walls keeping us in. We are working at removing the door to the boiler room which is, in our opinion, the safest place to be."

"What about taking the door off the computer room and shutting off the computer?" someone frustratingly asked.

"We can't do that. The pens are on the inside. We only have about an hour left, so unless there are any other ideas, let's get to the basement and stuff as many as possible into the boiler

355

room. The rest of you will have to find any place you can to protect yourselves. We do not know the intensity of the blast, but you can be assured they intend to level this place."

One by one, the specialists filed out of the conference room and down the two flights of stairs to the basement.

Nick Harton knew controllers would have never have given up so easily. These people are like sheep being led to the slaughter. Controllers would be digging at the walls with their fingernails until they died.

Arriving in the basement, they found two of the airway facilities personnel had just finished removing the door to the furnace room. Spilling into the room, the specialists and managers started crowding in.

"Don't be so pushy," someone yelled at the front of the line.

"Will this place save us?" someone else asked.

They quickly filled the room and shut the door. Everyone else kind of wandered around the rest of the basement looking for a place to die, hoping for the best.

Air France Flight 75

For the last two hours, Renee and Andre had been looking for some way to disconnect the data link and take back control of their aircraft. They weren't too concerned yet since they were still hundreds of miles from their new destination. Still, it bothered them that something else was telling them where they would be landing. Nothing they did seemed to work. Trying to send messages to the company resulted in messages returned undelivered.

Meanwhile in seat 23A and 23B, Carrie and Mitzy were busy reading magazines and chatting about Mitzy's upcoming wedding. Mitzy and Jason had met in college and decided to get married in April at the Beckler's church in Ely. This trip was a last-minute mother and daughter fling before they became

356

too busy with preparations for the spring wedding. Jason was from Atlanta and the couple had decided they would be living east of the city within a short drive of Mitzy's aging grandparents.

"We're only two hours from L.A.," Mitzy noticed as she looked at her watch. "I'm anxious to show Dad our pictures." They continued small talk about all the good times they had experienced over the last two weeks.

White House Situation Room

"What's the latest word?" President Banister asked as Secretary Riss got off the phone.

"We have all the controllers in place, and the old Centers are ready for the takeover. No one in the CATS facilities has gotten out, but we did hear WCATS personnel have all assembled in the basement trying to find a safe place from the blast."

"Will it work?" James Banister asked.

"Probably not, we are blasting them with two fifteen-hundred-pound bombs. If that doesn't take out the system, we will hit them with two more."

"Where are the bombers?"

Secretary Riss looked at a sheet of paper in front of him. "East coast has two bombers, a B-24 Liberator and a B-27 Marauder from Atlanta, which will be on station in time. We don't know how the Marauder will do because it's a high-altitude bomber. CCATS is in the sights of two B-28s from Dallas. They shouldn't have any trouble with that facility. As far as the West Coast, there are two different planes. One from Salt Lake is a B-24 Liberator and in route from Palmdale is a B-25 Mitchell. All aircraft will commence their attack at 2030 East Coast time."

President Banister had been through a lot, but this was the worst. Attacking his own country was more than any president should have to do. "What about the international flights?"

"The first will arrive at its rerouted destination at 2035 East Coast time. That gives us a five minute window." Riss replied. "If we could have gotten the bombers on target earlier, we wouldn't be sweating this narrow window."

The President shook his head and complained, "That is too close. We can only hope the pilots are on their toes when this thing gets terminated. What is the first target to get hit?"

"That would be the Hancock Building in Boston. It would be the first if the plan fails. It would be hit with Speed Bird flight 23 from London."

"Evacuate the building; we can't take any chances."

"What about the others?" This time secretary of homeland security, Penny Hankins spoke up. "We have the complete list here, Mr. President. It appears the program was planned for all impacts to happen within ten minutes. How anyone could build such a virus twenty years prior to the actual date of its activation is beyond me."

"Evacuate all buildings within a mile of all targeted locations," the president continued. "I understand it's a big undertaking, but let's do what we can to minimize casualties."

"Mr. President, you are aware that the White House is on the list along with the downtown of almost every major city?" Penny responded. "Yes, I understand the immensity of the job, but your people can handle it. We will transfer up to Camp David until this is through."

Los Angeles Center

Sean immediately got in touch with Charlie. "Charlie, I'm back. In theory the centers will be going off-line at 1730 West Coast time. Are you ready for a cold start?"

"Ready as we'll ever be," Charlie replied. "How are you going to get the centers shut down? Did you find a way in?"

"Your buddy, Billy Soother, is taking out WCATS. Four other bombers are slated for the other two centers."

"What do you mean, Sean?"

"You wrote it, Charlie, it's the Armageddon plan. The bombers are on their way now with four fifteen-hundred pound armor-piercing bombs."

"What about the specialists inside?"

Sean already despised the plan, and it was evident in his elevated response. "Charlie, this is a nightmare, but I know you understand the need of sacrificing the few for the many. As you are well aware, if we don't take out the system, all of the passengers on those ninety-two flights will die."

Charlie sat there quietly absorbing the reality of the situation he was experiencing.

"Are you still there, Charlie?" Sean asked.

"I'm scared, Sean. Carrie and Mitzy are on Air France flight 75. They're somewhere over the Midwest now."

"Sorry, buddy, that gives us all the more reason to make this plan work."

"I understand that, Boss. What bothers me is my selfishness in wanting my family to live while sacrificing those trapped in the centers."

"The good news, Charlie, is that it was not a decision you had to make. Take a walk and clean the cobwebs out of your brain. Be ready in forty-five minutes."

"What about the targeted impact areas? Have they been warned?"

"The president gave the order to evacuate everyone within a mile. My understanding is that it is moving forward rapidly. There has been some panic in the more populated areas."

"Thanks, Sean, I may do that. Can you tell me where Air France 75 has been redirected?"

"It looks like Hoover Dam. Its estimated impact time is fifty minutes from now."

"Five minutes to spare. That's running it close, Boss."

Mitchell bomber

"Mitchell bomber, Mitchell bomber, say position," Jeff Atwater called on the Guard frequency.

Billy keyed up his transmitter and answered, "Mitchell bomber to Mustang, we are just now flying over a dry lake bed with circles in it. Some kind of strange secret stuff, I'm sure."

"Roger, on the dry lake bed. There are only about a hundred of them out here. You got a navigator on board that can really help?"

Billy loved his flyboy friends, but this guy had some gall. "We're sixty-eight miles northwest of Indian Springs, bearing three-three-zero. How's that for position, Mustang, or would you rather have my lat/long at intercept point?"

"You guys always like to be precise in your navigation. Guess that's what happens when you've dropped too many bombs on the wrong target. We got you in sight, Billy. Do you think you can fly that thing any lower?"

Billy smiled over at Earl, whose knuckles were turning blue from gripping the yoke as he flew the old bird up another valley. "Earl has been mumbling since we left Edwards about wasting fuel at this altitude. I think he's more concerned about blowing up the TNT in the belly of this beast."

Within minutes, Jeff's P-51 pulled into position off the P-25's left wing. The slick design of one of the most recognizable aircraft from World War II made the Mustang fast and agile. It could top four hundred miles per hour and had been impressive many decades ago at defending the bombers making their runs into Germany.

"It does feel good having these guys out here flying escort." Billy told his slightly more relaxed copilot.

"What's the plan, Captain?" Jeff inquired.

"We are going to bomb the living heck out of the place then, if we're still alive, go back and land at Ely to clean out our pants. They have antiaircraft batteries around that place so I would recommend you guys stay clear while we do the bombing run."

"That isn't going to happen, bomber boy. We are here to kick butt too."

"What do you recommend, Mustang?"

"You set up your bombing run and let me and the boys go in to raise royal heck with the batteries before you slide in at ground level. If we do it that way, the systems will be too busy trying to target us and will miss the fat one."

"Sounds dangerous, but I'm okay with anything that gets the heat off us. Our bombing run will bring us around the hills to the southwest. We'll have six miles of real estate to cross in full view. That is almost a minute and a half for you to distract the defenses. Can you do that?"

"Consider it done, Billy. We could occupy those immature toy rockets for hours."

"Don't get too brave, Jeff. You know what they say about pilots?"

"There are old pilots, and there are bold pilots, but there are no old bold pilots. Okay, we will give you the time you need, then get out of there."

"Thanks, you do that and I'll buy you a drink in Ely tonight."

WCATS

Nick Harton stood in the back corner of the boiler room which was now crowded to capacity with a bunch of stone-faced specialists who looked like death warmed over. He could only wonder if this is how the Jews had felt when they had been crowded into the gas chambers during the Holocaust. This was no comparison, but the end would be the same.

"Move over," a young lady told Nick as she touched his arm. "There's a draft coming up from this grate and it's cold."

Nick moved back and let the girl move around him.

"Cold air," he mulled. "That can only mean one thing, fresh air, and that has to come from outside." He looked down to see a two foot square grate and felt the cool breeze.

"Move back, everyone!" Nick yelled as he pushed the specialists away from the grate. "I think this leads outside! Somebody help get this moved! "

A couple of the younger guys struggled desperately to remove the grate, and after it was shoved away, they looked down into a hole about ten feet deep. "Anyone in here know where this goes?" Nick asked.

"I think I know," ventured one of the women. "Out on my walks, I noticed a drain on the north side of the complex. It's right outside the fence, and it looked like it goes into a gully down to the road."

"Anyone have a flashlight?"

"No, but we have phones, and they have lights."

Nick saw how little time was left and ordered, "Someone open the door so those outside can follow us. We have about thirty minutes before this place blows up. Let's go!"

They rapidly descended the metal steps fastened to the side of the vertical shaft leading down to a five-foot culvert that led north and south. Total darkness gave way to LED lights as the trapped specialists turned on their phones. The dry climate had been good to the underground sewer. Other than a little water trickling down the bottom of the pipe, the ground was dry. The numerous cobwebs didn't slow them down as they raced through the tunnel.

Air France 75

The Airbus 340 had just crossed over Page, Arizona when the auto throttles slowly pulled back and the big jet started down. Looking out the window, Mitzy could see Lake Powell.

"Why are we starting down now?" she asked her mother.

"It could because of turbulence, or it could just be some controller getting his jollies."

"You know they don't do that anymore, Mom. It's the computer that stole Dad's job. Not only that, but the ride is smooth."

"Your father made the decision to leave on his own. I, for one, am glad he did."

"Maybe they're just going to give us a Grand Canyon tour. Where's your camera?"

Air France flight 75 now descended through twenty-five thousand feet. Up front, the Captain and the copilot were just passengers with a view. Everything they had tried to do failed to resolve the lockout. "The assigned altitude on the autopilot shows twelve hundred feet ASL. What's the altitude of Las Vegas?" Renee asked.

Looking at his map, Andre found what he was looking for. "I don't know about Las Vegas, but the autopilot is trying to land us on Lake Mead."

Renee sat there, quietly contemplating the future of their stricken flight, and then ordered, "Get Yvette up here. We need to brief the cabin crew. We have eighteen minutes until impact."

Washington D.C.

"How in the world are we getting to Camp David?" President James Banister asked his chief of staff as they were walking to the exit leading to the South Lawn.

"In an old Sikorsky H-34 used by President Eisenhower in 1958. It never even heard of a computer, so it should be safe."

"Where did they find this thing in such a hurry?" he asked.

"It was sitting over at Andrews in a hanger. It's on its way here now."

Walking through the door, the President noticed Sean heading towards the exit. "You coming with us?" he asked.

"Mr. President, as much as I would love to, I need to be in communications with my boys in the centers when this goes down. I will be at FAA headquarters where we have a communication network set up."

"What about the danger? This whole place could go up in flames."

"Sir, that is a risk I am willing to take. Charlie's family is on one of the flights. He could lose it all tonight. I will do everything in my power to prevent my friend from experiencing that agony."

"Good luck and God be with you," the president yelled over the racket made by the seven-decade-old helicopter landing a hundred yards away.

"Thank you, Mr. President. Tomorrow will be a new day," Sean replied.

Making his way into the Choctaw, The President sat down and strapped in. Looking around at his staff, he observed the nervousness of the Yale-trained self-proclaimed leaders of the free world. He should have chosen better when picking his cabinet. Old war veterans make better leaders. At least when the rubber meets the road, they will protect you. The urbanites make a lot of noise when they are protected, but let the shooting start, and they run for the fox holes. The rumbling old helicopter lifted off the lawn and headed north to Camp David.

Back patio at ZLA

Charlie stood up. "Jim, let's go for a walk. We have fifteen minutes." They walked in silence through the halls of their old workplace home down the steps to the cafeteria which was now dark and dingy.

"Remember all the tough times we gave the cooks? They made a great breakfast but never quite got dinner done right," Jim remarked wistfully.

Jim looked through the glass door. The lights were on in the dining room where many times the guys had taken their trainees and explained the day's events. Over in the corner sat an old computer that at one time had been hooked up to a flight simulator. "Remember all the times we use to crash that sucker?" Jim seemed full of memories as Charlie remained silent. "Charlie, you are really quiet."

Tears formed in Charlie's eyes as he shook his head. "I don't want to lose them." With that, the flood gates opened to his emotions, and Charlie could no longer hold back the agony he felt.

Jim put his arm around his old friend. "Let's go outside, Charlie."

Jim led his old friend out onto the patio where twenty years ago they had hung out and told tales. This night was different. This night there were no C-130s doing takeoffs and landings. Not one aircraft flew overhead towards Van Nuys or Burbank. This night was quiet and cold. The wind chilled the two men to the bones.

"I know it's cold, Charlie, but sit down." Sliding into chairs that had been vacant for the last thirteen years, they lay back and looked at the frosty sky.

"Charlie, eighteen years ago you and I sat on this patio, and you told me how Jesus had changed your life. I was not very perceptive to your point of view that day, but because of your willingness to share your faith, today I am a strong Christian with a strong marriage to a beautiful wife and have four incredible children who love the Lord. And you know what? That same God that you trusted back then is here today. Have you asked Him for help? Brother, we have ten minutes, let's not waste it."

Spellbound, Charlie looked at Jim. "You're right! How many times have we asked for help and he came through? Why have I been so prideful thinking I could save everyone?"

Together the two retired controllers knelt on the cold concrete patio and spent the next ten minutes asking, begging God to intervene in the affairs of their lives and save not only Carrie and Mitzy, but all those involved in the day's disaster.

Twenty miles southwest of Ely

"Mustang to Mitchell bomber, come in."

"Go ahead, Mustang."

"Billy, we're going to head east and come up from behind the eastern ridge. Maybe that will cause all the sensors to scan that direction once we pop the ridge. What do you think?"

"I think it will work, Mustang. Don't know if I like being left alone over here though."

"Come on, Billy. There aren't any fighters out here to take a shot at you. I really think that the less of a footprint you leave, the better."

"You're right, you just be careful." Billy and Earl watched as the fighters rolled over the top of them and headed due east.

366

"Five minutes to target," Scott Scholl called out from the bombardier's position. "We're four minutes early."

"Understand, bombardier, we will make a left three-sixty and should roll out right on schedule."

Fifteen miles east of their position, five World War II vintage fighters were full throttle flying just feet off the valley floor screaming northeast working their way to the eastern side of the White Pine Mountain ridge.

"Boy's, arm your guns," as Flight Leader Jeff Atwater ordered his pilots. Turning north, they climbed up the back side of the mountains.

Fifteen miles to the southwest of the Ely airport, the Mitchell bomber flew up a valley, climbed over a dam, and turning right flew low over the copper strip mine. Looking down at Riepetown, Billy could see workers stopping to watch the old bomber fly by.

"Enjoy the air show," he said out loud. "It may be the last time you see this old airplane in one piece." Earl just shook his head and grimaced. Intercepting Highway 50, they rounded the last mountain between them and their target.

"Ten miles to target, bomb doors opening," their bombardier's shaky voice intoned from the nose of the aircraft.

WCATS evacuation

Barney yelled at Tyrone as he walked into the control room. "Kid, quit typing and get out of here! They're about to bomb us!" Tyrone looked around to see the grizzled old manager growling at him to get going. Tyrone looked at the clock on the monitor. It read 2025, three minutes before the scheduled strike. Grabbing his jacket, he headed out the door. But he heard Barney say something as he turned the corner. "See you later, young man," Barney said, in a not so confident voice, as he slid into the operations manager's chair.

"Barney, come on, we don't have any time left!" he screamed.

"No, this is my life. I have spent my entire career working on getting NextGen to this stage. It is now time for the captain to go down with the ship. Now, get out of here."

Tyrone looked at his watch. Shaking his head, he ran for the stairs. He found the open doors and followed the others on ahead. As he crawled down the pipe, he could only think of Barney and why he would die for such a cause. He started running blindly towards the dim lights he saw flickering to the north.

Farther to the north, Nick Harton made it to the end of the pipe only to find a welded grate preventing their exit. Opening his cell phone, he hit 911 only to hear, "All lines are busy at this time. Please try again later."

"Great, trapped in a sewer drain and almost out!"

Then he heard it! It was the distinctive sound of a P-51. It was not alone. Nick could not make out the other aircraft, but he knew everything was about to change. "Get down!" he screamed at his followers. They all immediately sat down along the edge of the small stream of water running down the pipe and covered their heads.

Lake Mead

Yvette picked up the microphone and heard the click as the P.A. system activated. "Ladies and gentlemen, we have experienced an emergency. We do not have time to clue you in on the details other than to tell you that the Federal Aviation Administration is working on a solution to our emergency. In preparation for a crash landing, we are asking that you put your tray tables up and your seats in their upright position. If, per chance, it comes to a crash landing, we ask that you lean forward in your seats. If you have a pillow or a jacket, put it between your head and the seat in front of you. Put your hands behind your neck and your feet flat on the floor. Please remain calm and wait for further instructions."

Mitzy looked at her mother, who was as white as a ghost.

"Are you all right, Mom?"

"Mitzy, this is why your dad didn't want us to go. He told me many times this day would come. All we can do now is pray." And that they did. The two people most dear to Charlie were already leaning forward in their seats, hands clasped together as they did what they knew worked. They asked God to intervene in their situation.

Renee and Andre had resigned themselves to the idea that they were not the ones in control of this aircraft. Not wanting to give up completely, Andre continued to work his way through the aircraft operations manual, hoping to discover something that would keep them alive. "Maybe a water landing wouldn't be too bad," he suggested half-heartedly. "Remember the one that landed in the Hudson? They all survived."

Renee looked over at her copilot. "So, you think there will be ferries crossing Lake Mead in November? Andre, this is different. I really don't think this plane has any plans of slowing down."

Looking out the window, they watched the lake grow larger as the big jet continued its descent. Passing through five thousand feet, they were able to make out Las Vegas sixty miles to the west. Bringing in the range on the LCD navigational display, Andre made out the final route of their ill-fated flight. "Hoover Dam!" he exclaimed. "It's running us into Hoover Dam!"

Marine One

The old Sikorsky H-34 still had what it took, and twenty minutes after it had left the White House lawn it rounded Thurmont, Maryland and headed into the hills towards Camp David. Crossing over Hunting Creek Lake, it made a right turn onto final approach to the landing pad at the presidential retreat. Meanwhile, sixty thousand feet overhead, a small, unmanned aircraft had been tracking the vibration of the fifty-six-foot rotor as it churned the air. The RQ-4 Global Hawk was returning to Norfolk, Virginia from a routine mission monitoring the airspace between Havana and the Florida Keys. It had just started its initial descent when it received orders to extend its mission north. It had picked up the helicopter shortly after liftoff and continued to track it northwest. Within ten minutes of leaving Washington, the reconnaissance aircraft had plotted the potential routing of the unauthorized flight and sent its data to DHS.

Department of Homeland Security computers networking with the Department of Defense found what they were looking for.

Twenty pods of FIM-92 Stinger missiles surrounded Camp David. The defense system designed years ago was there to protect the President against attack. Now integrated into Homeland Security, these missiles were at the beck and call of the 4DT program. As Marine One started its descent into Camp David, the program sent a command through the DHS to the Department of Defense. The aging helicopter became an enemy of the president who was onboard. One and a half miles ahead, hidden in the trees, the missile battery computer received the command and acknowledged. Trap doors flew open and the pods rose out of the ground. Buried deep within the camp inside the bombproof bunker, monitors alerted the two naval officers to the activated Stingers.

"Wave off, Marine One!" one of the officers yelled into the mic. The controller at the landing pad heard the officer but questioned the reason, making a dreadful mistake. Onboard the

Sikorsky, the pilot concentrating on the landing zone never saw the missile streak up from the trees.

ZLA ATC-ready

Charlie and Jim quickly returned inside the old Los Angeles Air Traffic Control Center and stopped by the operations desk for the latest update on the mission. The computers were up and running, ready to start receiving data with the throw of a switch. In the control area, they found the rest of the controllers sitting in front of their scopes looking at maps of long ago.

"Things have changed a lot since we worked these sectors, Charlie. What are we suppose to do?"

"Take yourselves back a few years, boys. It's not like we're starting out with a thousand airplanes, just ninety-two."

Charlie didn't know if he wanted to do it but knew he had to. He sat down at the sector east of Las Vegas. This could be bitter sweet. Was Flight 75 going to be there when the radar came on? Would they have time to recover? *Just do your job* he told himself as he plugged in his headset. The clock on his screen showed 2029.

"One minute!" someone announced.

Chapter 54

Jeff didn't even bother pulling back the throttle as he crested the ridge. Letting all 1,720 horses do their job screaming for the compound below, he keyed his radio. "Look for the SAMs, boys. Let's take 'em out." Almost instantly, they watched puffs of smoke coming from the parameter of the compound. "Inbound!" he yelled. Dropping low against the terrain, he pointed the nose of his aircraft at the spots where he saw smoke. Pulling the trigger on his fifty caliber guns, he watched the tracers make their way to the missile launcher. A big explosion followed as Jeff broke right and flew north along the valley floor.

A mile away, and only twenty feet off the surface, he made a hard right turn and flew back toward the center. Smoke was rising from the compound as he approached at almost 300 miles an hour. Checking his wings he found only three of the four.

"Lightning, where are you?" he called to the P-38 which was nowhere to be seen.

"Sorry, Boss, kind of busy here," replied Greg, an old Iraq war veteran. "Took a hit back there, heading north to find a place to land."

Jeff didn't have time to contemplate what all that entailed; the compound was coming up fast.

Four miles south of the field, thirty feet off the deck, a cloud of dust formed a trough rising off the valley floor. At the controls Billy released directional control to Scott, their bombardier.

"Forty seconds to target. Stand by for altitude adjustment." Billy knew that once they climbed, they would be sitting ducks. He could see the smoke rising from the compound as they approached. "Look, Fred, they marked our target for us, and you know that if there's smoke, there's got to be fire. Be ready to hit the deck as soon as we release the bombs."

WCATS bomb shelter

Looking out through the grate, Nick could see fighter pilots making another run. "Who would think of bringing in antique aircraft to blow up one of most technically advanced air traffic facilities in the world?"

"It was someone with ingenuity, Boss."

Nick turned around to find Tyrone standing behind him. "Good to see you made it out. Did everyone else make it?"

Tyrone shook his head, "Barney refused to leave. I tried to talk some sense into his stubborn head, but he wouldn't hear it."

Nick frowned, "Some things never change. He always has been a thorn in the agency's side."

Tyrone looked out at the sky. "I thought they were going to bomb us, not fill us full of holes."

"Listen!" The sound of big radial engines grew louder. "They're here, get down!"

Everyone again took defensive positions as the rumble increased. Looking out the grate Nick and Tyrone saw the tail of the B-25 with bomb bays open for only a split second before the massive explosion rocked the culvert transformed into a bomb shelter.

Flaps down

The Airbus 340 with 295 passengers and a crew of ten continued its descent to just one hundred feet above the water. Mitzy looked out the window at the canyon walls rising not more than a few hundred feet away. The big aircraft made a hard left turn, bringing nothing but water into view. She screamed along with 294 other passengers. Up front, the two passengers who were supposed to be the pilots watched in horror as the autopilot had a mind of its own and continued to take them to their watery grave. Passing Sentinal Island, the aircraft started slowing down, and the flaps started to extend. Renee reached up and hit the crash alarm, alerting the cabin crew to an imminent crash. Looking at a canyon wall at their twelve o'clock position the pilots did not expect to live. At the last second, the aircraft made a turn to the right, just missing the towering walls along the water's edge. They could see the dam now just a mile ahead. The airspeed showed 180 knots. Renee and Andre, having accepted their fate, watched as the power was reduced and the aircraft started a slow descent towards the water.

Camp David

"Marine One! Marine One! Acknowledge and ident!" The navy controller working the landing pad knew the worst had happened, but he was not willing to admit it. He had been talking to the pilot from ten miles out and had vectored him for final. Reaching over, he hit the red crash button to alert the emergency units on the base. With his elbows on the console, he lowered his head into his hands and moaned, "God, help us."

On the ramp awaiting the arrival of Marine One, the ground crew saw the missile leave the tree line and a split second later the old helicopter go up in a ball of flames. Standing there in total shock, they watched as the leader of the free nation went down in flames. Sirens sounded as fire trucks and other first responders headed for the crash site. Everyone knew the worst but, as always with the human race, hoped for the impossible.

Ops desk - WCATS

Barney sat at the operations desk, stone faced and silent looking straight ahead at the room he had helped design and the system he had worked his entire career to create. Now it was down to this. It was a failed system, not because of what they had created, but because of the failure to protect it. "Why?" He said out loud with a feeling of painful resignation. "Now, with this agony, I enter eternity."

"That's not necessary."

Barney jumped at the voice coming from behind him. Turning, he saw Abdur standing at the counter.

"Abdur, I didn't even know you were here."

"Just got here early this morning to assist a young Tyrone locate a virus."

"Oh, it's too late for that. The virus found us. Haven't you heard they're bombing this place? If you hurry you can get out through the basement."

Abdur shook his head. "Barney, years ago you trusted me with fixing ERAMS, and boy, did I ever fix it. At that time, I did not know this would be the outcome of my actions. I should not have let the fate of my parents compromise my character. Now, so many peoples' lives are hanging in the balance. I just hope they know the Lord."

Barney looked at Abdur with disdain and smirked, "Don't tell me they got to you?"

"If your reference is to Jesus, then yes, He did get to me. And today I will be with him in glory."

Barney shook his head. "I guess it's all right for some people, but I'm not sure it's for me. I have my reasons for going down with this ship, Abdur. What's yours?"

"I am the one responsible for the virus being implanted in NextGen. In our culture, this is the only honorable thing to do. I know because of what Jesus did on the cross that I will be with Him today. It's that simple."

Barney scratched his chin and said, "Explain that again, how this transformation can be called simple."

Abdur looked up towards the ceiling, knowing that their time had nearly run out.

"Barney, you know what you were taught in Sunday School many years ago. Remember the story of a savior who lived without ever sinning and how he died on the cross for our sins? He never stayed in the grave, Barney. The resurrection of Jesus is real, and today he is in heaven with God. All you need to do is confess that you believe and accept Jesus as your Savior. Can you do that Barney?"

A smile formed on the face of the old man where for so many years there had been no smile. He opened his mouth to answer as the oxygen was sucked out of the room.

Bombs away

"Climb now!" Scott commanded as he stared through the lenses of the Norden bombsight. "Five seconds to target." He started his countdown as Billy pulled back on the yoke and climbed to three hundred feet. They were now vulnerable to attacks from the SAMs. They watched in horror as they saw four fighters coming straight at them.

376

"Mustang, we're on the target," Billy yelled into his mic.

"Roger, Mitchell, keep coming. We have you in sight!"

Billy and Fred watched as the four fighters opened fire on the complex and the complex defenses released four SAM's to meet the oncoming assault.

"Bombs away," Billy confirmed when he felt the thud of the bombs clear the racks and the lift of the reduced weight as three thousand pounds of American made bombs honed in on their target. Pushing hard forward on the yoke, the Mitchell bomber dropped as low as Fred could handle it. Screaming over McGill, they made a left turn back towards the target only to see a huge cloud forming over what use to be one of this country's finest air traffic control facilities.

"Wow! I'm glad they didn't load us up with a nuke," Scotty said as he crawled out from the bombardier's position. "Looks like a direct hit."

"Yes, Mr. Scholl, you still have it," Billy replied. He then turned towards Ely and started searching for his friends.

Billowing smoke shot down the culvert and out through the grate. Three hundred specialists and their managers, along with thirty of the airway facility personnel, hunkered down in the bottom of the pipe. Covering their noses and mouths with whatever they could find, they waited it out until finally, the cloud of dust and smoke cleared.

Looking around at the dust-covered specialists, Nick just had to laugh. "We made it, guys! Now if we can just get out of here."

"No problem, Boss." Tyrone was already on his phone. "It appears the virus has been terminated."

Chapter 55

"All systems are operational."

The call came over the intercom as the communications display lit up and the "Not receiving time" disappeared from the controllers' scopes. Charlie watched as targets started appearing on his scope. He was looking for one in particular. Although a few targets started appearing around the Center's airspace, there was no sign of the Air France. Communications were coming back on line as the controllers' broadcast on 121.5 for different flights to come up on their assigned sector's VHF frequency. Charlie located two aircraft coming in from the north, both headed for the Las Vegas Strip. The aircraft had been within two minutes of destroying one of the nation's costliest playgrounds, and they made one heck of a racket flying over the casinos as their pilots regained control. Putting both aircraft on fifty-five headings, Charlie set them up for Las Vegas approach to take over and turned them back onto the localizer for landing.

Air France 75

Just as the aircraft passed over a line marked "No boats past this point" a flashing alert startled them.

"Warning, warning," the speaker blared. "Autopilot is disconnected, caution terrain, caution terrain, climb immediately." Renee instinctively pulled back on the side stick and applied full power. All four of the big Rolls Royce engines responded to the command, and the Airbus started a slow climb. The Hoover Dam bypass bridge with its huge arch filled their vision as the lumbering jet's ascent seemed to take forever.

"Come on, baby, you can make it," Renee groaned as she pulled further back, raising the nose of the aircraft.

"Watch your speed," Andre spoke up as he pushed the throttles against the stops. The stall warning horn sounded as the air speed dropped below 145 knots. "We're not going to make it Renee. Go under it," Andre prodded.

"You're right, reduce power." She pushed hard forward on the stick, causing a lot of screams in the back of the aircraft as the g-force turned from positive to negative. Everything not strapped in became airborne as the aircraft started down. Just clearing the towers on the dam, Renee dropped the two-hundred-ton ton aircraft below the bridge.

Looking out the window, Mitzy had no idea what was going on as the roller-coaster ride continued.

The left wing tipped down as Renee tried to keep them in the middle of the river, and then they were clear.

"Full power," she requested as the feeling of pilot-in-command took over. Climbing above the rim of the canyon, they turned toward Los Angeles.

"There it is!" screamed Charlie. Jim looked over at his buddy who had tears streaming down his face.

"You find 'em?"

"Seven miles southeast of Boulder City, climbing southwest bound." He hit his foot pedal keying up his radio.

"Air France flight 75, Air France flight 75, Los Angeles Center on Guard, come up on frequency 134.65 and ident."

Five seconds later, the crackle in his headset was unmistakable. "Air France flight 75 with you, Center, on 134.65."

Charlie was so choked up he could not even respond.

Andre continued, "Center, we had a problem back there and are climbing out of six thousand five-hundred. At what altitude would you like for us to level off?"

Finally getting his wits together, he keyed up and answered, "Air France 75, it's good to hear from you. Sir, everyone had a problem back there. You were not alone. Climb and maintain flight level two-two-zero. If you want higher it's available, and Air France 75 cleared direct LAX."

"Direct LAX and maintain Flight Level two-two-zero, thanks Los Angeles Center." Then as an afterthought Andre added, "I thought they closed the LA Center."

"They did, they closed it way before its time, but don't worry Air France, we're back."

Releasing his foot pedal and leaning back in his rickety old chair, Charlie spun around one time and looked at his old friends. "Yes, we're back!"

Ely airport

"Yelland Field, this is Mitchell bomber straight in for runway one-eight."

"Welcome back, Mitchell bomber, you sure made a mess out of the neighborhood."

"Roger that, Ely, request permission to land."

"Sorry, Mitchell bomber, I got caught up in the moment. Cleared to land runway one-eight, winds are one-niner-five at fifteen knots, altimeter three-zero-zero-five."

"We're cleared to land runway one-eight. Thanks, Tower. You see any of our friends yet?"

"We had a Hellcat land a couple of minutes ago. How many friends did you have out there?"

"There were five fighters, Tower, two P-51s, two Hellcats, and a P-38 Lightning."

"Hold on, Mitchell bomber. You have traffic at your five o'clock and two miles closing fast. It may be your friends."

"Ely Tower, Mustang 51, four miles north of the field, has the bomber in sight, request permission for a flyby."

"Unable a flyby, Mustang, the bomber is landing. Do a right three-sixty, and space out your flight for landing."

Billy looked over at Fred, who was shaking his head and muttering, "They're going to do it. I just know it." Sure enough, the flight of four fighters blew right by the B-25 as it was touching down and did an overhead break from twenty-five feet off the deck.

"Sorry, Tower, we were a little slow on that turn."

"Mustang 51, you're going to get me fired. Maintain visual separation and land whenever you're ready. In the meantime, I will enjoy the air show."

Taxiing up to the ramp, they heard over the radio, "Ely Tower, this is Lightning 38, requesting a straight in for Runway one-eight."

"Lightning 38, say your position." the controller asked.

"We're about ten miles north of the field. I'm just about to go past a big hole in the ground, and it's still smoking."

"Roger, Lightning 38 cleared to land runway one-eight."

Fred keyed up his mic and just had to ask, "Where you been, Slick? We have been missing you."

"I was out there trying to find a place to land this beast. Missing half my tail, and had to shut down number two. You know there ain't an airport for a hundred miles up that direction. Not only that, I'm thirsty, and you owe me a beer."

The rest of the World War II fighter group watched as the P-38 made a very shaky approach and landing. Once that last airplane was on the ground and all the props stopped turning, they let out a collective breath of relief and began to recount the most memorable day in their flying careers.

Turning into the driveway, the firefighters were met by the gate guards and an additional contingency of ten agents from Homeland Security.

"Nobody got out of the center," said an agent who introduced himself as the one in charge. "It scared the heck out of us when they bombed this place. The explosions were deafening, even from the ditch down here." He was pointing to the deep ravine next to the drive.

"There was anti-aircraft fire going off, and it looked like old fighters shooting this place up."

The fire chief shook his head. "You're lucky they didn't blow you up. You guys do us a favor and guard the parameter. We have to put out some flames."

Within minutes, every fire truck from Ely and additional equipment from the copper mine arrived to assist with the huge fire. Gigantic streams of water sprayed what was left of the state-of-the-art facility. The water that didn't evaporate from the heat made its way to the basement and eventually down the drain to the sewer leading to the north ravine, a sewer line filled with 300 still scared specialists and managers waiting to be rescued.

"Say that again!" the fire chief barked at the 911 operator. "Where did the call come from? There is no way; it has to be a prank."

"I understand that possibility, but it's coming from your location, Chief," the emergency operator responded.

"We will check it out anyhow. Thanks." He motioned for one of the DHS onlookers who had been quick to respond. "Get your guys over along the north fence. We may have survivors in a drainage pipe over there."

Five minutes later, the out of breath agent returned smiling. "We found them! They say they're all in the pipe."

"Well, where are they?" the Chief asked.

"They're trapped in a culvert. Do you guys have anything to cut metal?"

"We have the Jaws of Life, it can cut anything."

He motioned for a couple of his boys and sent them with the agent. Twenty minutes later, a string of wet and dirty specialists and managers climbed their way up the ravine to look at a complex totally destroyed.

Tyrone walked up beside Nick, who was staring at the smoldering remains. "Hey, Boss, can I have tomorrow off?"

Charlie looked at his phone. It was Carrie. "Welcome home, darling." Without even thinking he added, "Did you have a good flight?"

Carrie chuckled, "If you only knew, my man. We have had an experience you would not believe. Where are you?"

"Well, it's a long story, and you would not believe it either. Did anyone say when they're going to resume flights out of LAX?"

"Some agent said something about waiting on Los Angeles Center to open up the airspace," Carrie answered with a questioning tone. "Do you know what they're talking about?"

Charlie laughed, "You might say I do. I'm at the center in Palmdale now. Rent a car and come on up. We have a lot of catching up to do."

Later that night, sometime around midnight, Charlie walked out the front gate at ZLA to a waiting car, where Carrie and Mitzy embraced the exhausted controller.

Chapter 56

Five o'clock the next morning, Charlie was back at ZLA, along with the other four controllers from Ely. It would be a big day with the welcomed arrival of fifty more controllers. Technicians had come in overnight from all over southern California and were busy cleaning and tweaking equipment. The goal was to have all sectors open within a week.

At lunchtime, he received the news about the president. Getting one of the other controllers to relieve him from his sector, Charlie went out to the flag pole and untied the rope, thinking of the tragedy. *Even if we did have our differences, he was a good man.* After lowering the flag halfway down the pole, he retied the rope. Taking two steps back, he saluted the Stars and Stripes and bowed his head in prayer.

Cold damp clouds descended on Washington. Charlie sat silently watching the people, all dressed in black, filling up the chairs. He was exhausted from the overnight flight. He had not slept well on the plane as his mind continued to replay the events of the last few days.

Sean slid into the chair beside his friend. "He was on our side, Charlie. We're going to miss him."

Charlie nodded, "James had the making of a great president, and I was looking forward to working with him. Has Hamel been sworn in yet?"

Sean smiled over at Charlie. "You should listen to the news a little more often. She was sworn in the night of the accident."

"Really? Guess I should have known. Have you had any contact with the acting administrator?" He was referring to Bob Burkhammer's replacement.

"It's all new, Charlie. It's not as if we had any leadership before, but now it's like a bunch of chickens with their heads cut off. You knew Secretary Laverne was with them?"

"Yeah, it's sad to lose 'em all. I feel for their families." Charlie nodded again, "What next?"

"Just wait and see. For now, we still have the contract to continue controlling the airspace. I have a meeting with the president in the morning. I would like for you to come along."

"Meeting about what?" Charlie whispered. "Does she even have the faintest inkling what's going on out there?"

"Not a chance, Charlie, but someone put a bug in her ear that she can trust you. Why do you think I flew you out here?"

"Well, I really thought it was for the president's funeral. I guess that was a little presumptuous."

Sean smiled. "Got to love you, Charlie. Welcome to Washington. It's the place where everyone wants you to do something to further their agenda. We'll talk over dinner. I have reservations at the Morton Steak House over in Georgetown."

The cold, blustery November wind bit through the observers as they walked up the hill to the burial site of the fallen president. The service had been one of remembrance for a soldier, governor, senator, and a president. From his youth had served his country well. Above all that, James Banister had been a role model to his children and grandchildren and a faithful husband to First Lady Isabel Banister. The funeral fulfilled his desires that he be laid to rest alongside his fellow soldiers who had died in the line of duty.

As the bagpipes played "Amazing Grace," Charlie's mind drifted to the day he had talked with President Banister. He had always respected the position of the president, even though many times they had disagreements with his handling of the controllers. Charlie had been humbled by the fact that this president had been inspired by his speech to the aviation community. He had been humbled by the phone call in Georgia that night not too long ago. Now here he was standing at the gravesite of the man he was just getting to know.

Charlie was almost starting to feel sorry for his loss when he witnessed the first lady with her three children and two grandchildren walk up and lay flowers on the grave. Ashamed, Charlie stood there, head bowed, asking God to forgive him for such selfish thoughts. Here was a wife who was now a widow, children who were now fatherless, and grandchildren who would ask about a missing grandpa. All of a sudden, a chill ran down his spine, and he felt very alone. He wiped the tears that made their way down his cold cheeks. How he missed Carrie at that moment. He knew he should have brought her along. The echo of the twenty-one gun salute across the Potomac River brought the funeral to an end.

Walking alone back down the hill, Charlie took a detour through a section of the cemetery where he saw row after row of government-issued headstones. These were men and women who died protecting our way of life. It had a sobering effect on Charlie as he stood and looked over the river at the Capital.

> *Vanity of vanity, all is vanity. What profit has a man from all his labor in which he toils under the sun? One generation passes away, and another generation comes; but the earth abides forever. The sun rises and the sun goes down, and hastens to the place where it arose. The wind goes toward the south, and turns around to the*

north; the wind whirls about continually, and comes
again on its circuit. All the rivers run into the sea, yet
the sea is not full; to the place from which the rivers
come, there they return again. All things are full of
labor; man cannot express it. The eye is not satisfied
with seeing, nor the ear filled with hearing. That which
has been is what will be, that which is done is what will
be done, and there is nothing new under the sun.

Charlie recalled the Old Testament passage from the book of Ecclesiastes.

Continuing down to the entrance, he decided to walk back across the Arlington Memorial Bridge to the National Mall. He stopped at the Lincoln Memorial long enough to look at the nineteen foot statue of President Lincoln before moving along the reflecting pool to the FAA headquarters. As expected, it was closed for the funeral, so Charlie walked up to his hotel where he cleaned up and waited for Sean to pick him up for dinner.

Chapter 57

The chauffeur opened the door to the black limo. "Good evening, Charlie." Sean greeted him as he slid into the soft leather seat.

"What gives with the formal ride?" Charlie asked.

"We've spent the day in mourning for the loss of a friend. Tonight, we are celebrating life as President Banister would have wanted. Charlie, I don't know if you noticed, but time continues to move on. Tomorrow, the skies will again fill with airplanes. We need to prepare for the day when the current system is filled to capacity. Yes, we took a big hit over these last two weeks, but the resilience of this country and our industry will bring back the airplanes. People like to travel, and flying is the preferred method. You and your friends did a great job in bringing your old facilities back online. Yesterday, nationwide we were up to the 80 percent level."

"You may be right, Sean, but these old controllers are paying a price. They're happy to be back, but they won't be able to maintain the current schedule. You have a plan?"

"Do I have a plan? You might say that. I'll tell you about it over dinner."

Sean dug into his medium rare Porterhouse, and Charlie sampled his yellow fin tuna as the plan came alive.

"Charlie, as you know, we have to bring in a system that will adapt to the current user interface. That means we have to work with the equipment the users have spent billions of dollars

388

acquiring. Now, I don't see that as a problem. We already have the infrastructure in place. The ADS-B is not a problem. The hardware is doing its job. Data link in itself is not a problem. It transmits what it is asked to transmit. ERAMS is another story. Regardless of the money that was invested in this platform, it does not work."

"So are you saying we need a completely new platform?" Charlie asked.

"Yes, this sounds like a huge order, but we will submit plans to the FAA that will blow their socks off."

"Okay," Charlie raised his eyebrows in a questioning fashion. "I don't know if I would use that term. They are kind of sensitive to blowing socks off right now."

Sean laughed, "Do you have to make jokes about everything? You know what I mean."

"All right I'm sorry. What's the plan?"

Sean sat back in his chair, wiping his face with his napkin. "Air traffic control has become too big of a job for the federal government. Over the past four decades, the talk has been all about contracting the job. As you know, this has already happened at some of the smaller airports around the country. Charlie, considering what has transpired over the last two months, it's time for that change."

"So what's going to convince the FAA to go along with privatization?" Charlie asked. "Don't you think they will say it's too big of a task for a company like ours?"

Sean motioned for the waiter and ordered more wine. "Too big for a job we are already doing? Now is the right time if there's ever going to be one. Look, a new president, a new administrator, a new DOT secretary. Now, I understand the Aviation Subcommittee will have a lot to say about how things move forward, and that is exactly what I'm counting on."

Charlie swirled his wine in the glass a couple of times, more for the time to think than to aerate the wine. "So, you think you have the subcommittee in your back pocket?"

389

Sean just smiled for a minute as he chewed down on a chunk of porterhouse. "Let's just say we look pretty favorable in their eyes right now. The FAA has one big black eye and our company saved them from another one."

"Yeah, a black eye we were instrumental in creating. Why hasn't anyone brought that up?"

"Whoa, Charlie, we tried to stop the program before the collapse. Once the administrator and the secretary overrode that decision, I feel we were vindicated."

"Okay, I can buy that logic. Please indulge me in this plan of yours." Charlie poured another glass of wine and sat back.

"Let's start with the thirty-five hundred controllers we now have. You have told me that they are only temporary and will shortly washout. So the first step is to find their replacements. For that, I'm bringing in some of the best recruiting practices out there."

"Like the Army uses?" Charlie interrupted.

"Yes, you could say that. I have hired an advertising agency, and they are working on an advertising campaign that looks more like we're selling a new game than a job."

"You know that all you will get is a bunch of pimple-faced kids looking for a game to play."

Sean chuckled. "That is exactly what we're wanting. From what you've been telling me about the air traffic specialists, they were out of their league controlling airplanes."

"That's right Sean. They just didn't have the right stuff."

"Okay, then who has the right stuff?"

Charlie looked up from his almost empty wine glass. "The kids who play the games the air traffic specialists design?"

Sean's eyes lit up, "There's your answer. We will bring in kids right out of high school. If you let these kids go to college, the way they process information changes."

Charlie was now sitting forward in his chair, starting to see the direction Sean was taking this thing. "So, you think we need kids who have not been tarnished by this change? Who can sit down with a game console and pick it up in a hurry?"

"I think so. For simplicity, we can set up initial testing at all the centers. Set a goal to hire your replacements over the next couple of months."

"Two months! The FAA can never process new hires that fast. It normally takes at least eighteen months," Charlie replied.

"Remember, this isn't the FAA. We can do it on a time line of our own choosing. What I haven't told you is that I have already hired thirty of the air traffic specialists who made it out of the WCATS."

"Why would you want the ATSs? They can't separate butter with a hot knife."

"You're right, but they are the future in aviation software design. They have had a taste of what we do and are overly educated in software design. We will start them off building a game to assist with the hiring process."

"A game for hiring, that sounds childish," Charlie commented.

"It is. Remember, we're hiring teenagers. Let's use a video game to determine the ability these kids have in learning the rules to the game but also in reacting to abnormal situations."

"Okay, so now we have determined how to replace the rag tag old guys. What's the next step?"

The waiter brought the chocolate soufflé, briefly interrupting their conversation.

"Charlie, I know you have no desire to stay at Los Angeles Center any longer than necessary. So, with your concurrence, I would like for you to come back here to Washington to assist with the replacement program."

"Not going to do it, Boss. As soon as I can leave ZLA in good hands, I'm going to retire for the second time. Carrie's already in Georgia, and I plan on joining her shortly. Mitzy and her fiancé will be living in Atlanta. I need to give up the life of twisting metal."

Sean shook his head. "Okay, fine then. Do it from Georgia. With the computer geeks we have on staff, we can set up a network so you can work from home. Whenever you need to come up for a face-to-face meeting, we will charter an aircraft. That way, my hen-pecked friend, you can be home for dinner."

This made Charlie laugh. "You only wish you had a hen pecking you. Sorry, Boss, continue."

"Very funny, where were we? Oh yeah, remember this is a private company. We will not have the constraint required within the federal government. Charlie, our company needs you close to Washington to help with this redesign."

Charlie scratched his chin and pondered what Sean had said. He would be at the farm with his wife, close to his daughter, and would be able to help Carrie with her aging parents. It was only a one-hour-and-fifteen-minute flight to Washington when he needed to go.

"I really need to talk to Carrie before I make this decision, but it would be my guess she'll approve. Even with that, I really need to spend another three months in Los Angeles to stabilize things there. Jim Gallagher is doing a great job and will make a great facility manager. He has already organized the schedule and developed a recertification plan for the controllers still coming in.

We have identified a handful of natural leaders and are setting them up to oversee the facility. We have not yet considered supervisors; so far the controllers are too busy to get into trouble. Sorry, Boss, I got off subject. Tell me more about the redesign and how we're going to develop it."

Sean looked around, making sure no one was eavesdropping in on their conversation. "I have been in contact with one of my old college buddies. He is the cofounder of Zedetech and is willing to help us with the development of the new program."

"Isn't Zedetech the number one video game developer?" Charlie asked.

"Yes, that's the company. He started the company with another one of our college friends right out of school. They have agreed to assign their top ten software designers to this project. That, along with our thirty new engineers, will make up the design team."

"That's a huge commitment. Where are we getting the funding?" Charlie questioned.

"Initial funding for our portion of the program comes from the contract we already have with the FAA for keeping the centers in operation. As far as Zedetech, they have agreed to assist in building and installing the program for the rights to use the technology in game development and 5 percent of the company's common stock."

"I must admit, a completely new program sounds like the best idea." Charlie sounded convinced. "What about the network? Are we going to replace the CATS?"

Sean shook his head. "Don't you think we learned our lesson? I'm of the opinion we go to a ten-facility layout with 100 percent overlap in airspace. The other thing I would like for you to consider is a complete airspace redesign. The airspace we currently use is so chopped up it doesn't make sense to anyone."

"Except for the controllers who work the airspace," Charlie interjected.

"But don't you think we can do better?" Sean replied.

"Yes, we can do a redesign, but, man, that's a lot of work and we will have to get the FAA to buy off on the new design."

"Charlie, they have wanted redesign for the last half a century. We will be the answer to their prayers."

"Okay, you haven't answered my question on hardware yet. Ten facilities with all the hardware will cost a pretty penny. Indulge me on that one, Boss."

Sean looked at the empty bottle of Pinot Noir. "That I will do, Charlie, but I think it's time for us to go for a ride.

Chapter 58

Back in the limo, Sean gave the driver instructions, 4rfgand then he plunked a couple of ice cubes in a glass and poured himself a scotch. "Have you ever been to the Steven F. Udvar-Hazy Center?" he asked Charlie.

Charlie shook his head. "It's the National Air and Space Museum out at Dulles. I have something I want to show you."

Looking at his watch, Charlie saw it was already after ten. "What time do they close?"

"They're already closed. That doesn't matter. I have friends."

"I have noticed," Charlie rolled his eyes. "Is this a private museum tour?"

"It's more than that, Charlie. Care for some scotch?"

Charlie shook his head. "No, I think maybe that wine was enough poison to last me for awhile."

Thirty minutes later, the car drove through the empty parking lot and up to the main entrance of the museum. A guard came out of the shadows and opened the back door. "Mr. O'Leary, welcome to my world." Noticing the Scotch in his hand he commented, "Am I to assume you had a good trip out from the city?"

"Listen, laddie, a little Scotch does a body well."

"Yeah, right ... a little maybe. Did you bring your friend?"

"I gather that would be me," Charlie answered crawling out of the car. "I'm Charlie Beckler, a friend of Mr. O'Leary's, without the scotch."

"Glad to meet you, Charlie. I have been a fan of yours for years. Was thrilled when Sean said he was bringing you out here to see your name."

"See my name?" Charlie questioned.

"Dog gone it, laddie, I told you it was a surprise! Now you gone and ruined it. You will see soon enough, Charlie. Let's go on that tour."

Their shoes echoed in the otherwise quiet museum. The lights in the normally well-lit building were turned down casting eerie shadows as the three men walked through the history of aviation. Exhilaration overwhelmed Charlie as they entered the James S. McDonnell Space Hanger coming face to face with the Space Shuttle. Spotlights reflected off the larger-than-life shuttle and a huge American flag hung from the ceiling behind it. He took it all in like a child in a candy store as he slowly walked around the *Enterprise*. He remembered as a preschooler watching on television when this shuttle sat on the top of a Boeing 747 as it climbed high into the sky over the Mojave Desert. He recalled watching as the shuttle lifted off the back of the jumbo jet and returned to the dry lake bed. Even if this shuttle never made it into space it definitely deserved to be sitting here in this aviation mecca.

They continued their abbreviated tour, not taking nearly as long as Charlie wanted to take in all the displays. From the J-3 Cub, to the prototype of the Boeing 707, there was just too much to see. "Come on, Charlie, let's go for a walk along the wall of honor."

Sean urged him along. Back outside, they crossed the drive and headed down a tree-lined walkway. The cold wind was now blowing through the bare trees, and clouds periodically covered the moon.

"You sure picked a great night for a stroll down memory lane, Sean. Where are we headed?" Charlie asked.

Sean didn't answer, but the guard pulled his flashlight out and shined it on what looked like stainless steel airfoils along the side of the path.

The guard offered, "It's right in here somewhere, Sean. Found it this evening when I came to work."

Charlie saw the names etched into the stainless steel as the guard ran the light across the bright reflecting wings.

"Surely you didn't?"

Before Charlie could even get the question out, Sean found what they were looking for. There, about halfway up one of the panels, in one inch letters it read, "Charles E. Beckler, ATCS."

"There you go, Charlie. It's not a star on the sidewalks in Hollywood, and not with the fanfare I would have liked, but I had to be the one to show you."

Charlie looked up and down the row of names. "Thank you for bringing me here to see this, Sean. I really don't feel I've done anything more than my brother and sister controllers. I was just at the right place at the wrong time."

Sean laughed. "That's what they say about luck. The harder you work, the luckier you will get. It's the least I could do after what you have done for aviation."

Chapter 59

"Gentlemen, welcome to the White House." President Sheri Hamel stood up and came around the desk to meet her guests. After shaking hands with Sean and Charlie, she offered them a seat as she herself sat down in one of the wingback chairs. "Mr. Beckler, it is my privilege to finally meet you. Anytime we had a discussion on aviation, James would always ask what Charlie would do in this situation."

Charlie blushed, "I'm humbled to be of service, Madam President."

Looking over at Sean, she quickly moved to the subject at hand. "Mr. O'Leary, my advisers tell me you and your people have done an excellent job in bringing the air traffic control system up to a satisfactory level. For that, I commend you. I have been assured you are willing to continue keeping it in operation as long as necessary."

Sean gave the newly sworn-in president an Irish grin. "Just depends on how long that may be. Not only do we have the organization in place to maintain a safe and expeditious system, we are within weeks of presenting a plan to the administration to completely privatize the air traffic control system."

President Hamel showed no emotion. "What is the cost to the taxpayers?"

Sean looked into the eyes of a lady who had the weight of the free world on her shoulders. "Madam President, we are talking of working within the current budget. We will seriously

398

consider a contract based on ticket tax and aviation fuel tax. Our company is standing by with the numbers and the details on how this will work. Furthermore, we are willing to finance the 4DT replacement, taking on complete responsibility for its success."

The president gave Sean a perplexed look. "Is the Aviation Subcommittee up to speed on this proposal?"

"I have approached them with the concept and have been given assurance they would give the proposal serious consideration." Sean answered.

"Mr. Beckler, you are the air traffic expert in the room. What is your opinion of privatization?"

Charlie looked over at Sean then back at the president. "As a senior controller, and a long time union member, I have always been opposed to privatizing. That was then, but now, considering what has transpired over the last three years, I am convinced it is the logical thing to do."

President Hamel stood up and walked behind her desk. Looking out the window at the garden, she stood there for a few moments. "Gentlemen, thank you for your visit. I appreciate what you have accomplished in these last few weeks. I am grieved at the loss of our president and am not sure I'm ready to make this kind of monumental decision. Please continue stabilizing the airspace system. Once we have a new secretary and administrator confirmed, we will work through the details of your proposal. I have to say, I am impressed." She returned to the two men and shook their hands, motioning to an aide to escort them out.

Chapter 60

"Come on Jim, you know you need to make the trip." Charlie had been on Jim all morning about returning to Ely for the weekend.

Jim shook his head. "That place is full of bad memories I have no desire to relive. With the family down here now, give me one good reason to go."

"You mean besides me asking? You know you need to wrap things up with your house. We can fly up on Saturday morning, take care of business, attend the ceremony Saturday afternoon and fly home that night."

"Don't you think I should stay close to Los Angeles Center? We've had it running for only two weeks now. Not all the bugs have been worked out."

Charlie smiled at his old friend. "Stop making excuses, Jim. We both know that the tech heads will keep the system up and running. Rich can run the place during the day, and the nights crews can take care of themselves." Jim finally consented to making the trip, against his better judgment.

On Saturday morning, the two boarded a chartered Falcon jet arranged by the newly formed O'Leary Aviation Group, owned by none other than O'Leary Aviation Consultants. Taking off out of Palmdale, the Falcon climbed east over Barstow, leveling off at flight level four-one-zero. Sitting comfortably in back, Charlie hit Jim with the news of the week before.

400

"I'm not so sure LA Center will be able to make it without your leadership," Jim expressed his concern.

Charlie looked seriously over at Jim. "We have identified a new leader to take my place. I think you will like him."

That did get Jim's attention. "Is it someone we know?"

"I didn't really want to tell you this, but your wife sleeps with this guy."

Jim's eyes got wide and then it hit him, "You want me to run LA?"

"That's right, Jim. Sean and I discussed it and decided you are the obvious choice, considering your background and desire to live in Palmdale. We are only asking you commit to at least four years. That will give us time to establish the new centers and bring them all up to speed."

Jim sat back in his seat, looking out the window at the curvature of the earth on the distant horizon. After a few moments, he looked back at the man who had been his mentor for so many years. Charlie could see the sadness in Jim's face. "Charlie, who would have ever thought twenty years ago we would ever be having this discussion? I will be happy to take the job, on the condition you and Carrie come out and visit periodically. Sandy and I miss the great times we used to have together."

"That is one thing you can count on, Jim."

The Falcon jet made a short trip of the flight up to Ely, Nevada. Charlie and Jim made their morning meeting with the real estate agent, who said she would be happy to list their homes but things didn't look promising that they could even get them sold. They continued to talk about the state of the local economy, and the guys soon realized they had blown up their cash cow. It had now become a boondoggle.

They drove down their old street to their empty homes. Since it had become evident that they would not be living here any longer, Carrie had packed up the house and moved all their

401

belongings to Georgia. The guys didn't even get out of the car as the homes only held memories

"Are you ready?" Charlie asked his friend.

"Ready as I will ever be. But do we have to do this?"

"It's good for the soul, brother. We have to have closure or it will eat at us forever. It could have been far worse. Think about how we would have felt if the kids hadn't gotten out. Can you imagine what was going through the pilots' minds as they flew the bombing run?"

Making their way up Highway 93, they turned onto the access road. The well-manicured entrance still stood as if nothing had ever happened, inviting those who entered.

"Western Center for Air Traffic Services," Jim read out loud as they passed through the entrance. There were a couple of guards at the gate, but they didn't even ask for ID. The men were silent as they looked at the burnt out shell of what used to be a beautiful structure. Even the parking garage was nothing but a pile of concrete with twisted cars protruding out of the rubble.

A White Pine County sheriff helped direct them to a makeshift parking lot where others who had arrived ahead of them were getting out of their vehicles. "They look pretty young. Were they the specialists?" Jim asked.

"I imagine so. I don't really know who all's going to be here."

A large tent had been erected on the rise overlooking the complex. The procession made its way around the debris and up the hill to the tent. They were the last to arrive.

"Looks like a revival meeting," Jim whispered to Charlie as they walked into the full tent. It was enclosed on three sides with the side open towards their old work place. On that end was a temporary stage with a podium and a portable sound system.

402

Nick Harton saw them arrive and ushered them up to the front of the tent. "Mr. Beckler, you are on right after the Governor gives recognition to the CAF pilots."

"Thanks, Nick. Who else is here?" Charlie asked.

"There are just a couple of Congressional leaders up for reelection. No one else thought it was important enough to brave the cold."

"I saw a lot of media trucks, expected some dignitary might be here" Charlie said looking around.

"That would be you, Charlie. I think someone leaked to the press that you would be the keynote speaker, and it not only filled up the tent, it brought national coverage. Thanks for coming."

Charlie's old pastor was sitting there all alone on the front row twisting his hands nervously. His eyes lit up when they slid into their seats beside him. "Welcome home," he said as he shook their hands. "Sure glad to see you guys. Can you give me some ideas on what to pray for?"

Charlie looked around at the hundreds of people behind them. "Pastor, in this circumstance it's not so much of what you pray for, but what you give thanks for. By the grace of God, these people are still alive. Let's give him the glory for the lives saved and ask his healing on this community."

"Thanks, Charlie. You always seem to know what to say. I have to say, I'm going to miss you." He stood up as Nick Harton introduced him to a quieting crowd.

After the Reverend opened the meeting with a gracious prayer asking for healing and guidance, Nick returned to the stage and introduced the facility chief. One by one he called each of the three hundred specialists up to the stage and shook their hands, giving them a certificate of appreciation. Then he introduced the managers and facility technicians, giving each of them the same certificate.

The Facility Chief looked out across the crowd and spoke frankly. "This next group of individuals was instrumental in the destruction of our facility. While they were only doing their jobs, I personally have not been able to overcome the emotional trauma of being bombed by my fellow Americans. So this afternoon, we are privileged to have with us Nevada governor Neil Achenbach." He motioned for the governor who took the stage dressed in his lieutenant colonel uniform.

"I, too, am appalled by the events that transpired here on this premise and across our nation. The loss of our nation's leader has been magnified in your lives by the loss of your administrator and the secretary of transportation. While this in itself is a traumatic event, those of you who escaped the certain death of the facility bombing now live with this haunting memory. Today we have in our presence twelve individuals who were required to carry out a very precarious mission. It was not one they chose, as you can imagine, but it was one that they carried out with bravery. For that reason I am honored to present these individuals with the Distinguished Flying Cross award."

It seemed to Charlie that the applause was half-hearted as the governor presented each of the pilots the award. The DFC had historically been given to men and women in the armed forces who distinguished themselves in actual combat while participating in an aerial mission. Charlie could only imagine what was going through the minds of those who were in the targeted building only moments before these pilots commenced the attack. Finally, all the awards were presented, and the governor took his seat.

Nick Harton returned to the stage and thanked the governor for his time and encouragement. "Many of you

404

personally know the last speaker we have here today. Charlie Beckler was a controller at Los Angeles Center before the consolidation. Later in his career, Charlie became an integral part in the testing and installation of 4DT. Having supervised Mr. Beckler for a number of years, I have nothing but good things to say about him."

That's not what he said the last time we met, Charlie thought as he got to his feet and stepped up on the platform.

The applause sounded like a rowdy rock concert. Charlie finally had to motion the crowd to sit down.

"On September 9th, 1978 in a remote village, a child was born. This child grew up in a home where fifty dollars was a month's salary. When he was a teenager, he dreamed of coming to America. He had read about the capitalist economic system and that a person could become successful if he desired to work hard.

At the age of nineteen, this young man's dream came true when he was offered a scholarship to come to the United States and attend the Massachusetts School of Technology. Taking full advantage of the offer, the young student studied with discipline and graduated with honors. Having dreamed of operating within the capitalist system, he was unwilling to spend his life as a servant, working for someone else. As a workforce of one, he worked hard building a software company. He did little jobs around the New York area, designing customized programs for small companies. When he was not writing software, he was busy doing research. It was during one of these sluggish times that he met an FAA manager who introduced him to our research and development team in Atlantic City. He solved the problems with the ERAMS software and was awarded a large contract to install it within our computers.

Unfortunately, he fell victim to those who desired to harm our way of life and succumbed to their threats. Only thinking of self-preservation, he failed to understand the

severity of his actions. After years of dissecting the virus he had installed within the program, he uncovered the potential devastation of the rogue program. As much as he tried to convince the FAA to shut down 4DT, it was to no avail. Two weeks ago, Abdur Rahman made the decision to remain within the walls of this doomed air traffic control center rather than live with the agony of his decisions. How easy it would be for us to blame him for the destructions we witnessed."
Charlie looked over the ruins and continued.

"Four years ago, after the Kansas City accident, the FAA administrator and the secretary of transportation were advised of our position to shut down 4DT until a fix could be found. After touring the crash site, we decided this would be the safest course of action. The late administrator, Robert Burkhammer and secretary of transportation, Terry Laverne overrode this decision. It would be easy to blame them for the aviation disaster that has forever changed our lives.

Two weeks ago, President James Banister signed an executive order authorizing the use of force against the air traffic control facilities around the country." Turning around, and again surveying the ruins, brought a lump to Charlie's throat. Chokingly, he continued. "It would be so easy to blame the president, for he is no longer alive to defend his decisions.

As you see, there are a great many people we can blame. Today, we are not here to blame others. As you will soon see, there will be enough blame laid on these individuals in congressional investigations over the coming months. Today, I am here to assume the responsibility for your near death experience."

Charlie hesitated for a moment as he again turned and looked across the complex. The crowd sat in stone silence. Turning back to his captive audience, he folded his notes and stepped away from the podium with the microphone in his hand. "After my untimely departure from the FAA, I became a consultant working to salvage the NextGen system. After the virus was discovered, our people worked day and night dissecting its contents. During this time, we formulated plans to handle all the different scenarios that could transpire from this infection. To our dismay, the worst possible became the inevitable.

"Ladies and gentlemen, I am the one who developed the plan we used in wrestling control away from the 4DT system. I am the one you can blame for the destruction of the center behind us. While I do apologize for the trauma you have experienced, I am here to tell you there was no other way. When we laid the groundwork for this plan, we never imagined that NextGen would be capable of locking down the facility, preventing your evacuation. Once this transpired, it became apparent a difficult decision had to be made - either destroy the three air traffic control centers with the potential loss of a thousand lives or allow the ninety-two aircraft to crash into as many targets around the country.

"While any decision of this magnitude is overwhelming, it became obvious this sacrifice had to be made. Your survival is nothing short of miraculous. As you know, your brothers and sisters in the other two facilities were not as fortunate. For them it was the ultimate sacrifice, and for their families, we grieve. Thank you for your willingness to serve. Now go home and hug your families, life is short, my friends." With that Charlie sat down in a very quiet tent.

After the ceremony was over, Charlie and Jim walked down the hill to the edge of the debris. They stared into what had been the control room floor with its twisted beams and jagged concrete. They could make out pieces of consoles scattered from the blast.

"Where did they find Abdur and Barney?" Jim asked.

"It wasn't pretty," Charlie replied. "Like the consoles, they were blown to pieces. Trust me, they didn't feel a thing."

"What a way to go. You have to feel sorry for Barney, he sure took things wrong. How's his family dealing with his death?"

Charlie shook his head. "I haven't heard. I'm surprised his wife wasn't here today. I know we never got along with Barney, but that doesn't mean we shouldn't have compassion. We should stop by and see her before we leave town."

"You're just too kind-hearted, Charlie. Guess that's what I like about you. Go ahead and take your time. I need to make some phone calls." Jim left Charlie standing there alone and headed for the car.

Continuing to look at what use to be a very impressive building overflowing with the latest in technology, tears rolled down the face of the man who had represented NextGen.

"If it makes you feel better, it tried to kill me too."

Charlie turned to see a man standing next to him. "Sorry, Mr. Beckler, let me introduce myself. I am Captain Kurt Hufford with Skywest. I was flying the CS100 in the Independence Day accident."

"Sorry, Captain," was all that Charlie could say.

"Is it true that you're back at Los Angeles Center?" the Captain asked.

"That I am, for the time being, anyhow." Charlie, wanting to be alone, was getting a little irritated. He tried to figure out what did this guy wanted. *Does he want me to beg for forgiveness? Could he just leave me the...*

"Mr. Beckler, it must be difficult to take on the burden of so many people, but I have listened to your speeches and read your articles. You don't have to take on the weight of the program. Neither I, nor my flight crew, blame you for our midair. We understand the complexity of the situation and accept it as an act of terrorism."

Charlie looked over at the balding Skywest pilot. "Thanks, Captain, I appreciate your understanding, but you didn't come here just to make me feel better. What is your reason for being here?"

Kurt was taken aback by Charlie's directness. "We have a mutual friend. Dan Winster told me I could find you here today."

The mention of his old friend brought a smile to Charlie's face. "How is the old boy? I haven't seen the old man for at least five years."

"He told me the same. He also sends a personal invitation for you and your family to visit the camp. As for my being here, from a pilot's perspective I have a few ideas I would like to share with you." Kurt decided if Charlie could be direct, so could he. "Would you be willing to take the time to listen?"

The ice broken, Charlie grabbed the pilot's shoulder. "If you're a friend of Daniel's then you're a friend of mine. Do you mind going to LA?"

November Two Two Three Foxtrot Juliet departed north and made a slow climb so the passengers could get one last view of the destroyed center before making a left turn back toward Palmdale. Once the aircraft leveled off at thirty-eight thousand feet, Charlie motioned for Kurt to join him and Jim at the table. "You drink?" Charlie asked.

"Not while flying." Kurt grinned. "Guess this time we can make an exception. What you got?"

"This thing has whatever you want, as for me, a scotch on the rocks after today's events."

"I think maybe a white wine would suite me better," Jim said as he jumped up to fill Kurt's order.

"I filled Jim in on our conversation. I think we're ready to listen to your ideas. You've got a captive audience for the next forty-five minutes, Captain. Give it your best shot."

"I won't waste time on my background, then," Kurt replied as Jim returned with his chablis.

Kurt tasted the wine, giving an approving nod. "Long before NextGen, I was flying all over the western half of the country. It was obvious in my day-to-day flying that the airspace had not kept up with technology. Once NextGen was introduced, I expected it to include a complete overhaul of the airspace. It never came."

"I'm sure you have ideas on how to accomplish this grandiose plan. Did you ever contact the FAA with your ideas?" Charlie asked.

"I tried, but all emails went unanswered."

"What makes you think things will be different this time?"

"The FAA is no longer controlling the airspace. The stone wall of bureaucracy has been broken. You are a revolutionary in redevelopment of the system. Why not revolutionize the airspace?"

Charlie scratched his chin and took another sip of his scotch. "Okay! Show me your plan for this revolutionized airspace."

Kurt gave the men a sheepish grin. "I really hadn't planned on getting this far on my first contact with you. Therefore, I came unprepared." Looking around, he found a pen and, on the back of a napkin, started laying out the future airspace system. The two veteran controllers immediately saw the benefits of the pilot's plan, and by the time they landed, there was a stack of napkins on the table.

Grabbing the napkins, Charlie stood up. "Your time is up, Captain Hufford. I have authorized the flight crew to take you home. We are fairly busy getting the centers back to full capacity at this time but will consider your proposal seriously." He handed his business card to a stunned airline pilot and departed the airplane.

Walking to the car, Jim had to ask, "Will it work?"

"Not only will it work, it will save the airlines millions."

410

DONALD L REAVIS

Chapter 61

Los Angeles Center

Charlie and Jim walked into the control room. Rich was sitting at the operation manger's desk with his feet up on the counter. Charlie shook his head. "I remember the days when this position was one of prestige. You have lowered it to a new standard."

"You're a lame duck anyway, Charlie. Why do you care?" Rich waved off the outgoing facility chief. "When you leaving?"

"The Falcon jet will be here in two hours. Are you happy to see me go?"

"Can't say that, just wondered who to put in charge of your flight. I was thinking about working it myself." Then Rich asked the question they all wanted to know. "When are we going to get the news coming out about the new facilities?"

"Don't have a release date, but you can count on it being before Memorial Day."

"Just wondering where we're moving to next. That's all."

Charlie laughed. "Hang in there, Rich. It's going to take every one of us to make this work."

"Even a hint on where we're going?" Rich asked, not letting it go.

"All I can tell you, my friend, is that it will not be in a desert."

Charlie continued through the control room, shaking hands with his old coworkers and promising them a better future. To the new kids, he offered words of encouragement.

"It's time to go, Charlie."

Jim pulled Charlie away from some of the veteran controllers telling old war stories.

Charlie gave Jim a don't-worry-about-it look and continued listening to his old friends. A few minutes later, he walked out of the center where twenty-seven years earlier his career had begun.

Charlie looked up at the huge trees. "Remember when we got here, Jim? These trees were nothing but newly planted tinder sticks. A light breeze could have blown them over. It reminds me of how we were back then. We were young and scared, transplanted into a strange environment at the mercy of others, but we grew. Now look at us - we need to be like those mature trees. Stand strong against the winds of adversity, shield the younger controllers from the stress that could destroy them."

Charlie gave his old friend a hug and crawled into the car waiting to take him to the airport.

Charlie picked up the in-flight phone and dialed Sean's cell. As he waited for an answer, he watched the San Gabriel Mountains disappear behind the clouds that covered their peeks.

"Greetings, ole boy, are you headed east?"

"We're homeward bound, Boss. Thanks for the nice ride. I don't think I'll ever get bored with this kind of flying. What's new on the eastern front?"

"I'm going home, Charlie. I have decided it is time." Sean hesitated for a moment, giving Charlie time to comprehend. "Think you can keep things moving on this side of the pond for a couple of months?"

"Am I to assume you're talking about Ireland?" Charlie responded. "I agree it's about time. Have you called your mother?"

"No, Charlie, I thought I would surprise her."

"Not always a good idea, the very knowledge of you even coming home would be enough of a surprise. How long's it been?"

"Since my dad died. That was twenty-six years ago."

Charlie could hear the sadness in Sean's voice. "Yes, Sean, it is time. We can keep things moving stateside as long as you keep your phone handy. Who do you have in place to run the day-to-day operations in Bethesda?" Charlie was referring to the new corporate office established in Maryland to build the 4DT replacement and run the air traffic control service company.

"I was hoping you would be willing to take the job."

Charlie laughed, "You know better. I'm heading home. Speaking of home, did they get my office finished?"

"I have been assured it will be complete before your arrival. Do you not communicate with your wife?"

"Not about you and your ill-conceived ideas. She's not too keen on having that high tech stuff in our home."

"You will like it, Charlie. Once you get home, take a test drive on your new toys, and we'll discuss the organization chart."

Charlie leaned back in his seat as the hum of the Pratt & Whitney engines quieted his soul. It had been a long hard road, and now he was headed home. As they crossed over northern New Mexico, his thoughts drifted back. It seemed like only yesterday he and Carrie were driving across the Badlands down there, just two young people with no idea of the future.

Now it was over. No longer did he have to take off for the "bad place." No more coming home late at night, exhausted from heavy traffic or adverse weather. No longer would Carrie spend the nights alone while he worked the midnight shifts. Yes, his career as an air traffic controller had been an honorable one, but, like Sean, it was time for him to go home. It had been two months since he had last spent the night with his wife. She had been busy taking care of her parents, and he had been working with Jim in the restoration of the Los Angeles Center.

He was so ready to hold Carrie in his arms as he looked down upon the farmlands of Kansas in the dwindling light. He remembered the terrible accident that had happened there. *Only another hour and I will be home,* Charlie reminded himself. At over five hundred knots, they crossed over northern Arkansas and down through Tennessee. He was very aware of the aircraft starting its descent into Georgia. He smiled and knew Carrie would be on her way to the airport. Twenty minutes later the slick Falcon 900 made a left turn onto final for runway four at Gainesville's Lee-Gilmer Memorial Airport.

Thirty minutes later, hand-in-hand, the very-in- love couple walked through the front door of the old homestead.

"Do you really have to call Sean right now?" Carrie asked as she attempted to prevent Charlie from going through the raised panel oak door into his new office.

"Trust me, it won't take long," he prodded. "You can even listen in."

Charlie could not believe what he saw when he turned on the light.

"You like it?" Carrie asked. "I designed the woodwork."

Charlie grabbed his wife and gave her a big hug. "Like it? I love it!" Two walls were lined with cherry bookshelves. On one side of the room, a couple of wingback leather chairs sat with a matching dark cherry table between them. An antique light hung from the punched copper ceiling illuminating the area. In the far corner, an old globe sat on a stand. In the middle of the room was a large dark mahogany desk. Charlie set down in the big leather chair, and Carrie jumped into his lap.

"Watch this," she told him as she opened the desk drawer. Pulling out a remote, she hit a couple of buttons. On the far wall, a large screen monitor lit up. "That is your new computer monitor. The technicians taught me how to use it. This is fun." A menu came up, and Carrie scrolled down to the contact list. "You said I could listen in, right?"

"That's right, girlfriend. That's the way it rolls from now on."

Carrie clicked on 'Sean O'Leary' and a little clock started spinning on the screen. Within seconds a popup message advised that contact was being made. Charlie wasn't paying much attention to the screen as Carrie had decided this would be a good time to catch up on the kissing she had missed out on the last two months.

"Excuse me?" Sean's voice caused them to jump. "Would you guys mind getting a room?" Charlie almost threw Carrie off his lap. There on the screen was Sean O'Leary, sitting in his office with his feet propped up on his desk. "Welcome home, Charlie. I see you've already started to adjust."

Charlie gave his boss a sheepish smile. "She never said anything about this being a video conference."

Sean got a good belly laugh out of Charlie's embarrassment. "It does a lot more than that. The technicians will be there tomorrow to show you how to work the programs. It should reduce your trips to Washington. Let's talk about my imminent departure."

"You saw the video, Sean. You have ten minutes, after that its tomorrow."

That made Carrie blush. "I'm going to leave you guys alone." She gave her husband a quick kiss on the cheek and left.

"When are you leaving?" Charlie asked Sean as Carrie left the room.

"I'll be flying across the pond in two weeks. That should give us enough time to get things moving smoothly here. I would like for you to make a trip up here before I leave." Charlie moaned, "I just got home. Can you give me a few days?"

"Sure, I just want you to meet our new program manager. You will be working closely with her. She's been selected to oversee the day-to-day operations here in Bethesda."

"Great you found us some emotional baggage to work around while you're gone," Charlie groaned.

Sean could see Charlie was perturbed. "Come on, Charlie, she's not that bad. She's one of your own, came from Kansas City."

A very numb feeling came over Charlie, surely not… "Do I know her?"

"Yeah, she was the girl who was working the midair we investigated four years ago."

Charlie's expression told a lot more then he was willing to share.

"She's working out real well, Charlie. Is there a problem I'm not aware of?"

Charlie shook his head. "No Boss, not at all. I'm sure she will do a great job."

"She already has. Got this place running smoothly and everyone loves her. She's beautiful, too." Sean added.

"That she is," was all Charlie could say.

Sean didn't pick up Charlie's remark and continued on, "I have more news that will make your night."

"I don't think that's possible. What's the news?"

Sean held up a document. "We have a signed ten-year contract."

"Good night, Sean."

Chapter 62

Over breakfast of cold cereal and English muffins, Charlie revealed their predicament to Carrie. "I had absolutely nothing to do with her getting hired. I haven't had contact with Denise since the accident, seriously."

Carrie smiled at her husband, "I believe you, dear. You have never given me reason not to. We will just have to be careful."

"Speaking of careful, can you go to Bethesda with me next week? We will only be gone for the day."

Carrie came over behind Charlie and put her arms around his neck. "I may trust you, but I'm not stupid. Save me a seat."

In his newly designed office, Charlie watched and listened to the technician demonstrate the high-tech system. First, he revealed two more large monitors behind hidden panels on each side of the one he had used to talk to Sean the night before. Charlie was amazed as the screens came to life, showing all the traffic flows from around the country.

"It does more, what sector do you want to see?" the tech asked.

Charlie directed the tech to Sector 6 at Los Angeles. The tech scrolled his mouse over a prompt and Sector 6 appeared live on one screen and data link started scrolling on another.

Over the surround sound speakers Charlie could hear the controller working the traffic and the pilots responding.

418

"What else will it do?"

The mouse moved over a menu, and up on the screen appeared the simulation facility in Bethesda. "You have over three thousand video and audio feeds available at your fingertips. Not only that, but you can access all the mainframe computers within the air traffic system."

Once Charlie was alone in the room, he scrolled down through his contacts. Finding Jim Gallagher, labeled 'ZLA-1,' he hit the enter button. Within seconds, the view of the executive boardroom appeared on the screen. It was empty. He was about to hang up when his old secretary stuck her head around the corner and looked at the monitor.

"Mr. Beckler!" she squealed. "How was your trip home?"

"It was wonderfully quiet, Janis." answered Charlie, forgetting she could see him roll his eyes. "Could you get Jim for me?"

Jim entered the room and immediately kicked back in the end chair of the conference room and threw his feet up on the table.

"No blasted way! Tell me it's not true!"

Charlie showed his disdain. "Does everyone have to put their feet on the table?"

"Only the cowboys do, Charlie. So is it true?"

"Yes, it's true, and I've already discussed it with Carrie. We'll be up there next week. I'll let you know how it works out."

Jim smiled and pulled his billfold out of his pocket. "I'm putting my money on Carrie in the first round."

"I am not a betting man, Jim, but I can tell you that I'm extremely happy nothing happened that night in Kansas. I have to let you go, Sean's calling."

Sean was sitting around a full conference table. "Top of the day, Charlie. Have you figured out all your new toys yet?"

419

Charlie immediately recognized Denise Derringer seated next to Sean. She was even better looking than he remembered. Focusing back on Sean, he answered. "I don't think there are enough hours in a day to figure all this stuff out. It will help keep me at home though. Who are your friends?"

"This is the management team here at the research center. I know you remember Denise. Like I told you last night, she will be running this facility."

Denise gave Charlie a little wave, "Looking forward to working for you, Mr. Beckler."

Charlie was baffled. How could she act so innocent? "Likewise," he replied.

Sean continued around the table, introducing each of the team. The only other one he recognized was Tyrone Cava from WCATS.

"If it suites you, Charlie, I'm planning on a conference meeting next Thursday with all the department leaders. It would be great if you could be here." Sean knew what was coming next. "And yes, we will send a jet to pick you up. I've got a surprise for you on that one too."

Thursday morning, Charlie and Carrie drove down to Jackson County Airport. Their ride was supposed to be there at ten, and Charlie wanted to be early. It never ceased to fascinate him watching a slick corporate jet land. Sure enough, at five minutes before ten an aircraft entered the pattern from the northwest. As it turned base Charlie recognized the profile of the Gulfstream G150. "Wow, sweet ride." Charlie commented as it rolled out on runway three-four. A few "airport rats" came out of the hangers to do a little gawking as the smooth jet taxied up to the ramp.

"Let me get this one," the Captain told his First Officer. He lowered the stairs just as the couple arrived at the door. "Welcome aboard, Mr. and Mrs. Beckler."

Charlie could not believe his eyes. "Captain Hufford, I thought you worked for Skywest."

"I did until last week. Thanks to you, Mr. O'Leary hired me to run your aviation fleet."

"Okay, you got me there. What aviation fleet?"

Kurt chuckled, "Guess your boss doesn't tell you everything. Have a seat; we will be airborne shortly. The flight time back up to Washington will be fifty minutes providing ATC doesn't slow us down."

It was smaller inside than the other aircraft but was well designed. Carrie was satisfied with the comfort level and had kicked off her shoes before they were in the air.

"Your seat back is not in the upright position," Charlie said mocking a flight attendant.

"I guess all these years of tolerating you has its benefits," she replied. "I need to get my rest."

It seemed no sooner they got to altitude that they started their descent into Ronald Reagan National Airport. A car was waiting for them at Signature Flight Support to take them to Bethesda, and by noon they were walking into Sean's office.

After the normal greetings, Carrie got a big hug from Sean as he thanked her for sharing her husband. "This place wouldn't exist without him," he told her. "Let me give you two a tour." Sean gave them a whirlwind tour of the research and development room which housed a majority of the software engineers and was run by Tyrone. The next department was the simulator where they would test all the new programs. There was only minimal staffing here since the programs to run were still in development. Finally, they moved into the administration wing where human resources took care of the thousands of employees from around the country. "This is where they process your paycheck, Charlie, so treat them nice," Sean teased.

"Yeah, I need to talk to them about that. They need to add a couple of zeros to my salary." Charlie jokingly grumbled.

They returned to the executive conference room, where Sean and Charlie started talking shop and Carrie quickly got bored and hungry. She was about to ask where she could find the vending machines when a very attractive young lady stuck her head in the door.

"The reservations are for one o'clock, Mr. O'Leary." She paid no attention to Charlie but instead looked at Carrie. "Hi, Carrie, could I speak with you for a moment?"

Carrie was stunned, but not as much as Charlie when Carrie got up and went out the door with Denise. He turned his attention back to Sean but had trouble concentrating.

Carrie followed the young lady to the office next to the conference room. Denise shut the door and turned to face Carrie with a look of tenderness and compassion.

"Carrie, I just want to say I am really sorry. Four years ago I was a young, lost girl at the lowest point in my life. It was right after the accident in Kansas, and Charlie was so kind and helped me survive the trauma."

Carrie looked the young lady up and down. "So you're Denise? Charlie's told me about you. To tell you the truth, you scare me."

Denise sobbed, "I am so sorry. You have a wonderful husband. If it weren't for him, we both would have made a big mistake. He was so strong and prayed for me."

Carrie listened to Denise open all those old wounds and had to ask, "So what else happened?"

"Seriously, nothing else happened. He told me to go find a good place to worship, which I did. I started attending my parents' old church where I met a guy my age and we got married. I am so happy now and am so thankful your husband showed me how a real husband should act. I am sorry for the date I had with your husband, but I am not sorry for the lessons

422

he taught me." Carrie could not hold back any longer and gave Denise a long hug and told her she was forgiven.

"You really think we can pull it off?" Charlie responded to Sean's excitement over the airspace redesign plan.

"I have looked this over from every angle. Now granted, I have never controlled airplanes, and neither has Mr. Hufford, that's where you come in. From the management and user standpoint, it's the greatest thing since sliced bread."

"Yeah, maybe so, but management is headed across the pond," Charlie reminded Sean.

"Oh, Charlie, you have proven you do not need me. The team is now in place. The future of aviation is on the fast track to recovery. While quality of management is paramount, so is quality of life. I am giving these people who have done the job, the opportunity to build a better system. You are to watch over them, not as a superior, but as a friend and partner in this development.

Over lunch Sean and Charlie continued to discuss the challenges that lay ahead for the company. Later, Sean and Denise rode with Charlie and Carrie back to the airport where Kurt had the airplane ready for the flight back to Georgia.

Sean gave Carrie a big hug. "Thanks for bringing your husband up here today. Seriously, as he is with you, he is my best friend. He is blessed to be married to such a wonderful person. Assure me you will make him keep his life in balance."

"Thank you, Mr. O'Leary. I will do what I can."

Sean turned to Charlie and warned, "Keep your priorities straight. While the past may be haunted with regrets and the job ahead seem so overwhelming, do not be discouraged. Live each day to its fullest, spending time with your family."

On the flight home, Carrie would not let go of her husband. She shared the conversations she had had with Denise and thanked her husband for maintaining integrity even at his weakest moment. "She's a very beautiful woman, Charlie. It must've been difficult."

Charlie knew that no matter what he said would be wrong, so he wisely only smiled at his wife and kissed her gently on the lips.

Going home

Sunday morning, just as the first hint of dawn was breaking over the Capital, Sean sat comfortably in the Global Express jet he had chartered for his return home. A lot of issues fought for his attention. Hearing the turbines start to spin, he opened the magazine lying in his lap. The advertisement in this Irish periodical brought back memories, faded with years of neglect, of the home he had abandoned. He could tell by the pictures that his home had not changed, but he knew he had. Would they, meaning his countrymen accept him as one of them? Would he be able to connect with the friends of his youth? It had not been his intentions to separate himself from his heritage.

Blaming no one but himself, he knew it had happened because he had submerged himself so deeply into his career. The bright rays of sunlight blasted through the window as the jet continued to climb northeast for its seven-hour flight across the North Atlantic. Sean pushed a button on his console and the shades lowered, darkening the lonely cabin. *Here, sitting in the lap of luxury,* he mused, *I may have all this world has to offer, but without friends, it is most miserable.*

"He's missing," Denise told Charlie with fear in her voice. Charlie's Sunday afternoon nap had been interrupted by her call. He rubbed his eyes as he listened to her explain, "Three-hundred miles east of Newfoundland the pilot reported electrical problems and said he was turning back to Gander for repairs. Ten minutes later they lost all contact with the aircraft."

Charlie sat down at his desk and turned on his monitors. "What flight is he on?" he asked.

"He didn't fly commercial, Charlie. Sean decided to charter a jet home. He said it would be the envy of all his old friends."

Charlie muttered something about pride before he started typing. "You got a call sign?"

Denise hesitated only for a moment, "November Five-Seven Lima Echo. What do you think happened?"

"Good gosh, Denise, how would I know? Let's take a look at the data." His hands flew across the keyboard and the monitors came alive with the data from the flight. Fast forwarding to the aircraft passing Nova Scotia he tracked the flight to the time and location the pilot had reported the problem. He watched as they made a left 180-degree turn and started a gradual descent. It was still over two hundred miles from the nearest airport, when the ADS-B stopped sending data.

Charlie sat, his mind numb from what he had just heard. He was frozen at his desk, waiting for the phone call that would give him the news. Reality started to take hold. He felt the empty gnawing of anxiety. This was not going to end well. What would they do? Did they have what it took to continue on with what Sean had started? Did he have it within him to take up the reins? All of a sudden, he felt overwhelmed as thoughts of the uncertain future toyed with his mind. Charlie bowed his head in prayer.

Conclusion

Spring wild flowers showed their vivid array of colors across the meadow. The lake was full of fresh rainwater, and the birds had built their nests in the trees full of leaves. Charlie and Carrie, hand-in-hand, looked out across the lake as the sun settled below the horizon. Slowly they walked up the path to the big farmhouse. Carrie grabbed Charlie's arm and laid her head on his shoulder. "Thank you for being my best friend, Grandpa."

"Did you say, Grandpa?" Charlie raised his eyebrows looking down at his smiling wife.

Carrie just giggled as any future grandma would.

DONALD L REAVIS

427

Lightning Source UK Ltd.
Milton Keynes UK
UKHW021824080620
364652UK00012B/3749